HIDDEN MYSTERIES

ETs, ANCIENT MYSTERY SCHOOLS AND ASCENSION

JOSHUA DAVID STONE, Ph.D.

HIDDEN MYSTERIES

ETs, Ancient Mystery Schools,
and Ascension

Joshua David Stone, Ph.D.

THE EASY-TO-READ ENCYCLOPEDIA
of the SPIRITUAL PATH
✦ Volume IV ✦

Published by

Light
Technology
Publishing

Cover design by
Fay Richards

ISBN 0-929385-57-8

Published by

Light Technology Publishing
PO Box 3540
Flagstaff, AZ 68003
1-800-450-0985
www.lighttechnology.com

Printed by

4030 E. Huntington Dr.
Flagstaff, AZ 86004
1-928-526-1345

Dedication

I would like to dedicate this book to my extraterrestrial brothers and sisters, to Pan and the nature spirits, to the archangels and angels, to friends from the inner Earth, and lastly to the hidden and lesser-known mystery schools of all faiths that grace this planet.

These less well-known friends and servants of the divine don't often get the gratitude and acknowledgment they so richly deserve for the tireless and often unseen spiritual work they do on humanity's behalf. My prayer is that in the not-too-distant future there will be much more open communication among us all and acknowledgment that we are all brothers and sisters in one universal and multidimensional family.

Contents

Introduction

As it has become clear to more and more people that humans are not the only intelligent beings in God's infinite creation, the need has arisen for an overview of the extraterrestrial civilizations that are currently contacting Earth. I have attempted to provide that, describing each civilization, along with its beliefs, characteristics, and reasons for being here.

It is also time for widespread awareness of information that is both ancient and Earthly. Many people are unfamiliar with the profound but hidden spiritual teachings of the Essenes, the Kahunas of Hawaii, Pan and the nature kingdom, the angelic kingdom, the Vedas and Upanishads, the Kabbalah, the Yoga sutras of Patanjali, the Egyptian mysteries, and the Keys of Enoch, even though they are some of the most profound spiritual teachings that exist on this beloved planet. It is my belief that a well-rounded study of all the world's religions, mystery schools, and saints and masters will accelerate your progress on the path toward Self-realization.

All in all, the contents of this book are guaranteed to expand your consciousness and change your perception of reality.

Namaste
Joshua David Stone

Part One

Extraterrestrial Activity in this Universe

1

Extraterrestrials and Other Governmental Cover-ups

*Ninety-five percent of all extraterrestrials visiting
our planet are of a positive nature.*

Vywamus

During the past five years I have developed an interest in understanding the nature and extent of extraterrestrial involvement with Planet Earth over the course of history. A thousand books would probably not cover the topic, but I will attempt to provide a brief overview of the subject, as I find it a curious phenomenon that a great many very devoted and spiritual people have very little knowledge about extraterrestrial involvement on Earth.

First of all, God's infinite universe is filled with life. It is the height of egoism to think that humans are the only life form to exist. Extraterrestrials have been visiting Earth since the beginning of time. There were the electrical wars in pre-Lemurian times and later, in Atlantis and Egypt, extraterrestrials visited in great numbers. In Atlantis they helped with crystal technologies and with the building of the great crystal, which was the power source for the entire civilization of Atlantis. Extraterrestrials have come from our galaxy as well as from distant galaxies.

It is important at this point to say that I believe, based on the guidance I have received, that ninety-five percent of all extraterrestrial contact with humans is of a positive nature. Most of the civilizations are far beyond humanity on technological and spiritual levels. One of the basic laws they follow is that of respecting the free choice of humans and never interfering unless they have been asked for help.

One of the reasons there have been so many sightings of UFOs in recent years is that the inhabitants of Earth have moved into a fourth-dimensional consciousness, and the planet has moved into sacred status. These are system-wide events. Each of the planets of this solar system could be likened to a chakra of the Sun or of the being that ensouls the solar system, Helios. When one chakra goes through a major transformation it affects all the other chakras. The extraterrestrials are aware of this transformation the Earth is going through and are very interested in watching it and in helping humanity to move into the new age. Many of the great advancements in Earth's past evolution have occurred because of extraterrestrial help.

One important thing to understand is that not all extraterrestrials have a human appearance. This particular kind of physical body is called the Adam Kadmon type; there are many other types of bodies that God has created.

Also let it be remembered that in past lives when humans have incarnated on other planets, they have inhabited some of these bodies themselves. Humans need to get beyond their egotistical attachment to this particular form and realize that humanity is part of a galactic, universal, and cosmic family of intelligent life forms — and most of them are far more advanced than this civilization.

One of the reasons extraterrestrials are not more overt in their visits to Earth — why they don't just make a landing on the White House lawn in full public view — is that Earthlings have been too warlike. Despite technological advancements, Earth has been a spiritually backward planet.

The Negative Extraterrestrials and the Dark Brotherhood

This brings me to the subject of the negative extraterrestrials. As I have already mentioned, at least 95% of all the extraterrestrial involvement on this planet is of a very positive nature. The 5% that is negative, though, is very negative. It is part of my purpose in writing this chapter to make you aware of what is actually going on behind the scenes. The information in this chapter has been confirmed over and over again by both Earthly and spiritual sources. Some of the information might even shock you. However, I ask you to keep reading and to keep an open mind, for I believe it is absolutely imperative that the people of the United States and of the world wake up.

Negative extraterrestrials were involved in the fall of Atlantis and they have been trying to control this planet and its people since the beginning of time. In God's infinite universe there are always two forces: those who serve the Law of One and those who serve more egotistical, selfish, fear-based principles. This is true for inhabitants of Earth; it is true for extraterrestrials.

By becoming aware of these egotistical factions humans are less likely to be controlled by them. If you are aware of what is really happening you can become even more empowered than you already are. You cannot solve a problem until you know what the problem is.

The problem, in its essence, probably goes back to the Dark Brotherhood. The Dark Brotherhood is an organization much like the Great White Brotherhood of the Spiritual Hierarchy except that these beings are working for a plan that is antithetical to God's divine plan. Both spiritually and on the material plane, these beings operate according to a plan that serves selfish interests rather than being for the good of everyone.

This dark force is nothing to fear as long as you own your power and don't walk around on automatic pilot; then they cannot affect you or harm you in any way. The problem is that a great many souls on this planet don't own their power and aren't attuned spiritually. They take drugs or drink too much alcohol or don't realize who they are and why they are here. Their lives are focused on hedonism and materialism and all these things leave them vulnerable to the influences of dark forces.

The negative extraterrestrials are obviously influenced by this dark, separative, egotistical, fear-based part of themselves. They have evolved technologically, which is obvious from their spacecraft, but they have not evolved spiritually. They are forcing their will upon the people of Planet Earth. They are breaking what *Star Trek* calls the Prime Directive — noninterference and respect for free choice.

The Secret Government

It is necessary to describe another group that continues to play a pivotal role in this drama, a group of men on this planet who make up the secret government, or the Illuminati.

There is a group of men who, because of their lack of attunement to their own souls, have, in a sense, been taken over by the Dark Brotherhood. These men have been overcome by selfishness, greed, and power, and they are attempting to control the United States and the world to suit their own deluded, materialistic values. These men have no respect for the United States government or any other government on this planet. Their basic game is to control the world in order to serve their own interests and values, which are clearly selfish to the core. There is an occasional scandal when they are caught, but the world as a whole does not realize the extent of their power and ruthlessness.

Some of the shocking activities attributable to this group are the assassination of John F. Kennedy, the assassination of Robert Kennedy, Watergate, Contragate, Iraqgate, the Savings and Loan debacle, the total control of the banking system, the control of the CIA, and the control of most of the presidents and governments of the United States. The group has financed a great many of their illegal projects through the CIA by selling drugs. This secret government is known by many names, some of which are the Illuminati, the Trilateral Commission, the Council on Foreign Relations, and the Olympians. They are, in essence, representatives or instruments of the Dark Brotherhood on Earth. A lot of these men have enormous financial wealth and hold positions of great political power.

It is time for the American people to wake up, reclaim their power and take back their government.

The secret government has perpetrated the greatest cover-up in the history of this planet. The most mind-boggling thing of all is that they have been, for the most part, successful.

The Modern History of Extraterrestrial Presence

Awareness of extraterrestrials began in 1936 when Nazi Germany recovered a crashed UFO. They had their top scientists working to copy and understand its technology. When the Allied forces invaded Germany in 1945, this entire project and its technology were discovered, and it sent shock waves through the United States government.

In the 1940s there was a great wave of extraterrestrial activity. The single most important event was probably the Roswell crash, which occurred on July 2, 1947, near Roswell, New Mexico. A UFO crashed and the dead bodies of four aliens were found. The corpses were of a smallish size, with large heads, and the beings were basically reptilian in appearance. This, of course, was an astounding event.

Between 1947 and 1952 the United States government obtained at least sixteen crashed or downed alien craft and sixty-five alien bodies. One live alien was recovered. An alien craft was found on February 13, 1948, on a mesa near Aztec, New Mexico. Another craft was located on March 25, 1949, in White Sands, New Mexico. It was over one hundred feet in diameter, and a total of seventeen alien bodies were recovered from the two craft.

Of even greater significance was the discovery of a large number of human body parts stored within both of these vehicles. This was coded as Ultra Top Secret because of the perceived panic that might occur if the information leaked out to the general public.

During the early years, the United States Air Force and the CIA controlled the secret of the aliens. The CIA was originally formed by presidential executive order for the express purpose of dealing with the alien situation. The live alien who had been found wandering in the desert after the 1947 Roswell crash was designated an extraterrestrial biological entity — Ebe, for short. Ebe had a tendency to lie and would give answers only to questions he desired to answer. Eventually, after the first year, Ebe began to open up. Then in 1951, Ebe became ill. American doctors had no idea how to deal with Ebe medically because his system was chlorophyll-based and he processed food into energy much the same way plants do. On June 2, 1952, Ebe died. The movie *E.T.* is based on the story of Ebe. In an attempt to save Ebe and to gain favor with his technologically superior race, the United States began broadcasting a call for help into the vast regions of space.

President Truman had been keeping America's allies, including the Soviet Union, informed of the developing alien problem in case the aliens turned out to be a threat to the human race. During Dwight Eisenhower's first year in office, 1953, at least ten more disks were recovered, along with twenty-six dead and four live aliens. Eisenhower did not reveal this secret to Congress. Instead, he turned to his friend and fellow member of the Council on Foreign Relations, Nelson Rockefeller. Eisenhower and Rockefeller began secretly planning a covert group to supervise the alien situation. This group became known as Majestic Twelve, or MJ12.

In 1953, astronomers discovered large objects in space that were moving toward the Earth. At first it was believed they were asteroids, but later evidence proved that the objects could only be spaceships. Project Signa intercepted alien radio communications, and by using the binary language of computers, it was possible to arrange face-to-face contact with beings from another planet. The movie *Close Encounters of the Third Kind* is a fictionalized version of this event. An alien was left on Earth after that meeting as a pledge that they would return and formalize a treaty.

This initial group of aliens was from Zeta Reticulum and has often been referred to as the Grays. They were small in stature, about four or five feet tall. They looked nothing like human beings of the Adam Kadmon type but had big heads, almond-shaped eyes, and long arms.

In the meantime, a race of humanoid aliens had landed at Homestead Air Force Base in Florida and had successfully communicated with the U.S. government. This group warned of an alien race that was orbiting the equator, mentioning both the Grays and a race from Orion with reptilian-looking heads and humanoid bodies.

The advanced, positive, human-looking extraterrestrials offered to help humanity with all the existing technological and spiritual problems, but they had one requirement: they demanded that all nuclear weapons be dismantled and destroyed. The U.S. government refused.

A third landing occurred at Edwards Air Force Base in 1954. The base was closed for three days and no one was allowed to enter or leave during that time. Eisenhower arranged to be in Palm Springs on vacation. On the appointed day he was spirited off to the base. The excuse given to the press was that he was visiting a dentist. Five craft landed, and Eisenhower met with the aliens. All these landings were filmed. This alien group was again the Grays from Zeta Reticulum.

A formal treaty between the alien nation and the United States government was signed, and the U.S. officially received its first ambassador from outer space who was the same being who had stayed behind after the first landing. He was called Omnipotent Highness Krill.

The treaty basically stated that the aliens would not interfere in the affairs of the United States, and the U.S. would not interfere in their affairs. The U.S. agreed to keep their presence on Earth a secret; they agreed to furnish the U.S. with advanced technological information and they promised not to enter into a treaty with any other nation on Earth. They were permitted to abduct humans on a limited and periodic basis for the purposes of medical examination and the monitoring of development, with the stipulation that the humans would not be harmed, would be returned to their point of abduction, and would have no memory of the event.

The Grays were supposed to furnish Majestic Twelve with a list of all human contacts and abductees on a regular, scheduled basis. It was also agreed that each nation would receive the ambassador of the other for as long as the treaty remained in force. It was further agreed that the alien nation and the United States would exchange sixteen citizens for the purpose of learning about each other. The alien guests would remain on Earth. The human guests would go to their planet and return, and then an exchange would take place. This was re-enacted in the movie *Close Encounters of the Third Kind*.

It was also agreed that bases would be constructed underground for the use of the alien nation and that two bases would be constructed for joint use of the alien nation and the United States government. Exchange of technology would occur in the jointly occupied bases. The bases would be constructed under the Indian reservation in the Four Corners area of Utah, Colorado, New Mexico, and Arizona and in the Mojave Dessert near Yucca, California. A secret military fund was put together to build seventy-five deep underground facilities. The excuse was that they were needed in case of nuclear war.

By 1955 it had become obvious that the aliens had deceived Eisenhower and broken the treaty.

The secret government had basically sold out the American people without their permission and in addition, abductions were occurring at hundreds of times the rate agreed upon. Records of them were not being provided. Animal mutilations were occurring all over the country, and there were reports of human mutilations occasionally happening also, although that was much rarer. It was also suspected that not all abductees had been returned. The Soviet Union was suspected of interacting with the Grays, and that later proved to be true.

The Grays were using humans and animals as a source of glandular secretions, enzymes, hormones, and blood plasma and for genetic experiments. The aliens said that it was necessary for their survival. They stated that their genetic structure had deteriorated and that they were no longer able to reproduce. They said that if they were unable to improve their genetic structure, their race would soon cease to exist. (I believe this is true.) The Grays were also found to be impregnating human females and somehow causing an early termination of the pregnancies to secure a cross-bred infant. They were also implanting humans with both mechanical and nonmechanical devices for biological monitoring and tracking purposes.

It is hard to believe that the United States government has provided these clearly selfish beings with underground military bases all over the country. In some material I obtained called *The Dulce Papers* it is said that over eighteen thousand Grays live at the Dulce, New Mexico, base alone. These papers say that the Grays and the reptilian beings are in league with each other.

Some of the technology on these bases was provided by the Grays and is way beyond the understanding of the United States government. There are apparently seven levels or more, with each deeper level requiring a higher security clearance. In levels six and seven there are apparently nightmarish Frankenstein-type experiments going on in the mixing of human and animal genetics.

Some reports of the things going on there are too disturbing to mention in this book. Needless to say, what is occurring is not in harmony with God's divine plan. As time has gone on, the Grays and the reptilians have become more and more bold in doing whatever they please to serve their own purposes.

The United States government has delineated over seventy species of aliens trying to make contact and has obtained and kept in its possession over forty flying disks, many of which have been reproduced and are being tested and flown by the U.S. military. The government has in its possession more than one hundred alien corpses.

Alternative 2 and Alternative 3

Alternative 2 and Alternative 3 are covert programs of the secret government having to do with the colonization of the Moon and Mars. Alternative 2, the program for the colonization of the Moon, was in operation long before the first official public landing on the Moon by astronaut Neil Armstrong. Long before that, the U.S. had already engaged in a joint venture with the Soviet Union and had set up bases there which continue to exist to this day. There are alien bases on the dark side of the Moon. There are also more gravity and atmosphere on the Moon than have been publicly acknowledged. For more information on this see the excellent book by Fred Steckling, *We Discovered Alien Bases on the Moon*, which includes one hundred twenty-five enlarged NASA photographs that show some of the strange things going on there.

The basic plan of the Alternative 2 program was to build a vast network of underground cities and tunnels in which a select representation of all cultures and occupations could survive in case of a nuclear holocaust on Earth.

Alternative 3 was also a joint Soviet Union-United States plan to set up a similar colony on Mars. A space probe landed on Mars and confirmed the existence of an environment that could support life. Not long afterward, the construction of a colony on Mars began in earnest. This information, obviously, was not released to the public.

This work went on for many years; however, it is my understanding that the project has been abandoned. You might have seen some of the NASA pictures of Mars that show previous alien civilizations. There is a clear picture of pyramids and a sculpted face that, beyond the shadow of a doubt, have been created by some form of extraterrestrial intelligence.

There was apparently an Alternative 1 plan that had to do with the idea of using nuclear devices to blast holes in the stratosphere to let the greenhouse heat and pollution escape. This plan was abandoned as ill-advised by the scientists in charge. (Thank God!)

Apparently the secret government's plan included depopulating the Earth. As part of this plan there was the implementation of birth control and sterilization and the introduction of deadly microbes to slow population growth.

The plague of AIDS was created by the United States government as a form of bacteriological warfare. It was purposely spread among specifically targeted populations including blacks, Hispanics, and homosexuals. One of the ways this was done was to lace hepatitis vaccines with the virus. It was a bacteriological warfare experiment done on the people of the United States that has gone out of control.

Another one of the great lies of all time is that it is passed on primarily through sexual involvement. According to all the sources of information I have, this is a blatantly false lie, just as is the World Health Organization's statement saying that the AIDS virus came from a monkey in Africa. The AIDS virus *can* be passed in saliva. It is not a homosexual disease.

Condoms don't always protect you because the AIDS virus is so infinitesimally small. It has been proven that the AIDS virus can live in an open-air petri dish for ten to fourteen days.

One of the things killing people faster than the AIDS virus is the present treatment for the AIDS virus. From the information I have received, AZT, the common drug for the treatment of AIDS, is absolute poison to the human body and is killing people much faster than even AIDS itself.

Lastly, the biggest cover-up of all is that there is no cure. People *are* being cured of AIDS. Hanna Kroeger, an herbalist from Colorado, has come up with a cure for AIDS, and many other doctors dealing with energetic medicine and holistic medicine are having marvelous results, too.

The most important thing I can say in this entire book I will say right now: You are not a victim of AIDS. You are not a victim of the Dark Brotherhood. You are not a victim of the Grays or the reptilian race. And you are not a victim of your mind, your emotions, your physical body, or anything else in God's infinite universe. You are God. God created you perfectly. God has given you personal power and free choice.

The only effect anyone or anything can have on you is the effect you let it have on you. No alien can abduct you if you own your God-given power. The same principle applies across the board. You are not a victim of disease; there is no such thing as a contagious disease (this is another myth of the Dark Brotherhood, and it applies to AIDS, also), there are only people with low resistance. If you eat well, exercise, get sunshine and fresh air, think right, spiritualize your emotions, and stay attuned to God and your own true identity as the Christ, the Buddha, the Atma, and the Eternal Self, then nothing can touch you, including AIDS.

The Secret Government and Politics

The one president who wasn't under the thumb of the secret government was John Kennedy. When he found out about the secret government's activities, he planned to blow the whistle on some of them. That is why he was assassinated. His murder was part of a widespread conspiracy of the secret government, as was Robert Kennedy's death. Again, the American people bought the cover-up. It is amazing to me how the secret government is able to get away with the things they do.

One of the main ways the secret government has financed all its projects is with drug money. George Bush was one of the original people who was approached to help the CIA start its program of selling drugs. Bush's Secretary of State, James Baker, is even higher up on the secret-government ladder than George Bush is. George Bush, as you know, had been head of the CIA. The fact that these men and the entire corrupt staff were voted out of office marks a great step forward for the American people and the beginning of the end for the Dark Brotherhood's reign of control, according to Djwhal Khul.

The secret government, or the Council on Foreign Relations and the Trilateral Commission, is currently in complete control of the alien technology this country has obtained and is also in complete control of the nation's economy. Eisenhower was apparently the last president to have had a complete overview of the alien presence. The extent of the secret government's control is evident in the fact that even the presidents of the United States are often not told what is going on; succeeding presidents have been told only what Majestic Twelve wanted them to know.

These greedy servants of the Dark Brotherhood must be stopped. It is time for the American people to fully wake up to what's been going on and to reclaim their government. The people who run the government are supposed to be the servants of the American people, not servants of their own selfish interests. To take back the government, Americans must reclaim their power and use it to change the world.

A great many spiritual people don't take enough responsibility politically for changing the Earthly institutions of this world. God's divine plan does not intend for you to ascend to God and forget about the Earth; God's divine plan is to make Earth a heavenly place to live. That means changing the institutions and ego-oriented structures that have governed the planet. The time of living in a cave and meditating is over. This situation will obviously be helped by the coming of the Lord Maitreya and the externalization of the Hierarchy that are now taking place. However, it is not for them to do it. It is for the people to do it, the common people. For they, in truth, are the externalization of the Spiritual Hierarchy. It is time for the people to claim power and take action, to support the president and elected representatives on all levels of government. If the people don't take an interest, then the only information they receive is from the greedy lobbyists whose only cares are for their own particular interest groups. More spiritual politicians, lawyers, bankers, counselors, doctors, and real estate agents are absolutely essential so that they will take responsibility now. People who abdicate their power deserve what they get.

Nikola Tesla

Another one of the great cover-ups of the secret government and the military-industrial complex was the inventions of Nikola Tesla.

Tesla was one of the greatest inventors in the history of this planet. Recent channelings have said that he was actually an extraterrestrial who was brought here as a young child. The Tibetan Foundation channelings say he was a soul extension of the great cosmic being known as Melchizedek. He was raised in Yugoslavia and came to the United States in early adulthood. The secret government has systematically tried to strike his name from the history books because it is so frightened that the public will learn about his inventions.

Nikola Tesla was actually a channel. Inventions would come into his mind in perfectly clear pictures and diagrams. He could create prototypes of his inventions right away, based on what appeared to him in his consciousness. In his biography it was said that he was in telepathic communication with extraterrestrials.

He was definitely here on a mission of service. The problem was that he ran into the Illuminati and selfish, greedy men in the late 1800s and early 1900s who blocked the manifestation of his inventions.

One of his inventions that would have revolutionized this world was a small antenna that would have been attached to the top of every house, office building, shop, and factory. This antenna would have supplied all necessary electricity without meters or wires of any kind. The antenna tapped the limitless universal supply of cosmic energy. Then people like J.P. Morgan told him to forget the idea because there would be no way to make money. Tesla was blocked at every turn. If this invention had been implemented, just think of the money people would have saved, the pollution that would have been avoided, and the absence of any need to fight wars in the Middle East over oil. This was far too threatening for the secret government, the military-industrial complex, and the greedy power elite.

Tesla invented a machine that could place an energy beam, or a wall of light, around the United States that would prevent any other country from attacking. He also built a machine that could be used for interplanetary communication. He invented a method to counteract gravity. He invented technology that could make planes and battleships undetectable by radar and actually invisible. He invented a system of alternating electrical current that far surpassed Edison's inventions. But he was blocked again and again.

It has been said Tesla created over twelve hundred inventions. He designed what he called the sphere, an aircraft that could have rivaled the jets of 1958. In 1891, Tesla built a cosmic ray engine, a free-energy device to utilize the cosmic rays. Tesla actually contacted spaceships on his interplanetary communication device.

With Tesla's inventions in operation, no TV towers, telephone poles, or wires would be required. His anti-war machine would have made Reagan's Star Wars project completely unnecessary. His antigravity machine, which would have allowed the U.S. to begin interplanetary travel, was similar to that used by the UFOs that come to Earth.

Nikola Tesla was a humanitarian and a selfless servant of humankind. Can you imagine what this world would be like if the governmental and industrial leaders had accepted his inventions?

This is only one example of how the secret government and greedy industrialists prevent this world from evolving. What happened to Tesla is happening every day of the year to inventors, even now. You might hear news about some car that gets two hundred miles to the gallon or runs on water or runs on solar energy, but the car and oil companies buy the patents and somehow prevent it from ever being produced.

Do you wonder why more of this kind of information doesn't come out on TV? Well, guess who owns the three main television networks. You guessed right: members of the Trilateral Commission and the Council on Foreign Relations. Any time a controversial story surfaces, the powers that be go into action to stifle it.

Other Governmental Cover-ups

One of the most disturbing governmental cover-ups is the systematic, conscious effort by the secret government, the Illuminati, and the Dark Brotherhood to poison the American people. First of all, the enormous amounts of canned, processed, and frozen foods that fill 90% of the supermarket shelves are made with chemicals and preservatives that are poisonous to the human body. Then on every street corner is a fast food restaurant serving food filled with the same chemicals that systematically and gradually poison the liver and weaken the immune system. "Fresh" produce is covered with pesticides. The air is polluted because of lack of strict environmental controls of cars and factories.

A gaping hole has been ripped in the ozone layer, allowing ultraviolet rays from the Sun to enter Earth's atmosphere, causing cells to mutate or die. Dental cavities are filled with mercury which is an extraordinarily toxic substance to the human body. Usually within ten or fifteen years the fillings begin to crack and this toxic substance leaks into the system.

In Los Angeles and probably in other cities they spray malathion to get rid of the medfly. It is such a toxic substance that the nights they spray, the entire population has to cover their cars because the malathion will actually take the paint off your car. Yet that incredible advocate for the American people, the FDA, says it is not harmful to the human physical body! A process like that systematically destroys the immune systems of everyone in the whole city.

In many cities the water supply is fluoridated because they say it helps to prevent tooth decay in children; but fluorine is poisonous to the human body.

They vaccinate children, which the average mother and father think is an incredible service the government is providing but which, in fact, is just the opposite. Vaccinations break down the immune system. Then the children are fed all kinds of sugar at school which continues the process of weakening the immune system.

Then too, because inventions like Nikola Tesla's have not been used, there are incredible numbers of electrical power lines surrounding homes and in cities. They have a much more negative effect on the physical body than most people realize. People are getting serious illnesses from sitting in front of computers all day. Police officers are getting cancer from using the police radar guns. This is why there has been recent popularity of inventions like the Tesla watch, which protects an individual from these low-grade electromagnetic frequencies.

There is an entire new field of technology called radionics or psychotronics which uses machines to transmit currents of positive energy for healing purposes. Of course, it has been stifled by the government and the AMA and instead, the technology is being used by the Pentagon and the war machines in both the United States and the former Soviet Union for military purposes. They actually build gigantic towers to send negative electrical frequencies to destroy individuals and groups of people. This type of warfare is very insidious because the people being attacked cannot even see they are being attacked. This, unfortunately, is the warfare technology of the future that is being developed now. It must be stopped.

The secret government and the Illuminati have no respect for the environment. All they care about is power and money, so they allow the environment to be systematically destroyed which continues to compromise the health of the people of the world. The ocean, rivers, and lakes are polluted. The deforestation of the rain forests and of the forests in the United States is screwing up the oxygen balance on the planet. A greenhouse reaction is occurring because of the burning of fossil fuels.

The minds, emotions, and bodies of children and adults are being poisoned by all the violence and lowlife activity on television.

The Federal Drug Administration has said it is okay to shoot radioactivity at fruits and vegetables to kill microorganisms. The only problem is that radiation is the single most poisonous substance to the human body in God's infinite universe. The secret government loves this idea for it is a way for the Department of Energy to get rid of radioactive waste. To add insult to injury, it has been decreed by the FDA that irradiated food does not require labeling except in a few cases in which all they are required to do is print a sweet-looking flower symbol with the words "Pico Wave."

The Dark Brotherhood has such a hold on the health system that there was even legislation on the docket that would have taken away people's right to buy vitamins, minerals, and herbs in health food stores without a doctor's prescription.

Another one of the major blunders of the FDA was allowing Nutrasweet on the market. This low-calorie sweetener's scientific name is aspartame. Dr. Woodrow Monte, head of the Food Science and Nutrition Laboratory at Arizona State University says about Nutrasweet, "If you tried to design a food additive that could cause problems for humans, you'd have to try real hard to design one as bad as aspartame." He goes on to say, "This stuff is a drug but is being used as a food additive."

As for the fluoridation of water, Dr. Robert Harris, professor of biochemistry of nutrition at Massachusetts Institute of Technology says, "Fluorine is a toxic element . . . which has been shown to interfere with important processes in the body." Dr. Charles T. Betts, D.D.S., states, "Fluorine is a poison which is cumulative in the body, similar to radium. No antidote is known."

In regard to all the health-related statements I have made in this chapter, I want to state that I don't claim to be a medical doctor, and for legal purposes I will say that these statements are just my personal opinion. You should consult your holistically oriented medical doctor in all cases. However, as a concerned citizen, I believe that if you research for yourself what I have been saying you will find it all to be true.

The secret government and the Illuminati have taken power and control because the people have given it to them. But the power of the people can be seen in American elections, in the end of Communism in the Soviet Union and in Germany. People are waking up. The time is now. People must wake up from their apathy, laziness, and indolence. The first step is knowing the problem. It has been clearly stated. The second step is being part of the solution.

What is the solution? The solution is manyfold: talk about these things with people, raise consciousness, support the right political leaders, write letters to congresspeople, vote, give money to causes, write books, give lectures, educate people, pray, affirm and visualize. Take action in any way you are guided to. No one can do everything, but God has given each of you a gift and piece of the puzzle only you can add to the picture.

The Philadelphia Experiment

Another of the great cover-ups by the United States government was a secret military program called the Philadelphia Experiment which was based on an invention by Nikola Tesla. It began as an attempt by the U.S. Navy to achieve the radar invisibility of its battleships during World War II. Some of the greatest scientific minds in the world were involved in this experiment, including Albert Einstein and Tesla.

They did a test run on an empty battleship and the ship not only became invisible to radar but actually disappeared from view completely. The U.S. Navy was very excited about this success and immediately wanted to put Naval personnel on the ship for the next experiment. Nikola Tesla was dead set against this and it turned out he was right. The ship disappeared and when it returned many of the crew members had burst into flames or had become frozen into the steel structures of the ship itself. Many of the other men went insane. The Navy was dealing with a technology it had no business dealing with yet. According to Al Bielek, one of the crew members, the ship was actually transported in time and space from Philadelphia to a grassy area on the Montauk Army Base on Long Island, New York, in the year 1983, forty years in the future. Al Bielek's account states that a UFO craft was sucked along with the battleship and was later dismantled on Long Island.

The Navy tried the experiment one more time, even after these disastrous results, but without personnel. Once again, the battleship Eldridge completely disappeared without even a waterline to mark its invisible presence. When it finally reappeared to physical vision the ship was damaged and half of its equipment was "missing." The powers that be decided that they had had enough of such experiments.

I have included this account just to make you aware of some of the technologies the government is working with that are totally hidden from the American people. It is time for the American people to really know what is going on behind the scenes instead of being treated like sheep. The ability to make a gigantic battleship completely disappear, teleport through time and space, and return again is quite extraordinary. If this technology could ever be truly understood without harming the people involved, and if it could be placed in the hands of spiritual scientists rather than the military, some of the possibilities and potentials are mind-boggling. Many of the alien spacecraft are able to travel such long distances in such a short period of time using technologies such as this.

The Secret Government and a Staged Alien Attack

There is a scenario that many UFO researchers have uncovered and that Djwhal Khul has confirmed to be a potential: a staged alien invasion. With the end of the Cold War and Communism, the country has been left without an enemy. There is no longer a reason to build weapons. There is no longer a reason to let the CIA and FBI have free rein in their secret government activities. There is no longer a reason to take away rights and manipulate and control people as they have been doing. They no longer have a reason to keep people in fear, and if they can't maintain the fear level, they can't control people in the same way.

The secret government is very frightened of the prospects of peace and is certainly afraid of a world of spiritual people involved in the New Age movement. Their areas of expertise are domination, control, manipulation, exploitation, and deceit, so one idea they are tossing around is to stage a fake alien invasion to create a new enemy. The panic that would be created would allow them to continue their illegal activities under the guise of a world crisis. This plan might be a little more difficult to implement with Bill Clinton and Al Gore in office. It would have been much easier with George Bush as president. It could be a last desperate attempt to stay in power, because on some level, I think they realize that the world is changing so fast they can no longer control it. I think they unconsciously realize that their reign of terror might soon be coming to an end. Do not underestimate their desperate attempts to remain in power. They murdered John F. Kennedy and Robert Kennedy and there has been an assassination attempt on every other president who has tried to cross them. A video tape I got from Bill Cooper clearly shows that the man driving the car John Kennedy was riding in is the man who killed Kennedy. It is as plain as day. You can see the gun, and you can see him shooting it.

These are desperate men who will do anything to stay in power. Their influence is coming to an end as the New Age approaches, but please be on the lookout for their deception.

The secret government is also frightened of the good aliens, who are involved in at least 95% of all extraterrestrial activity. They are quite aware of those beings' desire for a more loving and spiritual society free of nuclear weapons. They realize that if the positive extraterrestrials get the public's attention, it means the end of their power. That is another reason they are covering up what is really going on and another reason they might try to stage a fake invasion — to try to stigmatize all alien contacts as being negative.

There is no way the secret government can stay in power much longer. There are too many spiritual forces at work that make their destiny inevitable; but that doesn't mean you can be passive and wait until it happens. They will be removed when humanity collectively awakens to the need to eliminate their power.

Vywamus on Negative Aliens and the Secret Government

One of the finest channels on the planet was Janet McClure, the founder of The Tibetan Foundation. In my research I came across a channeling she did in Sedona, Arizona, on August 31, 1989, and which was published in a wonderful magazine called *Sedona Journal of Emergence!* In this article Vywamus made some statements that confirmed information I had found elsewhere in my research.

He confirmed that only about 5% of the extraterrestrials are causing

problems. Of this 5%, many have been scientists who have no understanding of the emotional body. The type of invasion Earth has been
experiencing, he said, has occurred seven or eight different times in the
history of the planet. Humanity has always won out, usually because of help
from the higher forces.

He said another very interesting thing about the secret government
and the Trilateral Commission: he said that ninety-five individuals are
controlling the whole planet. They live all over the world and usually are
connected to wealthy families of long standing. They are also connected to
great banking conglomerates and large holding companies. These ninety-
five people and their families are also connected into thirty-five other
planets. What this means is that the Trilateral Commission exists not just
on this planet; it is a galaxy-wide problem.

The negative extraterrestrials are not very well united as a group, and
that makes them a lot easier to deal with. The fact that they are run by their
negative egos makes them very fragmented and most concerned with their
own self-interests. That will be what causes their fall. There are only a
couple of groups of them that are connected into any real power on Earth.
Vywamus refers to them as not black or white but more like gray in terms
of their psychological makeup. What this means is that they have a whole
range of mixed intentions. It is interesting that Vywamus should use this
expression, given that the beings from Zeta Reticulum are often referred
to as the Grays.

Vywamus also confirmed that the CIA and its power structure do
control the selling of drugs, and the money is used for the underground
bases and the secret government's activities. Vywamus also said that the
negative extraterrestrial invasion didn't begin in 1947 when the alien craft
crashed in Roswell, New Mexico; it has been going on for five hundred
years, and 1947 was just when the time the United States discovered actual
proof.

The Grays who are having all the health problems are sick because, as
Vywamus termed it, they are "wearing the energy from another universe."
Apparently you can't just change universes, because each universe has its
own unique source and energy matrix. Vywamus says that these beings
could be helped by spiritual masters from the Galactic Core or by healers
on Earth who allow masters from the Galactic Core to work through them
to change the Grays' energy matrix. He has been amazed that they have
been able to survive as long as they have.

Vywamus also said that there used to be a physical civilization on Mars,
although it has now departed, and he confirmed that humans had a base
on Mars, too. He also confirmed that the secret government and its
henchmen actually kidnapped people and forced them to go to Mars to

work. The information about Alternative 3 is all true. The colony has been dismantled in recent times, however.

I would like to acknowledge Milton William Cooper's book, *Behold a Pale Horse*, as the source of much of the information in this chapter. The book is fascinating, as are the two videotapes his organization has put out. Cooper is a true patriot who has done a tremendous service for humankind.

2

Agartha in the Hollow Earth

*Our interest rightly begins just after
your race exploded the first atomic bombs over
Hiroshima and Nagasaki, Japan. It was at that
alarming time we sent our flying machines, the
flugelrads, to your surface world to investigate
what your race had done.*

The King of the Hollow Earth

I've spoken of the greatest cover-up of all time being the suppression of the fact that extraterrestrials have been visiting Earth from other planets. If that is the biggest cover-up of all time, then the second biggest cover-up of all time is the attempt to keep secret the fact that there is a civilization of people living in the center of the Earth. The civilization is known as Agartha. This might be hard to believe; I know it was difficult for me at first. However, I now have an absolute knowingness of the truth of it.

To begin with, Buddhist theology fervently affirms its existence. It is believed to be a race of supermen and superwomen who occasionally come to the surface to oversee the development of the human race. It is also believed that this subterranean world has millions of inhabitants and many cities, its capital being Shamballa.

The king of this world is believed to have given orders to the Dalai Lama of Tibet, who is his terrestrial representative. His messages are transmitted through certain secret tunnels connecting the inner world of Agartha with Tibet.

The famous Russian channel Nicholas Roerich, who was a channel for Ascended Master El Morya, claimed that Lhasa, the capital of Tibet, was connected by a tunnel with Shamballa in the inner Earth. The entrance of this tunnel was guarded by lamas who were sworn to secrecy. A similar tunnel was believed to connect the secret chambers at the base of the Great Pyramid at Giza with Agartha.

The *Ramayana*, one of the most famous texts of India, tells the story of the great avatar, Rama. It describes Rama as "an emissary from Agartha" who arrived on an air vehicle. It is quite extraordinary that both the Buddhist and Hindu religions refer to Agartha.

The first public scientific evidence of Agartha's existence occurred in 1947 when Rear Admiral Richard E. Byrd of the United States Navy flew to the North Pole and instead of going over the pole actually entered the inner Earth. In his diary, he tells of entering the hollow interior of the Earth, along with others, and traveling seventeen hundred miles over mountains, lakes, rivers, green vegetation, and animal life. He tells of seeing monstrous animals resembling the mammoths of antiquity moving through the brush. He eventually found cities and a thriving civilization.

His plane was finally greeted by flying machines of a type he had never seen before. They escorted him to a safe landing place and he was graciously greeted by emissaries from Agartha. After resting, he and his crew were taken to meet the king and queen of Agartha. They told him that he had been allowed to enter Agartha because of his high moral and ethical character. They went on to say that ever since the United States had dropped atomic bombs on Hiroshima and Nagasaki, they had been very concerned for their own safety and survival. They had decided that it was time to make greater contact with the outside world to make sure humanity didn't destroy the planet and their civilization with it. Byrd had been allowed in so they could make contact with someone they trusted.

To make a long story short, when their visit was finished, Admiral Byrd and his crew were guided in their plane back to the outer world, their lives having been changed forever.

In January of 1956, Admiral Byrd led an expedition to the South Pole. On that expedition he and his crew penetrated two thousand three hundred miles into the center of the Earth. Admiral Byrd states that the North and South Poles are only two of many openings into the center of the Earth. (I can't help thinking about Jules Verne's famous science "fiction" book, *Journey to the Center of the Earth*.) Admiral Byrd also states that the inner Earth has its own sun. Byrd's theory is that the poles of the Earth are concave, rather than convex, and ships and planes can actually sail or fly right in.

The American press announced Admiral Byrd's discovery, but it was immediately suppressed by our good friends, the secret government. Ray Palmer, the editor of the magazine *Flying Saucer*, published a detailed story about Admiral Byrd's discoveries. The United States government bought, stole, or destroyed almost every copy and then destroyed the plates at the printing office. I have been told that exactly the same thing happened to an article about Admiral Byrd's discovery published by *National Geographic*. The magazine was released, and the U.S. government gobbled up almost every issue. If the story weren't true, why would the government be so nervous?

It is interesting to note that the United States government does not allow planes to fly over the poles. All flights are directed to go around the poles, and any airline pilot flying in those areas will confirm this. Another interesting point is that icebergs are composed of fresh water, not salt water. It is also curious that it is warmer near the poles than it is six hundred to one thousand miles away from them. The opening at the poles might also explain why there are so many UFO sightings in those areas.

In his book *The Hollow Earth*, Dr. Raymond Bernard tells of a man who has confirmed Admiral Byrd's story. Dr. Nephi Cotton of Los Angeles reported that one of his patients, a man of Nordic descent, told him the following story:

I lived near the Arctic Circle in Norway. One summer my friend and I made up our minds to take a boat trip together and go as far as we could into the north country. So we put a month's worth of provisions into a small fishing boat and set to sea.

At the end of one month we had traveled far into the north, beyond the pole and into a strange new country. We were much astonished at the weather there. It was warm, and at times at night it was almost too warm to sleep. Then we saw something so strange that we were both astonished. Ahead of us on the warm open sea was what looked like a great mountain. Into that mountain at a certain point the ocean seemed to be emptying. Mystified, we continued in that direction and found ourselves sailing into a vast canyon leading into the interior of the Earth. We kept sailing, and then we saw what surprised us . . . a sun shining inside the Earth.

The ocean that had carried us into the hollow interior of the Earth gradually became a river. This river led, as we came to realize later, all through the inner world, from one end to the other. It can take you, if you follow it long enough, from the North Pole clear through to the South Pole.

We saw that the inner surface of the Earth was divided, as the outer one is, into both land and water. There is plenty of sunshine and both animal and vegetable life abound there. We sailed farther and farther into this fantastic country — fantastic because everything was huge in size as compared with things on the outside. Plants were big, trees gigantic. Finally we came to giants themselves.

They were dwelling in homes and towns, just as we do on the Earth's surface, and they used a type of electrical conveyance like a monorail car to transport people. It ran along the river's edge from town to town.

Several of the inner Earth inhabitants, huge giants, detected our boat on the river and were quite amazed. They were, however, quite friendly. We were invited to dine with them in their homes, and so my companion and I separated, he going with one giant to that giant's home and I going with another giant to his home.

My gigantic friend brought me home to his family and I was completely dismayed to see the huge size of all the objects in his home. The dinner table was colossal. A plate was put before me and filled with a portion of food so big it would have fed me abundantly for an entire week. The giant offered me a cluster of grapes and each grape was as big as one of our peaches. I tasted one and found it far sweeter than any I had ever tasted outside. In the interior of the Earth all the fruits and vegetables taste far better and more flavorsome than those we have on the outer surface of the Earth.

We stayed with the giants for one year, enjoying their companionship as much as they enjoyed knowing us. We observed many strange and unusual things during our visit with these remarkable people and were continually amazed at their scientific progress and inventions. All of this time they were never unfriendly to us, and we were allowed to return to our own home in the same manner in which we came. . . . In fact, they courteously offered their protection if we should need it for the return voyage.

An additional account of a visit to the hollow Earth was told by another Norwegian, Olaf Jansen, and was recorded in *The Smoky God*, written by Willis George Emerson and published in 1908. (The term "smoky god" refers to the central sun in the hollow interior of the Earth, which is smaller and less brilliant than the outer sun and so appears smoky.) The book relates the experiences of a Norse father and his son who, in their small fishing boat, attempted to find "the land beyond the North wind," which they had heard about. A windstorm apparently carried them through the polar opening into the hollow interior of the Earth. They spent two years there and upon returning through the southern polar opening, the father lost his life when an iceberg broke in two and destroyed the boat. The son was rescued, but when he told his incredible story, he was placed in a prison for the insane because no one would believe him. After being released and spending twenty-six years as a fisherman, he moved to the United States. In his nineties he befriended Willis George Emerson and told him his story. On his deathbed he also gave Emerson maps that he had made of the interior of the Earth along with a manuscript relating his experiences.

He said that the people live for four hundred to eight hundred years and are twelve feet tall or more. Their scientific technology is very advanced. They can transmit their thoughts to each other using certain kinds of radiation and they have sources of power greater than electricity. They make "flying saucers" that are operated by this superior power, which is drawn from the electromagnetism in the atmosphere.

It is notable that in 1942, Nazi Germany sent out an expedition composed of some of its leading scientists in an attempt to find an entrance to the hollow Earth. Göring, Himmler, and Hitler enthusiastically endorsed the project. The führer was convinced that the Earth is concave and that humanity lives on the inside of the globe.

In *The Hollow Earth*, Bernard also tells of a photograph published in 1960 in the *Globe and Mail* in Toronto, Canada, which shows a beautiful valley with lush green hills. An aviator claimed that the picture had been taken from his airplane as he flew "beyond the North Pole."

Earlyne Chaney's Channelings about the Hollow Earth

Earlyne Chaney (channel for Kuthumi, the Virgin Mary, and Zoser, an Egyptian pharaoh) gives a fascinating account of how Agartha came into being in her book *Revelations of Things to Come*. She had a hard time accepting the truth of Agartha's existence, but her guides were absolutely adamant about it and its importance to human civilization both now and in the future.

Earlyne's channelings state that ages ago, very advanced souls came to Earth from other planets. She calls them the Anunnaki; their offspring on Earth are the Annu. It was these beings who brought the arks of the covenant that were used as laser guns and gravity control devices for the uplifting of the Earth's civilization. The Anunnaki and the Annu helped to build the great civilizations of Atlantis and Lemuria.

Eventually, the Anunnaki departed, leaving Earth in the hands of the Annu who had mated with Earthlings. As time went on, Atlantis began to be taken over by the Sons of Belial, or the Dark Brotherhood. The Annu, realizing destruction of Atlantis was approaching, fled to other lands, especially Egypt. They helped to build the pyramids with their arks of the covenant. However, they also used these instruments to bore deep underground, building underground tunnels and cities. When the deluge and pole shift were about to demolish Atlantis and Lemuria, the Annu entered their inner-Earth cities through the Great Pyramid. They then sealed the pyramid, preventing Earthlings from discovering their underground passages and keeping out the waters of the flood.

Agartha consists of vast continents, oceans, mountains, and rivers. Shamballa is its central city. The population there is highly evolved. She says that the civilizations of the Yucatan, Peru, Brazil, Cambodia, and Tibet also went underground and that many UFOs come from the inner Earth. She confirms that the Earth has an inner sun; the aurora borealis is a reflection of it. She also confirms that there are openings at both poles, as Admiral Byrd said.

It is interesting to note that the Egyptian government has found many of these tunnels and has tried to explore them over the past thirty years but they are so complex and extensive that they have recently been sealed for fear tourists would venture into them and get lost forever.

In another fascinating book by Chaney called *Beyond Tomorrow,* Robert Stacy-Judd, a noted archeologist from California, tells of being in the Yucatan and entering the stupendous cave of Loltun with a party of six researchers. They descended far into the depths of the Earth and then realized they were lost. They became very concerned when all of a sudden, from farther down in the depths, a light came toward them. The light turned out to be a torch carried by an old blind hermit who told them he had seen them clairvoyantly and knew they were lost. Even though blind, he proceeded to lead them back to the Earth's surface.

The men were exceedingly grateful and asked the hermit where he lived. The hermit told them that the cave was his home and that he came to the surface only every few months. When asked how he survived, how he found food and drink, he said that he was cared for by the friends who lived in the beautiful inner city in the depths of the Earth. He paused long enough to have his picture taken, then disappeared back into the cave.

Telos, beneath Mt. Shasta

I attended a lecture given by a woman named Sharula and her husband, Shield, who stated that she was something like three hundred fifty years old and that they came from the underground city of Telos, which apparently is a couple of miles beneath Mt. Shasta. I listened very intently to their teachings and have to admit they were both very sharp and knew their stuff, in a spiritual sense. I agreed with everything they said. However, I have to admit I did question her statement about being over three hundred fifty years old!

The next day, when I was receiving a healing treatment from a friend who is exceedingly clairvoyant, I told her about the lecture. She said that she could tell from a picture if what Sharula had said were true. I happened to have the advertisement for the lecture in my car, and it contained a picture of both Shield and Sharula.

Upon looking at Sharula's aura in the picture, my friend said that it was totally different from a normal human aura and that she felt that there was a good possibility that Sharula had been telling the truth about her age and home. My own intuition and inner guidance had felt it to be true; it was interesting to get this confirmation.

There are apparently underground tunnels and cities at various levels of the Earth's crust throughout the planet. Many of the beings who live there are apparently coming to the surface now, just as extraterrestrials are coming to Earth in great abundance.

Djwhal Khul's Channelings about the Hollow Earth

Whenever I research a subject I like to get Djwhal Khul's feedback on the information I have come up with. I told him what I had learned, and he had a number of interesting things to add.

First of all, he confirmed that Admiral Byrd had indeed traveled to the inner Earth as he had claimed. He said that there is a sun in the inner Earth, but that it is different from the outer sun. He said that the aurora borealis is not caused by the sun of the inner Earth but by a different light source. He said that the openings at the poles are very wide, so ships and planes can fly into them, but that they are naturally protected by an energy field. People can find them if they really search, even though they are camouflaged by the energy field. He confirmed that there are entrances to the inner Earth in Egypt, Tibet, and the Yucatan and added that there are other entrances in the Bermuda Triangle, the former Soviet Union, and Africa. He said that there are different races in the inner Earth, just as on the surface, and that some of them are quite tall. He also confirmed that the United States government and those of other countries are aware of the inner Earth and are hiding the information about it just as they are hiding their connections with extraterrestrials. He also confirmed Earlyne's story of the Annu and their escape into the tunnels just prior to the flood. However, he added that beings had been living there long before the Atlanteans came.

Among the Native American peoples, the Navajo legends teach that the forerunners of man came from beneath the Earth. The ancient ones had supernatural powers but were driven from their caverns by a great flood (Atlantis?). Once on the surface, they passed on their great knowledge to the human race before once again seeking their secret sanctuary.

The Pueblo Indians' mythology also places their gods' place of origin in the inner Earth. The inner world was supposedly connected to the surface people by a hole in the north.

The ancient writings of the Chinese, Egyptians, and Eskimos speak of a great opening in the north and of a race of people who live under the Earth's crust. The writings say that their ancestors came from the paradise land in the Earth's interior.

In the Buddhist tradition, ancient philosophy states that Agartha was first colonized many thousands of years ago when a holy man led a tribe that disappeared under the ground. The present population of that underground kingdom is believed to number many millions and the people are believed to possess a science, far superior to any found on the surface of the Earth, that includes cars that run at tremendous speeds through underground tunnels.

In the ancient legends of Quetzalcoatl, the great avatar of the Aztecs and Toltecs, it is told that he vanished on a flying saucer for eight days and visited the subterranean world.

Russian explorer Ferdinand Ossendowski, author of *Beasts, Men and Gods*, relates his own experiences in Mongolia. In his travels he came across Mongolian legends of the subterranean world of Agartha, ruled by the king of the world who resides in the holy city of Shamballa. The legend says that in ancient times, a Mongolian tribe seeking to escape Genghis Khan hid in a subterranean land. They were shown a door that turned out to be the entrance to the kingdom of Agartha. According to Ossendowski, who was considered a great authority on the subterranean worlds, Agartha extends through subterranean tunnels to all parts of the world. These tunnels run under both major oceans and under all continents of the Earth and there are swift vehicles that move through them. He believes that the inhabitants of both Atlantis and Lemuria found refuge there.

Hidden Cities

There are over one hundred subterranean colonies underneath the Earth, all but one of them quite close to the surface. These underground cities have been referred to as the Agartha Network. Their customs vary, but they follow a common, spiritually oriented structure of living – the Melchizedek teachings. (The Melchizedek are an ancient priesthood that disseminates the teachings of the Great White Brotherhood throughout the universe.) The average population of these cities is five hundred thousand, but Telos, beneath Mt. Shasta, has over 1.5 million inhabitants. A second colony of approximately the same size is located beneath the Matto Grosso Plains of Brazil. This Atlantean outpost is called Posid. Although Atlantis and Lemuria have become myth to most people on the surface of the Earth, in reality they are just continuing their evolution underground.

There are other inner world cities, including Shonshe, a refuge of the Uighur culture, a branch of the Lemurians. The entrance is guarded by a Himalayan lamasery and the population is three quarters of a million. Rama is a remnant of the surface city of Rama, India, and is located near Jaipur. The population is one million and the inhabitants are known for their classic Hindu features. Shingwa is a remnant of the northern migration of the Uighurs and is located on the border of Mongolia and China. It has a population of three quarters of a million.

Admiral Byrd's Diary

I would like to quote Admiral Byrd's own description in his diary of his experiences after entering the opening at the pole and traveling by plane to one of the main cities in the center of the Earth.

They were flying over a beautiful lush terrain of mountains, rivers, and streams. Byrd saw what at first looked like an elephant, but he then realized it was a mammoth prehistoric dinosaur. The external temperature was seventy-four degrees. The radio was not functioning. Suddenly before them was a beautiful rainbow-tinted city, and off each wing was a disk-shaped flying saucer. The engines of the plane stopped and their craft fell under control of the flying saucers. The plane was landed for them, and Admiral Byrd was taken to meet the king of the civilization living in the hollow Earth:

> "We have let you enter here because you are of noble character and well known on the surface world, Admiral." I half gasped under my breath! "Yes," the master replied with a smile, "you are in the domain of the Arianni, the inner world of the Earth. We shall not long delay your mission, and you will be safely escorted back to the surface and for a distance beyond. But now, Admiral, I shall tell you why you have been summoned here."

> "Our interest rightly begins just after your race exploded the first atomic bombs over Hiroshima and Nagasaki, Japan. It was at that alarming time we sent our flying machines, the flugelrads, to your surface world to investigate what your race had done. This is, of course, past history now, my dear Admiral, but I must continue on. You see, we have never interfered before in your race's wars and barbarity. But now we must, for you have learned to tamper with a certain power that is not for man, namely that of atomic energy. Our emissaries have already delivered messages to the powers of your world and yet they do not heed. Now you have been chosen to be witness here that our world does exist. You see, our culture and science are many thousands of years beyond your race, Admiral."

> I interrupted, "But what does this have to do with me, sir?"

> The master's eyes seemed to penetrate deeply into my mind, and after studying me for a few moments he replied, "Your race has now reached the point of no return, for there are those among you who would destroy your very world rather than relinquish their power as they know it." I nodded, and the master continued, "In 1945 and afterward, we tried to contact your race, but our efforts were met with hostility. Our flugelrads were fired upon, yes, even pursued with malice and animosity by your fighter planes. So, now I say to you, my son, there is a great storm gathering in your world, a black fury that will not spend itself for many years. There will be no answer in your arms, there will be no safety in your science. It may rage on until every flower of your culture is trampled, and all human things are leveled in vast chaos. Your recent war was only a prelude of what is yet to come for your race. We, here, see

it more clearly with each hour . . . do you say I am mistaken?

"I do," I answered. "It happened once before; the dark ages came and they lasted for more than five hundred years."

"Yes, my son," replied the master, "the dark ages that will come now for your race will cover the Earth like a pall, but I believe that some of your race will live through the storm. Beyond that, I cannot say. We see, at a great distance, a new world stirring from the ruins of your race, seeking its lost and legendary treasures, and they will be here, my son, safe in our keeping. When that time arrives, we shall come forward again to help revive your culture and your race. Perhaps by then you will have learned the futility of war and its strife . . . and after that time, certain of your culture and science will be returned for your race to begin anew.

"You, my son, are to return to the surface world with this message."

After this conversation, Admiral Byrd and his crew were led out of the great city and taken back to their plane. The plane was lifted into the air by some unseen force and transported back toward the opening at the North Pole on the surface of the Earth. The plane was released back into their command, and before they knew it they were again flying over vast areas of ice and snow.

On March 11, 1947, Admiral Byrd attended a staff meeting at the Pentagon and was ordered to remain silent in regard to all that he had learned on behalf of humanity. He was reminded that he was a military man and that he must obey orders. It was not until the end of his life that Admiral Byrd finally decided he could keep his experiences secret no longer, and his diary and recollections were made available to the world.

Harley Byrd, a nephew of Admiral Richard Byrd, has continued his uncle's work. He revealed that seventy-seven alien bodies were taken from an underground city and were being secretly studied by the U.S. government in holding tanks. He said he saw the photographs as well as the bodies in the holding tanks when he worked in the offices of the U.S. Air Force's Blue Book project in the 1950s.

I would like to acknowledge Raymond Bernard's book, *The Hollow Earth*, as one of the sources of the information in this chapter.

3

Walk-ins

*The transfer is very much like
major surgery on an electrical level. There are
teams of spirit guides who help in this transfer
just as one would have during major
surgery in a hospital on Earth.*

Ascended Master Djwhal Khul

W alk-ins are soul extensions, or personalities, who take over the body of an adult human being who has chosen to leave his or her physical body. Djwhal Khul has told me that this is an occurrence that has not been very common in the history of this planet. However, it has been occurring much more frequently recently because of the amazing shift this planet is going through as it moves into the new age. Djwhal said that there are as many as one million walk-ins on the planet at this time.

It is important to explain that this process is usually governed by and controlled at the soul level. The soul extension, or personality, who is walking out of the body usually has no conscious awareness of the procedure. It is usually the soul who has made the decision, although in some rare instances the personality has requested it.

In most cases the new walk-in who takes over the body has no conscious awareness of the change, either. The transition period can take anywhere from three months to six years to transpire. It is usually very disconcerting to the walk-out's emotional body because there is a process of sharing the physical body with the other entity for a period of time, and, in most cases, the walk-out is not conscious of what is occurring.

Entities of all levels and states of consciousness can be walk-ins and it is not limited to sixth-dimensional beings, according to the information I have received from Djwhal Khul. The walk-in will come into the new physical body only, of course, if the walk-out has agreed to it on a soul level.

The second important ingredient is that the souls, or higher selves, and the spirit guides of the walk-in and the walk-out feel that the physical vehicle is strong enough and the emotional vehicle stable enough for the process to work effectively. Such a transfer is very much like major surgery on an etheric level. Teams of spirit guides help in the transfer. It is a very delicate procedure.

It is very important to point out the difference between a walk-in and a possession: a possession is a forced entry into a person's auric field that can cause the entity living in that body to be booted out. Djwhal has told me that the negative extraterrestrials have attempted possessions and have even succeeded at times. Most possessions, however, do not result in the existing entity's being booted out of its body. This is very rare and nothing to be fearful about if you have a spiritual belief and any sense of your own personal power, and as long as you are not a drug addict or an alcoholic.

Djwhal Khul has told me that Adolph Hitler was a walk-in. The Dark Brotherhood facilitated the shifting of one of their high-ranking members into Hitler's body. Adolph Hitler was on the dark path himself before he left, but the new entity was even darker in consciousness.

There is no karmic penalty when a walk-out chooses to leave his or her existing body.

The concept of a walk-in is sometimes hard for people to believe. If you think about it, everyone is a walk-in in the sense that everyone walks into a baby's body. The only difference is that the walk-in moves into an adult body rather than an infant body.

A walk-in gets to skip the whole childhood phase, which at first glance sounds pretty good. Djwhal has told me, however, that being a walk-in is no piece of cake. It is traumatic to the entity who is coming in as well as to the entity who is walking out. The walk-in is, in a sense, taking on some of the karma of the walk-out — both the karma in the physical vehicle and all the brain memories of the walk-out remain with the new walk-in. Part of the responsibility of the new walk-in is to balance and clear the personal karma that was left behind by the entity that has left. In most cases the entity that leaves has been very depressed and suicidal or has just had a major accident. A new entity walks in to a preexisting complex of marriage, children, and friends. Because the brain memories are left by the walk-out in the physical structure of the brain, the walk-in is able to function in such a way that the wife or husband and family might not realize they are not dealing with the same entity. They will in most cases notice a big change, but they will attribute it to a change in attitude, not a change in entities.

Since walk-ins are not consciously aware, in almost all cases, that they are walk-ins, because they have all the brain memories of the walk-out, they are disoriented for a time, but they also feel that they are where they belong.

Djwhal told me that the ascended masters are not usually involved in this process. It is more the soul and spirit guides and the soul extension who make such a decision. Once the exchange has taken place, walk-ins live normal lives. The motivation to be of service to the planet will depend on their levels of spiritual evolvement.

If you think about it, the concept of walk-ins is rather expedient, for if an entity wants to leave the physical body, it is a shame to waste that physical vehicle if someone else could use it for spiritual growth. However, it takes a very bold soul and soul extension to make this choice, for it is not an easy or glamorous path to take. This period of history on Planet Earth is such an exciting time in a spiritual sense that many entities are willing to take on the karma and risk in order to be a part of the action. Physical bodies of all kinds are at a premium during this period of time.

Ruth Montgomery's spirit guides have said that the following people were walk-ins: Abraham Lincoln, Gandhi, Benjamin Franklin, Emanuel Swedenborg, Meister Eckhart, Shankara, Moses, Quetzalcoatl, and Christopher Columbus. I have not confirmed the truth of this information, but I bring it forth for your discernment and consideration.

Before a walk-in enters the new body, the entity spends a great deal of time studying the Akashic Records and physical behaviors of the walk-out to determine how to master the physical body, personal lessons, and karma it is about to take on. The actual moment of exchange usually occurs during sleep. A person who is contemplating suicide might consider being a walk-out as a better alternative if it truly is his time to leave his body.

I want to emphasize that walk-ins are not ascended masters. They are soul extensions who are still on the karmic wheel of rebirth at varying levels of initiation and spiritual awareness. Lord Maitreya, who came into Jesus' body at the baptism, would not be called a walk-in. The esoteric term for this process in which two entities, in a sense, share the same body is "overshadowing."

At some later date a walk-in might begin to remember that he or she is a walk-in. This can be an emotionally traumatic experience. Walking in can be additionally difficult because the transfer has often taken place during a serious illness or near-death experience of the walk-out. A walk-out is really donating his physical body to another soul to use instead of letting it die of natural causes or destroying it through suicide.

In the transition period during the changeover there are also, very often, physical health problems as well as emotional problems. Very often, on subconscious levels, there is a kind of ego battle that is taking place between the walk-in and the walk-out. The soul, or higher self, is conscious of the process, but since the personality in embodiment is not conscious of what is going on, it can be extremely confusing and a very wrenching process. The entire fiber of the soul must be completely removed from every cell of the physical body and four-body system and replaced with the soul fiber of the incoming entity. It can be likened to having major heart surgery.

Even though the walk-in has all the physical memories of the walk-out, the entity doesn't have the same feelings since it is a different entity. For example, in the case of a walk-in coming in to the marriage of the walk-out, the walk-in will retain all the physical memories, so everything will seem normal in that sense, but the entity will feel somewhat distant, strange, and out of place. Physically, everything will seem normal, but the new emotional body will not have adjusted yet. The fact that the walk-in doesn't realize he is a walk-in helps in the adjustment process since he or she still has the physical memories of being married and so forth.

After going through an adjustment period the walk-in will literally begin a new life. Walk-ins tend to be of a highly evolved nature, although there are exceptions to this. Walk-ins usually don't awaken to the fact that they are walk-ins unless a spiritual teacher tells them of it, which does happen and which is happening with greater and greater frequency. What also helps in the adjustment process is the fact that the entity has had a long time to prepare for this event on the inner plane.

It is often a bizarre and difficult situation for a spouse and family to deal with. At the same time, it often happens that people who know the walk-in and notice a change say something like, "She hasn't been the same since her accident" and let that be the extent to which they take the train of thought.

When the actual changeover takes place, it occurs during a one-night period while the physical body is sleeping. The soul, the spirit guides, and the specialized spirit guide team of walk-in and walk-out experts perform the metaphysical operation of slipping one soul extension out of the physical body and slipping the new one in.

It is only in the past two or three decades that the phenomenon of walk-ins has really expanded. Previous to that it was a much rarer occurrence. Djwhal has told me that this increase in walk-ins will continue for the next twenty to thirty years and then will begin to taper off again and become less common. Some walk-ins have the specific focus of helping other walk-ins, and they are the ones who advertise themselves as such in metaphysical newspapers.

4

Extraterrestrial Activity

If the average person had any idea how many extraterrestrial civilizations have contacted or are currently contacting Earth, he/she would be astonished.

During his training to become a Planetary Logos, Sanat Kumara incarnated into nine hundred thousand different planets in this Milky Way Galaxy alone. God's universe is filled with life forms both on the material plane and in all other dimensions of reality. The notion that Earth is the only planet supporting physical life is just about the most egoistical notion a person could possibly believe. There is so much extraterrestrial activity occurring on this planet that I will be able to touch only the surface in this book.

There are a number of systems that have been intimately involved in Earth's history since humanity's physical inception upon the planet. These primary extraterrestrial contacts have come from:

1. Lyra
2. Vega
3. Zeta Reticulum
4. Arcturus
5. Sirius
6. Orion
7. The Pleiades

The United States government is aware of seventy different extraterrestrial civilizations that are contacting the Earth; in reality, there are thousands. To begin with, I would like to look at visitors to Earth from within Earth's own galaxy, the Milky Way.

5

The Pleiades

*The activation of the twelve strands
of DNA coincides with the activation, spinning,
movement, and opening of the twelve
centers of information.*

through Barbara Marciniak

The Pleiades is a star cluster in the constellation of Taurus, which lies approximately five hundred light-years from Earth. There are two hundred and fifty to five hundred stars within this cluster, although only nine of them have been named by humans on Earth. The Pleiades is often referred to as the Seven Sisters.

We have received a great deal of information about the Pleiades from numerous sources. Billy Meier of Switzerland has had the most profound contact and has made more documented accounts of extraterrestrial activity than almost any other person on the planet. He was first contacted by a female from the Pleiades by the name of Semjase. She has said that she comes from the planet Erra, which looks something like the lower Swiss Alps. Her race is human-like in appearance; however, they are far advanced, both technologically and spiritually. On her planet, her profession is that of communicator with other races. She has actually trained for this job. Her people contact a civilization only when its members have developed into thinking, rational beings. She has said that she has many purposes in coming here:

    1. To share with the Earth people the information that they are not alone in this universe;

    2. To help guide Earth people in terms of religions and their repression of the human spirit;

3. To warn Earth people that there are a few negative extraterrestrial races visiting this planet whose purpose is to try to take over the planet for their own selfish purposes;

4. To warn Earth people that their animalistic nature is destroying the ecological environment within which they live;

5. To help Earth people both spiritually and technologically, as long as that help is used in the service of the Creator.

The Pleiadians are able to travel vast distances in their spacecraft by entering hyperspace. They are able to overcome space and time and enter what they call null time. In that split second they can travel millions of light-years. The entire trip from Earth to the Pleiades takes only seven hours. It would occur even faster, but they cannot enter or leave hyperspace too close to an existing planet. Their average life span is over one thousand years of Earth time. Semjase is still quite young, for she is only three hundred and thirty, which would correspond to thirty-three years of age on Earth.

She and her crew studied the Earth languages while on her planet. This was accomplished by using a machine that facilitated a hypnosis-like state which allows the programming of the language skills into the subconscious mind. To learn a language on their planet takes only twenty-one days, plus nine or ten days to be able to speak it correctly.

Semjase has said that her craft are crash-proof because of a built-in automatic device that calculates the probability factors of failure of a mechanical apparatus days before it happens. On some of the motherships they actually have androids, which are half mechanical, half organic artificial beings that resemble man to a large extent. (*Star Trek's* Data might be much more true to life than you realized!) Semjase's planet is three thousand years ahead of Earth in terms of its technology. The craft have cloaking devices that prevent them from being seen, even if they are right in front of you.

The Pleiadians believe in God and in reincarnation and are here only to be of service. They do not see themselves as perfect and superior to humans, but rather as brothers and sisters in a greater spiritual family. They teach that clock time is a mental construction of Earth humans, and that humans will never be able to travel very far in space until they fully realize that.

The Pleiadians belong to a union of planets reaching far out into the universe and involving somewhere around one hundred twenty-seven billion people. They are also connected to an even larger group called the Association of Worlds. This is a group of both physical and nonphysical beings from many different levels of consciousness. It has also been called a galactic confederation of planets. It is their hope that humanity will soon rise above its barbaric, animalistic nature and be able to join this association. All the galactic civilizations mentioned in this chapter are under the auspices of a council based in the star system Andromeda.

Very often Pleiadians are present in everyday life, even though the average person on the street would never know it. They are able to breathe Earth's air, but prolonged exposure results in sinus problems due to the pollution level. If they get into a jam for some reason, they can usually get out of it easily because of their ability to influence the thoughts of the average human being on Earth.

They have viewing devices on their spacecraft that allow them to see into solid material. For example, they were able to see inside of the American and Soviet spacecraft during their maneuvers in space. Their motherships are almost like small planets which more than one hundred forty-three thousand Pleiadians can inhabit comfortably. Everything that is necessary for life is produced aboard the craft. The motherships are able to travel billions of light-years in a second. She said that this mothership, which is over 10.6 miles long, was used for intragalactic patrol to oversee law and order.

When Semjase was asked if there were an end to the universe, she said that there is no end but that there is a barrier where this universe touches the next one. She referred to this next universe as the Dal universe. The people of the Dal universe are about three hundred fifty years more advanced than even the Pleiadians, technologically. The Pleiadians have become quite friendly with these beings, and they helped the Pleiadians with the building of their most recent motherships.

The Dals are a handsome Nordic-looking race, much like the northern European Caucasians. They are able to breathe Earth's atmosphere without special equipment. It must be understood, however, that many, if not most, extraterrestrials do not have the Adam Kadmon style of physical bodies humans have. It is important that humans not be frightened by the differences.

Billy Meier had the opportunity to meet Semjase's father, who was able to speak with Billy Meier in German because he wore an apparatus around his waist that was a language converter. They also have devices that allow them to teleport themselves, much like the apparatus on *Star Trek*. Once, during some picture-taking, Meier noticed that a particular tree was missing, yet the ground where it had once stood was completely normal in appearance. When asked about this, Semjase said that it had been moved by changing its time.

The Lyran Civilization

In 1977, a different spacecraft landed in front of Billy Meier's home. This craft carried three beings aboard, one of whom introduced herself as Menara from the star system Lyra. She said that their planet had a population of fourteen billion and also belonged to the Confederation of Planets. She said that her people worked closely with the Pleiadians and with the people of the Dal universe. She said that her ship was constructed three hundred years in the Earth's future and had been used for over two hundred fifty years already. The Lyrans' technology is apparently several thousand years ahead of even that of the Dals.

Alena, a member of the crew, returned another time in her own ship. She said she came from the star system Vega, which is a part of the Lyran constellation. The Vegans are apparently descendants of the early Lyrans, as are the Pleiadians.

The Lyrans were the original ancestors of humanity's galactic family. Many thousands of years ago, their civilization reached a very high technological level; however, they fell into disagreement, and factions developed within the culture. These factions went to war and destroyed much of the society. Many of the beings from Lyra left in their starships to colonize the Pleiades, the Hyades, and the Vega system.

Some of these Pleiadians of Lyran ancestors also came to Earth during the Lemurian and Atlantean periods. The Lyrans have long since evolved past the conflict and past the war-like stage of evolution. The other civilizations could be looked at as humans' galactic cousins.

God has created different kinds of bodies for different types of gravities and climate conditions but all are brothers and sisters in a universal family, even if from an average human perspective, others appear to be ugly, strange, or distorted. It is important to remember that beauty is in the eye of the beholder, and humans can look just was weird to others. There are extraterrestrials who are small, tall, reptilian-like, insect-like, crocodile-looking, and with slanted eyes, no hair, big heads, long fingers, and so forth. The *Star Wars* bar scene is more truth than fiction.

The Lyran races began evacuating their home planet over twenty-two million years ago, at which time they visited Hyperboria, one of the earliest continents on Planet Earth in Pre-Lemurian times. (Madam Blavatsky writes about it in *The Secret Doctrine*. The earliest societies on Earth learned from the visiting Lyrans.

Vegan technology is about two hundred fifty years ahead of Pleiadian technology. Vegans are also in contact with the Dal universe and are being assisted by them. The Vegans are darker in skin color than the Lyrans, and they have higher cheekbones and more triangular faces. The Vegans also helped to colonize star systems such as Altair, Centauri, Sirius, and Orion, among others. Altair lies around fifteen light-years from Earth. The Altair civilization is quiet and contemplative, given to peaceful philosophic pursuits. They are not currently involved in space exploration. All these civilizations are guided by nonphysical beings who sit on the Andromeda Council. Andromeda is a large spiral galaxy, the closest to the Milky Way at a distance of 2.2 million light-years.

More about the Pleiadians

All Pleiadians have small gardens in which they work with their own hands. For them it is a way of staying in touch with the Creator. They all work for two hours each day in their factories, overseeing their automated machines and robots. The Pleiadians go to school until they are in their seventies. Every person must be familiar with twelve to twenty professions. They mature in body in twelve to twenty-five years but do not marry until they are at least seventy years old and have completed their chosen education. The median age for those who marry is one hundred ten. Both spouses must pass strict mental and physical examinations before they are allowed to marry. No one is forced to marry and many don't.

The Pleiadians have, apparently, a number of ground stations on Earth, one of them in the Swiss Alps which has been in existence for seventy years. It is in an enclosed valley between some very high mountain peaks and has no vehicle access. It is totally protected and cannot be seen from the air.

Life on the planet Erra is peaceful and harmonious. The buildings are circular in formation and are sometimes made of glass or even quartz crystal which creates rainbow patterns of light. Each home has land around it, and horticulture is a popular activity. Some of the flowers on Erra actually change color throughout the day to get maximum benefit from the sun. The environment and atmosphere are quiet and serene with none of the noise pollution that exists on Earth.

The Pleiadians vibrate to the color blue. They are, hence, attuned to the ideals of truth and justice. The Pleiadian civilization is one of the most advanced in this galaxy when it comes to music and dance. The new forms of music they are presenting to Earth will raise the vibrational frequencies of all who listen to it. This music of the spheres will help to open the higher chakras, which will open humanity to greater creativity and knowledge. The Pleiadians are also experts in the use of light. They will be helping to bring forth on Earth great advancements in the use of holograms and laser technology.

Wendelle C. Stevens' wonderful book, *UFO: Contact from the Pleiades,* has served as a source for much of the information in this chapter.

6

Orion

*The Orion civilization was one of the
very few that evolved into a state of technological
advancement while still being in a state
of intense spiritual conflict.*

through Lyssa Royal
in *The Prism of Lyra*

Civilization in Orion, according to information channeled by Lyssa Royal, was unusual in that advanced technology was developed before internal conflict was resolved. In the Orion conflict there were two groups: the negative side, which believed in the concept of serving the self, convincing themselves that the whole would be served thereby, even though it actually translates into seeking domination over others; and the positive side, which held the ideal of being of service to others. Does this sound familiar? It is the exact same conflict that occurred in Atlantis between the Sons of Belial and the believers in the Law of One. It is the exact same conflict that occurs in the present world today — serving ego or serving God.

This Orion conflict played out for eons in a most destructive and disturbing manner. Three groups formed: the dominators, the victims, and the resistance. The dominators were the Orion Empire; the Black League was the resistance to the evil domination of the empire. Does this sound familiar? The movie *Star Wars* was actually based on this Orion conflict. The Empire attempted to dominate mentally, emotionally, and technologically and even devised methods of control using the psychic arts.

A great spiritual avatar came forward and awakened the inhabitants of Orion to the Law of Love and Forgiveness, which facilitated the beginning of a mass awakening for the civilization. There are parts of the Orion system that have awakened and parts that are still trying to dominate. One of those still trying to dominate in the Orion system is the reptilian race.

The positive Orions who are visiting the Earth are contributing their advanced mental power for the development of smoothly running systems of organization on Earth. These Orions resonate to the color yellow, and they beam this frequency to Earth for the purpose of stabilizing the intuitive powers within human consciousness.

This information is from Lyssa Royal's *The Prism of Lyra*, a book that is well worth reading.

7

Ummo

*Extraterrestrials from the planet Ummo have
bases on Earth in at least eight countries.*

Antonio Ribera

Antonio Ribera tells, in *UFO: Contact from Planet Ummo*, of his contact with a group of beings from the planet Ummo who arrived in
1950, established their bases, and acclimatized themselves. In 1965 they
began to make contact with twenty people in Spain. Most of these people
had some openness to the possibility of extraterrestrials, for they all belonged to a group called The Society of Friends of Space. The Ummites
said they also had contact with other groups all over the world.

They claimed that in 1948 they picked up a strange radio signal which
they were unable to decipher. They eventually traced it to this solar system.
The actual transmission had occurred in 1934 and had taken fourteen
years to reach their planet; later Earthly investigations confirmed that the
transmission had occurred.

The Ummites were surprised at there being intelligent life on this
planet and decided to investigate this civilization. They first landed in La
Javie in Les Basses Alpes in France. The landing was unobserved and an
investigative party of four men and two women was left on Earth.

The Ummites told Antonio Ribera that their planet orbits a star
astronomers refer to as Wolf 424 which is fourteen light-years from Earth.
The planet Ummo is quite similar to Earth. The Ummites are extremely
telepathic. They very much believe in the existence of the soul and in a
Creator God. At the age of 13.7, Ummite children leave their families for
teaching centers where they are prepared for adult life. They make practical use of at least ten dimensions of reality and are aware of far more. They

say one of the reasons they are able to travel such far distances in such a short time in their spacecraft is that they use folds and warps in the space continuum. They have sophisticated technology, and their craft can exceed the speed of light. Although similar to humans in appearance, one marked physiological difference is that their fingers are very sensitive to light and other forms of radiation. For this reason they find it difficult to use light switches and electrical apparatus of all kinds.

It was in 1967 that the group in Madrid began to receive an extraordinary number of phone calls and letters from the Ummites on Earth. They hired a typist to type all the letters and told this person they were Danish doctors. When the typist became uncomfortable with the content of the letters, the Ummites produced a tiny sphere, just an inch or so in diameter. This sphere was placed in midair, and as the typist looked into it he saw a scene that had occurred the preceding day when he had been at home with his wife. There was no logical explanation for how this could have been done unless the Ummites were telling the truth about themselves.

They eventually opened bases in eight other countries. Researchers have received over one thousand seven hundred forty pages of written material from the Ummites in Spanish and French and over six thousand in all languages combined. Their ships have been photographed six different times with scores of witnesses of each sighting. Landing tracks have been found on the ground, and metal artifacts have been recovered.

I am grateful to Antonio Ribera for recording this information in *UFO: Contact from Planet Ummo.*

8

Iarga

*The people of Earth do not have
the values or ethics of an advanced civilization
and this is blocking the way for the people of
Earth to achieve cosmic integration.*

The Iargans

The planet Iarga is about ten light-years from Earth's Sun. I first became aware of this advanced civilization when I read *UFO: Contact from Planet Iarga* by Stefan Denaerde and Lt. Col. Wendelle C. Stevens. Denaerde's first contact occurred while on his boat with his wife. In the middle of the ocean they bumped into a flat metallic object floating in the water. Then he saw a body and dived in to save the person. To his surprise, the individual was wearing some kind of metallic suit. Upon pulling him to safety, Denaerde noticed that the metallic fabric that remained under the water had lit up.

Coming toward him was another being with a human body but an animal's face. Denaerde tried to escape, but his boat wouldn't move. The extraterrestrial beings got the body and then left. From the platform on their craft, they politely bowed.

Denaerde began to relax when they spoke to him in English and thanked him for rescuing their crewmember. They proceeded to tell him that they came from another solar system. That began a long discussion which ended up in an agreement between them that Denaerde would spend two days with them on their ship while they told him about life on their planet.

They are a very advanced society, both technologically and spiritually, and they began by saying that they had not made themselves known to humanity because those of Earth do not know the laws of higher civilization or have the values and ethics of an advanced civilization, and that is preventing Earth from achieving cosmic integration. To share advanced technological information with a spiritually and socially undeveloped planet would be a crime and would be against cosmic law. They noted that humans are carrying on probes to Mars when half the world's population lives in poverty and hunger. Cosmic isolation can be lifted only when a minimum level of ethics has been reached. This communication with Denaerde was their first open physical contact.

They invited Denaerde into their spacecraft and showed him a sort of holographic film of their planet and civilization. Their planet has a much thicker atmosphere, so the people of Iarga do not see bright sunlight, and they see nothing of a moon or stars. Iarga is a green planet with a misty light (they refer to Earth as the blue planet) and the bright green ocean covers most of Iarga's surface. The temperature range is much smaller, but rain and snow can be ten times greater. Since the population is one hundred times larger than that of Earth, and the amount of dry land is much less than that of Earth, they have to be extremely efficient in how they run their society.

Denaerde viewed amazing house facilities and transoceanic rail connections. There is no money on Iarga. They have an entirely different kind of political and economic system based on total equality for all. They call this system cosmic economics; it is not like either communism or capitalism.

They hold selfless service, immortality, and cosmic integration as their highest goals. There are no class distinctions, and chores are shared by everyone. Females and males are equals. Their society is entirely based on a sort of Christian love. The Iargans stand approximately five feet tall. They were originally amphibians and still have webs between their fingers and toes. Their sex drive is totally different from sexuality on Earth, for theirs is born completely of love and never of lust. A male-female relationship based only on sex would be considered completely degrading. Their consciousnesses function according to the principle of mind over matter. They view Earth's isolation as being not only isolation from extraterrestrial intelligence but also isolation from God and the goals of His creation. Earth's isolation will end when the masses of humanity acknowledge God and their true purpose for being on Earth.

There is much more I could say about this fascinating civilization, but I just want to give you a sense of an interesting galactic neighbor. These beings might look strange in appearance, but there is nothing strange about what lives in their hearts and consciousnesses. For more information, I recommend reading *UFO: Contact from Planet Iarga*; this book by Denaerde and Stevens is the source of the material in this chapter.

9

Mars

*The purpose of my coming
is to help man return to God.*

Valiant Thor,
Martian visitor

O ne of the most amazing extraterrestrial contacts I have come across
in my research was a physical visitation to Earth by a being from
Mars. This being was a guest of the United States government for over
three years! His name was Valiant Thor.

His first known contact with government officials occurred in March
1957 when the Alexandria (Virginia) Police Department notified the Pentagon that two on-duty police officers had picked up an alien. His physical
appearance was similar to that of a human.

He was immediately shuttled underground to meet the Secretary of
Defense and President Dwight D. Eisenhower. He warned President Eisenhower that the world was in a very precarious state and that if it continued
to move in the direction in which it was going, it was headed for self-destruction. Besides the dangers of nuclear war there was also worldwide
economic collapse to be concerned about. He indicated that his race lived
underground. (As I have mentioned, bases have been set up on Mars, and
NASA photos show past civilizations there.)

When I first came in contact with this story through Dr. Frank
Stranges' book, *Stranger at the Pentagon*, I immediately asked Djwhal
Khul about the truth or fiction of Valiant Thor's existence, and Djwhal told
me the information is true.

Valiant Thor was immediately liked by those who met him. His ability
in thought transference and his goodwill were notable. He and his people

offered to help the human family. The President stated that he thought that if he accepted the help of Val, along with that of the High Council of Mars, it would throw the economy of the United States into chaos.

NASA scientists found Val's spacesuit to be indestructible. Diamond drill bits and even lasers couldn't affect it. In private conversations with Dr. Frank Stranges, a UFO researcher, Val said that his purpose in coming was to help man return to God. He said that seventy-seven of his crew were walking among the people of the United States. One thing that astounded scientists was that he had no finger prints.

Val was instructed by his High Council on Mars to leave on March 16, 1960. In the three years during which he was a guest of the United States government, very few people took advantage of his guidance. On that date he dematerialized and departed from his Earthly mission.

Dr. Frank Stranges, who had befriended Valiant Thor and had listened to his guidance, was driving in his car in Beverly Hills, California, a year later when Valiant Thor appeared in the back seat. Meetings such as that continued for the next several years.

Communication bases began to be set up in people's homes around the world, using equipment far beyond normal technology. One of the instruments was a holographic communicator that allowed you to see the person you were communicating with so realistically that you couldn't tell if the holographic image was real or not.

Val told of a mothership, his home base, which currently orbits this planet. Dr. Stranges had the opportunity to visit Val's spacecraft. He was served a food of high protein value and a drink that was green in color and tasted like papaya. The ship had no square corners, and the crew was briefed each morning only after a kind of worship service.

Subsequently, Dr. Stranges had a number of run-ins with what people in the extraterrestrial movement call the Men in Black. From what I have been able to gather, they are a group of people on Earth who physically intimidate and sometimes kill those people who are openly discussing the UFO phenomenon. I have read of hundreds of cases of this kind of harassment. Some believe that they are from other planets. Djwhal Khul told me that they are from this planet. These men are very evil, and any person openly involved with extraterrestrials needs to be aware of their presence.

At the time of the writing of *Stranger at the Pentagon* in 1967, there were, according to Val, one hundred three victor-class spacecraft from Mars on or near the surface of the Earth, at some two hundred eighty-seven locations. The first victor-class craft visited Earth nearly six thousand years ago. The total number of crew on one victor-class craft is two hundred. Many classes about Earth are taught aboard the craft, including Earth sciences, Earth people and their habits, the fall of humankind and the salvation by Jesus Christ, the psychology of the human being, the reason for the human being, the history of humankind, and the ultimate position of humankind in the universe.

With gratitude, I thank Dr. Frank Stranges for recording the information in this chapter in his book *Stranger at the Pentagon.*

10

Venus

*Their mission is to help the Adamic race
(humans) develop on mental, moral,
and material levels.*

Extraterrestrials from Venus

People on Planet Earth have been being contacted by beings from Venus for at least the past 18.5 million years because Sanat Kumara, Earth's Planetary Logos, came from Venus with one hundred five brother kumaras to initiate the Spiritual Hierarchy for this planet. Venus is a sister planet that embodies the love focus. She is a sacred planet and serves as an elder sister in a planetary sense. You might not know that Jesus came from Venus, as did Buddha, for they are also kumaras.

This extraterrestrial contact story is from a book called *The White Sands Incident*, by Dr. Daniel Fry. The book tells the story of Mr. Rolf Telano and his extraterrestrial contact with a Venusian named Borealis. Borealis is a member of an extraterrestrial race called the Nors, who are one of the elder races, or guardian races, of Planet Earth.

The story begins on a deserted country road in 1950 when Rolf Telano saw a spacecraft land about seventy feet in front of him. The craft was spheroid in shape and flattened on the top and the bottom. The dimensions of the craft were sixteen feet high by about thirty feet wide. Rolf went up to get a closer look and had reached out to touch the craft when a voice sharply said, "Better not touch the hull, pal, it's still hot! Take it easy, you're among friends."

It turned out that the craft was a remote-controlled cargo vehicle, and there were no extraterrestrials aboard. The Venusians who were controlling the craft were in a mothership nine hundred miles above, watching Rolf and talking to him through the communication system on the craft. The cargo craft was on an exploratory mission to collect samples of the Earth's atmosphere so that Borealis could get accustomed to the atmosphere before embarking on his mission to actually live on Earth.

Rolf was invited to go for a ride and was told that if he wanted to, they would travel to New York and back in thirty minutes. Given the fact that New York was two thousand miles away, that meant they would have to travel at a speed of eight thousand miles an hour. He was told he would not feel the acceleration in the slightest. He accepted their offer and they were true to their word, giving him one of the great experiences of his life.

The Venusians said that tens of thousands of years ago, their ancestors had actually lived on the Earth in the civilization known as Lemuria. They built a great empire and developed science and technology on the planet, but eventually they had to leave.

During a second contact, the Venusians requested Rolf's help in their mission to be of service to Planet Earth and its people. They told him that it would not be easy, that he would probably not be believed and would be ridiculed, but that he would receive great satisfaction for assisting the survival of his race and would also gain considerable knowledge and understanding. They also told him that if he refused, there was no penalty, but they would have to erase his memories of meeting them. Rolf agreed to help. Since this contact occurred in 1950 when the masses of humanity were not quite as open to the idea that extraterrestrials exist as they are now, they wanted Rolf to write a book and share his experiences and the Venusians' message with the inhabitants of Earth — that Planet Earth is not alone in the universe.

Borealis was actually a High Priest of the Mother Temple on Venus. They are monotheists and refer to God as "the Unnameable," which, interestingly enough, echos Judaism. Borealis' present home is not on Venus but on a higher-frequency world that is somewhat larger than Venus, much as Sanat Kumara and his brother kumaras first came to Earth from Venus as etheric beings.

The Nors are mortal beings even though they are not physical in the sense that humans are physical. They are etheric beings who are able to make themselves physical either with their own mind power or by using special instruments they wear on their belts. They can materialize into any race of being or any animal form. They regard themselves as brothers and sisters of humans. According to Borealis, in 1950, the Nors were the largest group of extraterrestrials operating in this solar system. Their actual appearance is similar to that of Earth's Nordic races who, they say, took their name from them.

This particular race of Nors lives in several different solar systems.

They have bases and colonies on Mars and Venus. They also have a base on the Moon, as do several other groups of extraterrestrials. Other extraterrestrial groups often use Mars and Venus as check-in points since they are the planets closest in proximity to Earth.

Their spacecraft is controlled manually, automatically, or by mind power. The Venusians who operate the craft are much more skilled in the mental sciences than are the rest of their people. Many craft are operating in the vicinity of the Earth even though most people don't see them unless they are clairvoyant or unless the Venusians choose to materialize their ships.

They use seven different types of ships besides the motherships that transport the smaller craft. Five of these carry crews while two are robotic in nature. Two kinds of craft are crescent in shape like a disk from which a bite has been taken. Another one is cigar-shaped and is about one hundred feet long and twenty-five feet wide. Yet another type of craft is doughnut-shaped. The other three types are spherical, or ball-shaped.

Their space patrols work under a Galactic Council composed of representatives from all the advanced planets. The space patrol executes the orders of the Galactic Council and can serve as an armed force in extreme cases. The craft are heavily armed with disintegrator rays that make an H-bomb look like a bow and arrow. These weapons are hardly ever used but are available in an emergency. They guard backward planets such as Earth from outside threats. They also teach ethical and scientific information where appropriate under universal law. The crews are made up of men and women, and often families travel together.

The people on Venus have a much higher ethical and moral standard than the people on Earth have. Their highest ethical foundation is that of universal brotherhood. They regard all intelligent beings on all planets throughout the universe, no matter what type of physical bodies they might have, as their brothers and sisters; they might be on a low level of evolvement, but they are still brothers.

Venusians teach that each being's inner self is part of the Unnameable One. To hurt a brother or sister is no different from biting off your own tongue or gouging out your own eye in a fit of anger. In a spiritual sense, Venusians know other people are a part of themselves to the same extent that humans perceive their physical bodies to be part of themselves.

The people on Venus are highly telepathic. Moral pressure, hence, becomes a powerful instrument, for it is hard for anyone to conceal anything. Divorce is almost unknown. Their life span is several thousand years, and then they do get old. Since everyone believes in reincarnation, they choose two trusted friends to be parents for their next body. Wouldn't that be nice!

The population is relatively stable because of their long lifespan, and children are much rarer than they are on Earth. Children are not seen as possessions but rather as friends who require a temporary amount of care and protection until they have regained their previous memory.

The mission of the Venusians is to help the Adamic (human) race develop on mental, moral, and material levels. They have been working with Earth since its inception; however, they are usually present in greater numbers during times of crisis. The present transition of this planet from the Piscean to the Aquarian Age is one of those times. Since the dropping of the atomic bombs on Hiroshima and Nagasaki, they have been especially focused on Earth, for obvious reasons.

11

The Ashtar Command

*The Ashtar Command is the airborne division of
the Great White Brotherhood.*

Commander Ashtar

One of the most intriguing extraterrestrial groups of them all is the Ashtar Command. Commander Ashtar is the being who is in charge of the airborne division of the Great White Brotherhood, or the Brotherhood of Light. He and his vast extraterrestrial army of over twenty million beings work in conjunction with the ascended masters. Besides the twenty million personnel under his command in this solar system, there are another four million members and workers on the physical plane.

Commander Ashtar himself is a great and noble being approximately seven feet in height, with blue eyes. His body is of the Adam Kadmon type. He evolved on the planets Ashtar and Venus and has never had an embodiment on Planet Earth.

Although Commander Ashtar is in charge of the space fleet in this solar system, he is not restricted to this sector of space in terms of his service. He represents this solar system in the council meetings of this galaxy and of universes throughout the greater omniverse.

One of the important things to understand about Commander Ashtar and his army of workers and fleet of extraterrestrial craft is that they are etheric in nature. Even though they do not have physical bodies, they are able to manifest their bodies and their craft onto the physical plane any time they want to. A human seeing them would not think of them as being any different from another human. Indeed, members of the Ashtar Command walk among humanity on the streets of this world without anyone's being aware of it.

Most of the life on the other planets in this solar system is etheric in nature. Sometimes for this reason these beings have been called "etherians"; they would not be considered discarnate beings, for they do have bodies. They are in a state of evolution just as humans are, and their lives are not that much different from those of humans, except that they have transcended much of the lower-self and astral desire that the people of Earth struggle with so frequently.

Commander Ashtar also works closely with the angelic kingdom, specifically with Archangel Michael. Commander Ashtar is an extremely loving and gentle being but is stern and adamant in his mission to serve, educate, and protect humankind throughout the solar system.

Commander Ashtar and his crew do not wish to be seen as gods but rather as comrades and equals on the paths of ascension and beyond. Two of his main missions are to spiritually educate humans as to their true reason for being here and to defend and protect the Earth and the solar system from hostile and selfish extraterrestrial groups. Much gratitude is owed him and his tireless workers.

Ashtar's First Contact

Commander Ashtar's first open contact with Planet Earth came in the 1950s through a man by the name of George van Tassel. On July 18, 1952, George was given a telepathic message from a space intelligence by the name of Portla that his chief was about to enter this solar system for the first time. Then the first message from Commander Ashtar was broadcast. The following are some fragments of that first message:

> Hail to you, beings of Shan [Earth]. I greet you in love and peace. My identity is Ashtar, Commandant Quadra Sector, Patrol Station Schare. . . . The purpose of this organization is, in a sense, to save mankind from himself.

> Some years ago, your time, nuclear physicists penetrated the Book of Knowledge. They discovered how to explode the atom. Disgusting as the results have been, that this force should be used for destruction, it is not compared to that which can be. . . . We are concerned, however, with their attempt to explode the hydrogen element.

> When they explode the hydrogen atom, they shall extinguish life on this planet. They are tinkering with a formula they do not comprehend. We are not concerned with man's desire to continue war on this planet, Shan. We are concerned with their deliberate determination to extinguish humanity and turn this planet into a cinder.

This is quite a powerful message, I am sure you would agree. The full message can be read in a book by Tuella called *Ashtar, a Tribute,* which I recommend. It is no accident that extraterrestrial activity increased one-hundredfold after atomic bombs were dropped on Nagasaki and Hiroshima.

In developing this dangerous technology, humanity was endangering the entire solar system and, hence, even the galaxy. It was upon that occasion that the extraterrestrial forces throughout this solar system, galaxy, universe, and even universes were mobilized to help Earth and prevent further destruction from occurring.

In the sacred teachings it is said that a planet in this solar system called Maldek did obliterate itself through just this process of tampering with nuclear technology. The real battle that the Ashtar Command is fighting is for the minds of the people of Earth. Will they serve the soul and spirit or the lower self, negative ego, and astral materialistic desire?

Commander Ashtar works very closely with the Christ and also with Jesus, who on the higher planes is called Sananda. Commander Ashtar has literally millions of spaceships at his disposal for emergency purposes. He has not only his own fleet but also unlimited numbers of craft available from the galactic fleets and even from the universal fleets, if he should make the call for help.

In many of the Ashtar channelings there has been mention of an evacuation by these fleets if Earth should go through massive changes or any other kind of catastrophe. From the information I have received, that danger has now passed and the project of evacuation is no longer necessary.

The Ashtar Command has motherships anchored in space that are as much as one hundred miles in diameter. These motherships contain entire cities populated by millions of people in a thriving society. The Ashtar Command is part of a great confederation of planets that includes this solar system and this galaxy. In the center circle is the Ashtar Command which is in charge of this solar system. Then there is the Interplanetary Confederation which includes a larger group of planets in this sector of space. Then there is the Galactic Confederation of Planets. Beyond that is the Interdimensional Federation of Free Worlds. Each of these councils works in conjunction with the planetary, solar, galactic, and universal spiritual hierarchies.

The universe is divided into different sectors of space and different dimensions of reality. Commander Ashtar is the representative from this solar system to the various council meetings throughout the universe. Each of the confederations is accountable to the one above it in terms of the hierarchy of authority.

These confederations have not openly accepted Earth into their circle because of humanity's egocentric, materialistic, war-like nature. The Ashtar Command has most definitely made physical contact with leaders of the U.S. and the former Soviet Union and has been listened to to some extent. However, the bottom line is that Earthly government leaders are always more interested in military technology than in spiritual growth. It is hoped that will begin to change.

The confederations and the Ashtar Command are not allowed to interfere with humanity's free choice unless humans interfere with other members of the universe, which atomic and hydrogen bombs certainly do. So eventually, instead of the United Nations on Earth, there will be the Federation of United Worlds. Human thinking will move from a one-world attitude, which hasn't even been achieved yet, to a one-solar system, one-galaxy, one-universe, and finally to a one-omnniverse attitude. That will be a great day in the evolution of Planet Earth. Then Earth will be able to take its rightful place in solar, galactic, and universal affairs.

It is important to understand that each planet has its own spiritual hierarchy, just as each solar system has its own solar hierarchy, and on up the ladder throughout the galaxies and universes. These hierarchies work in perfect unison and harmony with the confederations.

The Ashtar Command's entire function is to be of service, and it goes wherever it is needed throughout the sector to fulfill this function in all possible ways. Many of the crewmembers return to their home planets for vacations and shifts rotate. The Command's craft have been patrolling this system for many ages, since long before contact was made in the fifties.

The Ashtar Command and the Negative Extraterrestrials

There are many extraterrestrial civilizations throughout the galaxy, universe, and omniverse that have come to Earth to collect data and perform experiments for their own selfish purposes. They are not here to be of service. Some of these extraterrestrials are of what might be termed a neutral nature, and some are serving the dark forces.

There are also negative extraterrestrials who openly oppose the Great White Brotherhood and the Ashtar Command. They would seize the planet and take it over if they could. It is the Ashtar Command and civilizations like that of Arcturus that have protected Earth so that does not take place. Just as in *Star Trek*, there are bands of renegades in starships that are escorted out of this sector. The Ashtar Command serves in a certain sense as Heaven's police force. In her channelings, Tuella has said that beings from six planets in the Orion system and a group called the Deros from inner space have had to be cordoned off. As a general rule, the cigar-shaped craft are the potentially dangerous extraterrestrials, although there are a few exceptions.

One of the problems the Ashtar Command has is that if an Earthly government makes legally binding agreements with negative extraterrestrial groups, the Command is not allowed to interfere. Free choice is a tenet of cosmic law unless the solar system and galaxy are being endangered.

The number of negative extraterrestrials is small compared to the vast number of positive extraterrestrials; however, the negative ones are quite dangerous if not controlled. Thank goodness for the Ashtar Command.

The Motherships

The Ashtar Command's motherships, or space cities, usually have twelve levels. The first level is for the entry and exit of craft. The second level is a vast stockroom of supplies for all the other levels of the ship. The third level is a zoo, with animals from many worlds. The fourth level is used for agricultural research, farmland, gardens, and orchards. The fifth level is the housing center for technicians and other persons working on the first four levels. The sixth level is the recreational level, with vast parks and landscaping. The seventh level is the medical complex. The eighth level is housing for evacuees, should it ever be needed. The ninth level is the university compound, complete with libraries, halls of wisdom, concert halls, and areas for other cultural activities. Level ten is where visiting dignitaries from all dimensions go. The eleventh level is the headquarters for the Ashtar Command and the Great Rotunda Meeting Hall. Level twelve is referred to as the dome. It is the pilot control center and officers' observation deck. Visitors are allowed to observe by appointment and in groups. Down through the center of the mothership is a circular shaft that is a power reactor for the entire craft. Ashtar has described one particular mothership called the Shan Chea as the largest of the orbiting cities that encircle the solar system. This is the ship that Commander Ashtar apparently lives on most of the time.

Trapped Essences

In an absolutely fascinating transcript from The Tibetan Foundation, Betty J. Dix channeled Ashtar on the subject of "trapped energy in the Earth." In this transcript, Ashtar speaks of the later days of Atlantis when the Sons of Belial (egocentric people and lords of materialism) trapped many people's "essences within pseudo-crystals." I don't mean to say that the soul extension or incarnated personality itself was trapped, but rather that a certain portion of the soul extension's energy was trapped. The pseudo-crystals are not true crystals; true crystals would not allow that to happen. The Sons of Belial created the pseudo-crystals to look like regular crystals, and some of them are coming to the surface of the planet now. Ashtar says that these crystals don't feel right when you pick them up. The energy in them feels dead.

In order for these souls to go to their next level of evolution, their trapped essences need to be released. Souls on the inner plane are requesting that this work be done now because of the great transformation that is taking place on Earth. Ashtar is requesting that all Lightworkers help in this important work. The crystals don't have to be physically broken to release the energy, just worked with energetically. Some of the pseudo-crystals can be placed on crystal clusters and asked to heal and release the energies that have been trapped inside. It can also be requested that the pseudo-crystal heal and become a true crystal.

Interestingly enough, when the trapped essence leaves, many pseudo-crystals just disappear. Some transmute into another form and others into a true crystal in its beginning stages of conscious development.

Ashtar states that these pseudo-crystals are all over the planet, but are found especially in Africa, South America, and the United States. Once it is released, the essence will usually return to its soul. In some cases, the trapped essence may need some guidance to return to the soul.

In Atlantis, toward the endtime, the Sons of Belial actually created entrapment machines to accomplish the process. They were able to do it without the machines, but the machines did it faster. He also says that implants were used to pull out the essences.

It is very important to make people aware of this phenomenon, for most people have never heard of it. Ashtar says that out of twenty pounds of crystals, as many as five pounds could be pseudo-crystals. Working with pseudo-crystals in meditation to release the trapped essences and transform the pseudo-crystals is a great service that can be rendered to many souls.

The pseudo-crystals can also be worked with without coming into physical contact with them, although some will have to be physically touched to facilitate the releasing process. The more Lightworkers focus on releasing the trapped essences, the more others will be able to come to the surface, for many are trapped in the Earth.

Ashtar says that in the future the Earth will be of such a great magnitude of Light that the essences will be unable to stay. Most of the pseudo-crystals look like clear quartz, smoky quartz, and a lavender shade of amethyst. You will not be able to know a pseudo-crystal by just looking at it; you will have to feel it to know for sure, although when viewed clairvoyantly, the distinction is obvious. Ashtar says that there are hundreds of thousands of pseudo-crystals.

Major Grid Points that Need Clearing

Another service that Lightworkers can render the Ashtar Command and the Great White Brotherhood is in the cleansing of certain grid points on the planet. The Earth is covered with energy meridians called ley lines, much in the same way that humans have acupuncture meridians. When one of these points gets blocked in the physical body, stagnation occurs in the energy flow and that eventually leads to disease. The same is true of

Planet Earth.

Commander Ashtar points out in the same transcript that some of the grid points on the Earth need clearing: a major one is in the center of the Pacific Ocean; another is in the northern part of Canada, close to the Arctic Circle. Unstable forces have been stored there since the time of Atlantis. There is another one directly below New York City that is tied to the chaotic energy of the city itself.

Ashtar is requesting humanity's help in releasing these unstable forces which will also help to heal the Earth Mother herself. Some additional points are south of the Hawaiian Islands, almost on the equator; off the coast of Africa, also close to the equator; in Russia, where there are two points; at the North and South Poles; underneath the tip of South Africa (which is partly why there has been so much dissension there) and beneath Columbia, Ecuador, and the Gulf of Thailand.

The best way to help in the cleansing of these points is to use a group dynamic. This can be done by following a grid line until you come to a blockage. Calling for the help of the soul, the monad, the Great White Brotherhood, and the Ashtar Command, a laser light can be visualized shining into it. Ask for the soul's and monad's help in focusing the correct amount of laser light.

Underground Ashtar Command Conferences

One of the ways the Ashtar Command can be contacted is to plan to join them while sleeping. Large conferences are held which are attended by physical beings, etheric beings, and beings from other planets. These conferences occur at least twice monthly; many Lightworkers attend five or six conferences a year. One of them dealt with how to clean up the pollution in the air, sea, and ground. Sometimes these conferences meet every night for as long as two or three weeks. Many beings attend in their astral bodies. Commander Ashtar is very pleased to see how fast the Light is growing on Earth and to see the unfolding spiritual commitment of so many Lightworkers.

Tuella's wonderful book, *Ashtar: A Tribute*, is one of the best sources for information about the Ashtar Command.

12

Arcturus

*Arcturus is one of the most
advanced civilizations in our entire galaxy.*

Edgar Cayce

Edgar Cayce has said in his channelings that Arcturus is one of the most advanced civilizations in this galaxy. It is a fifth-dimensional civilization that is a prototype for Earth's future. Its energy works as an emotional, mental, and spiritual healer for humanity. It is also an energy gateway through which humans pass during death and rebirth. It functions as a way station for nonphysical consciousness to become accustomed to physicality. *The Book of Knowledge: The Keys of Enoch* describes it as the midway programming center used by the physical brotherhoods in this universe to govern the many rounds of experiments with "physicals" at this end of the galaxy.

Arcturus itself is the brightest star in the Boötes constellation, which is approximately thirty-six light-years from Earth.

Some fascinating information comes from a book by Norma Milanovich called *We, the Arcturians*, which I highly recommend. Of all the extraterrestrial civilizations, I feel most drawn to Arcturus, probably because of their total focus in every aspect of society on the path of God-realization. For that reason I will go into detail in describing their wonderful civilization.

I also have the good fortune to know someone from Arcturus who is living on the Earth plane. She is one of the most spiritually gifted people I know. My connection with her and her work has greatly enhanced my own life and spiritual path.

The Arcturians teach that the most fundamental ingredient for living in the fifth dimension is love. Negativity, fear, and guilt must be overcome and exchanged for love and Light.

The Arcturians work in close connection with the ascended masters whom they call the Brotherhood of the All. They also work closely with what they refer to as the Galactic Command. The Arcturians travel the universe in their starships, which are some of the most advanced in the entire universe.

One of the reasons Earth has not been attacked by warlike negative extraterrestrials has been those civilizations' fears of the advanced starships of the Arcturians. Their ships are state-of-the-art technology, far beyond anything I have mentioned so far. One of the starships circling the Earth is called the Starship Athena, after the Greek goddess.

Arcturian society is governed by the elders, who are revered by the people of Arcturus for their advanced knowledge, wisdom, and extremely high vibrational frequencies. The higher the vibrational frequency, the closer one is to Light, or spirit, or God.

The Arcturians are short in physical stature, about three to four feet tall, and slender. They look very much alike, which they are happy about because it erases the pettiness of comparing looks which is so predominant in Earthly society. The Arcturians are the most loving and nonjudgmental beings you can possibly imagine. Their skin is a greenish color. They have very large, almond-shaped eyes. They have only three fingers. They have the ability to move objects with their minds and are totally telepathic. Their source of nourishment is an effervescent liquid that is highly vitalizing to their entire being.

Their eyes are dark brown or black. Their main organ of seeing is actually their telepathic nature, not their physical eyes. Their sense of hearing transcends even their telepathic nature. They also have an ability to sense with the backs of their heads.

The average life span is from three hundred fifty to four hundred Earth years. Their highly developed spiritual nature has allowed them to avoid aging, since they have the ability to transcend time and space. They terminate life when the contract that has been arranged for their existence is finished. There is no sickness in Arcturus; it was eliminated centuries ago.

In the Arcturian system there are no extreme temperatures. Their civilization is one that has transcended duality and lives in oneness. Professions on Arcturus are determined by a person's vibrational frequency and the colors in his or her aura. For example, those who are in charge of taking care of the children must have violet as the predominant color in their auras, for only the wisest souls are allowed to associate with the young.

The same is true for those who are allowed to give birth. They are screened and tested in terms of their auric and vibrational frequencies, and when chosen by the elders to give birth to an Arcturian child, people go through an amazing process. The vibrations of both individuals involved are raised to a seventh-dimensional frequency for the birthing process to insure bringing in the most highly evolved souls. (The seventh-dimensional frequency is that of an ascended master.) Reproduction is an honor on Arcturus and one of the most highly regarded professions. The actual reproductive act is not performed in a physical sense as it is understood on Earth. On Arcturus it is done through a kind of mind link in which the male and female energies are perfectly balanced. Through this procreation process, some kind of electron force flows through the two beings, and it creates another being that is a replica of the link.

The new life form is then taken to a special room that emanates the proper vibrational frequencies until the being is ready for integration into a family unit on Arcturus. Many beings from Arcturus are seeded onto other planets because the high council has ordered this as a great act.

On Arcturus there is no competition. Every thought, word, deed, and product is judged by its ability to raise the vibration closer to God. If it does not, it does not exist on Arcturus. A person's frequency of vibration is directly related to the mastery he has over his body, emotions, thoughts, actions, and creations. Arcturians have total mastery over these aspects of self. They have developed the ability to transcend the ego, the separative, lower, fear-based self. Success is judged only in terms of the measure of Light frequency. There are machines that constantly check the vibrational frequencies each individual on the planet is manifesting. If one particular Arcturian receives feedback that he is not meeting his own goals for evolution, then immediately the elders send teachers to help that individual.

There is never any comparison with others, only measurement against one's own goals. All scores registered by the frequency-measuring machines are kept private from all but the elders and ascended masters. The only way to evolve on Arcturus — or anywhere in the universe, for that matter — is to be of service, so fellow Arcturians are happy to help in any way they can.

Arcturians live very much in a group consciousness, since they recognize all are one. If one individual is having problems meeting his goals, then that affects everyone. On Arcturus, everyone truly is his brother's keeper. Each person grows at the speed he feels comfortable with. These machines might measure the amount of love, patience, tolerance, and lack of judgmentalness. Human society would do well to receive this kind of feedback.

In the Arcturian system there are no liquids like rivers, lakes, and oceans, so they are fascinated by humans' use of water for recreation and power, even though they have many elements on their planet that Earth doesn't have. Their basic energy form is liquid light. Arcturus can provide a glimpse of Earth's future.

The Arcturian Starships

The Arcturian starships are the finest in the entire universe. They are propelled by crystals that do not come from that planet but from a planet in the Milky Way that has not been discovered by Earthly scientists. These crystals have a way of conducting light energy from the Great Central Sun.

The Arcturians say that they no longer use computers because they long ago outgrew the need for them. They have other systems that are far more advanced. One section of the starship is a replication of Arcturus. It has the ability to take any crewmember back to Arcturus in his etheric body. This helps to strengthen and rejuvenate crewmembers who are away from home for long periods of time as they traverse the universes. Earth's frequency is very harsh for Arcturians because of their fifth-dimensional frequency.

Arcturians don't eat but are able to ingest energy. The Arcturians sleep for only a short time once a week, but for them it is a sacred time to soul travel and connect to higher realms of consciousness.

Another room in an Arcturian starship has a complete data bank containing every aspect of Earth life and of life on other planets as well. Arcturians are able to ingest information by means of their telepathic abilities and through their nervous systems. This process is similar to ingesting food but it occurs on an energy level. They are able to assimilate information one hundred times faster than the average human being on Earth.

An Arcturian ship has a room that strengthens the vibration of all who enter it so they will not be overwhelmed by even the strongest vibrations of Planet Earth. The Arcturians are able to travel through time. They also have shuttlecraft that are global in shape which are used for activating energy points and grids on Earth that have been lying dormant for many centuries. The Arcturians have been working with Earth since life first started on this planet. They have many bases on Earth, and they also have three bases on the Moon. Many of their bases on Earth are inside mountains. Arcturians can manifest physically, but they also exist in the etheric state, so physical matter is not an obstacle to them.

There is a vaporizing section in a starship that can instantly make any person or object disappear. They use it on a person only if he has died. The amazing thing about this machine is that whatever is vaporized can be resolidified at any time in the future just by checking the ship's records.

The more I learn about Arcturus, the more *Star Trek* seems realistic.

Many souls are brought to the Arcturian starships during the dream state where they are worked on and helped, although the Arcturians never invade a person's free choice as the Grays are doing. The Arcturians are here to assist humans in entering the fourth and fifth dimensions of reality and in raising their vibrational frequencies. They stand as the guardians and protectors of higher consciousness in the universe.

They are based in every country on the planet and, in fact, have bases all over the universe. They are here to educate humanity but have had a difficult time dealing with the government and the military, who are primarily interested in military technology, not spiritual enlightenment. The Arcturians could help in an even greater and more open capacity than they are now, but the people who govern the United States and the world are so materialistically and egoistically oriented that they resist the help of these incredibly advanced beings. Instead, the U.S. government made a deal with the Grays who are very selfish beings interested only in taking over the world for their own greedy purposes.

This is a sad commentary on how the people of the United States have allowed themselves to lose control of their government. The government has sold out to the dark forces for the purposes of greed and power, but it has backfired. If it were not for the ascended masters and other selfless beings such as the Arcturians and the Ashtar Command, humanity would be in deep trouble.

Other Arcturian Technology

The vaporizing machines and the machines used to transfer a person into another dimensional frequency are also used to decode a person's entire genetic structure and physical body. The Arcturians have said that there is not a being in any galaxy or universe they have visited whom they could not heal by using these machines to diagnose the problem and then to make the most minute corrections. These machines can also be used to teleport beings from one location to another.

Another mission of the Arcturians is to transfer gigantic beds of crystals to certain locations in the Earth's crust. Doing so usually results in much activity around those areas and in an energizing of Planet Earth herself.

There are machines throughout the starship that are constantly monitoring each crewmember's vibrational frequencies to make sure that no depletion is taking place and that each person is growing and emanating love and Light as his soul has intended. This information is, again, kept private except for the elders who will then design programs to help that individual make the needed corrections so he and the group may realize

God more fully. Since Arcturians see no separation between themselves and others, to help another is to help oneself, and vice versa. The basic curriculum of the Arcturians involves teaching each person to know his Godself. This is done through education, medicine, healing, arts, and entertainment.

The Arcturians have met with the presidents and premiers of many countries and have exchanged some information on an equal basis. They have made an interesting observation: every time they make contact with governmental leaders, they are immediately introduced to the military commander. That makes the Arcturians wonder who is really in charge. Nonetheless, they are currently working in thirty-three countries and have also made contact with the beings of the hollow Earth.

One of the ways they communicate with Earthlings is to write letters which are then teleported to the place they are to be found. Sometimes the Arcturians appear physically. Other ways they make contact are through telepathy or channeling and by bringing soul extensions aboard their ships, although that is done only if the person has given his permission in the etheric state. They also communicate with people in their dreams.

The Arcturians follow a code that is much like the Prime Directive of *Star Trek* fame: the code prohibits them from interfering with a civilization unless they are specifically requested to come. Prayers from people on Earth and requests from the ascended masters, angels, and celestial beings have brought them to Earth during this critical turning point in history, as humanity moves into the Golden Age.

I would like to fully acknowledge Norma Milanovich's book, *We, the Arcturians,* as the main source of the material in this chapter. She is a fantastic channel, and this is the best book available on the subject.

13

Sirius

*During many of the Egyptian dynasties it was
quite common to have a visitation from a Sirian in
the disguise of one of their gods. . . . The Mayans
were, in a sense, tourists from the Sirius realm.*

Lyssa Royal

Sirius was one of the first areas to be colonized by beings from the Lyran star group, and it is very advanced, in a metaphysical sense. Djwhal Khul says Sirius is one of the more advanced training centers, or universities, to which ascended masters may travel. The Path to Sirius is one of the seven paths to higher evolution among which each soul must choose upon achieving the sixth initiation, or ascension.

Sirius is known as the Dog Star and is a member of the constellation Canis Major. It lies approximately 8.7 light-years from Earth and is one of the most brilliant stars in the night sky.

Sirians are a group consciousness of both a physical and a nonphysical nature. The third-dimensional Sirians visited both the Egyptian and the Mayan civilizations. They gave the Egyptians much advanced astronomical and medical information. The Mayans apparently had a very personal relationship with the Sirians in which much information was shared. The Sirians left behind time capsules for future generations to discover, one of which is supposedly the crystal skull.

Robert Temple wrote a very interesting book called *The Sirius Mystery* in which he studied tribal cultures in present-day Africa whose most sacred and secret traditions are based on a cosmology of knowledge they say they received from the star Sirius. He traces the Dogon and three related tribes back over five thousand years, showing that they were civilizations of great wealth and learning that embraced knowledge of physics and astrophysics. The Dogon tribe also had a whole system of spiritual initiation that reminds me somewhat of the Western esoteric tradition.

Another group of extraterrestrial beings visiting us from Sirius is referred to by Ruth Montgomery's spirit guides (in *Aliens Among Us*) as the Kantarians. They are interdimensional extraterrestrial beings who apparently had physical contact with humanity in its beginnings, having been particularly helpful during the cataclysmic period of Atlantis, at which time they mixed with humans genetically. At this time they are working with humanity without direct intervention and will not consider a more active partnership again until humans outgrow the tendency as a people to be exploitive, judgmental, and manipulative.

They say that Sirius is a remarkable star in that it gives free rein to the development of all talents that are usable for the common good. The Kantarians serve as protectors of their people who are incarnated here and with whom they have had previous ties. Their fleet of starships is much smaller than the Ashtar Command's but is equally dedicated to helping Earthlings. They refer to themselves as the Kantarian Confederation.

Montgomery's guides also say that those who live in the Sirius system are seldom permanent residents. It is a meeting place for those who have mastered their own planetary systems and are preparing for further duties and missions. They talk about it as an important way-station for Earthlings who wish to continue their spiritual development.

The beings from Sirius who are visiting Earth are very good at the practical application of very advanced theoretical ideas that are being brought forth by other advanced extraterrestrial civilizations. They are here to ground and make usable these ideas and technologies.

Sirians helped to build the great pyramids and temples of Egypt. They also helped in the building of many of the tunnels and pathways to the inner Earth. In the future, they will be involved in establishing the Golden Age on this planet.

Along with Robert Temple and Ruth Montgomery, Lyssa Royal, in *The Prism of Lyra*, has served as a source of the material in this chapter.

14

Hydra

There is another extraterrestrial civilization that is visiting Earth, this one from the planet Hydra. These beings are skilled in the areas of agriculture, archaeology, and creating with their hands from the substances of the Earth. They excel at creating products of great beauty from the Earth's energy. These beings are the sensitives and artists of this galaxy, and they have a deep connection to the land.

Each civilization that is visiting Earth carries a specific vibration and a particular focus of energies. Each civilization has a different area of expertise. The combined input of all the different groups contributing to Earth in a positive manner is helping to propel the Earth into the New Age in a holistic and well-rounded manner.

Again, I am indebted to Lyssa Royal and *The Prism of Lyra* for the above information.

15

The Grays

I have mentioned the secret deal the Grays made with the United States government to abduct human beings for research and breeding. In this chapter I would like to provide an in-depth understanding of the Grays' culture — where they come from and why they are doing what they are doing.

The Grays are commonly divided into three different types: the Orion Gray type 1; the Orion Gray type 2; and Gray species 3. Besides these three categories of Grays, there are also twenty-two subspecies coming from such star systems as Rigel, Ursa Major, Draconis, and Zeta Reticulum. It is essential that the Grays be understood, for they are one of the main negative extraterrestrial groups trying to take over this planet for their own selfish purposes.

There are apparently two kinds of Grays from Orion, who might be referred to as the larger Grays and the smaller Grays. The smaller Grays have actually been cloned by the larger Grays and that is why they all look the same. The abductions are for their genetic experiments which include cloning, DNA enrichment, and crossbreeding with human beings.

The Grays have a genetic weakness in their digestive systems which is one of their main motivations for all the genetic work. The Grays are part of a kind of group consciousness rather than having individual consciousnesses. Their religion is science, not true spirituality. Their social structure is based on obedience and duty.

They are attempting to take over this planet not by military force but rather through covert mind control. Since the U.S. government sold out to these negative aliens, even they have realized the fix they are in. If they try to attack these aliens with military force, it would be suicide, as the Grays are far more advanced technologically than is the U.S.

One of the primary methods of protection against confrontation with the Grays is to stay attuned spiritually and to stay in your power. The Grays look at fear and victim consciousness as permission to intrude.

The tall Grays seem less prone to frailties than the smaller Grays. Their basic program is service to self. They are using this planet as a supply depot for biological materials, as is evidenced by mutilations of people and cattle. They are very telepathic. Earth is not the only world they have tried to conquer. The Grays from Zeta Reticulum have the ability to magnify their mental fields in order to maintain control over humans. The different species of Grays are members of a network which is a sort of loose alliance within which all have common purposes and aims.

The Grays from Rigel were the ones who made the secret deal with the U.S. government. They are small with yellow-greenish skin. When they are lacking a specific glandular substance in their bodies because of the digestive problems, they appear grayish. They are from a solar system that revolves around Rigel, which is a double bluish-white star about eight hundred light-years from Earth. The digestive problems were caused by exposure to radioactivity during a nuclear war many thousands of years ago. They derive nourishment from the glandular secretions and enzymes they extract from animal mutilations.

The Rigelians are almost entirely devoid of emotions. They are not capable of direct interbreeding with us but can do it in laboratories. They have the ability to disintegrate matter into energy, which is how they pass through walls and roofs and transport abductees from their homes.

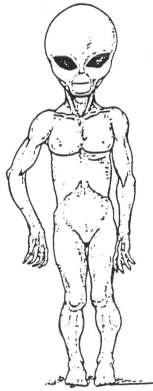

Part of their mind control over humans is based on a sort of telepathic hypnosis they are able to induce. One facet of this is their ability to make people forget consciously that they have been abducted. They also use this ability to try to control the country's leaders. Control is also exerted through the placing of implants, both mechanical and etheric.

The Grays have bases all over this planet, especially in the United States, and also on the dark side of the Moon. They have made clones of human beings, as well, which are cloned into android-type bodies. The degree to which the Grays have interpenetrated society is extreme.

They are impregnating human females on a massive scale and later extracting the fetuses. Most of their biological materials come from the cattle mutilations; however, it is a fact that at times they have performed human mutilations. These materials have been found on their crashed spacecraft. There are some books on the market saying that they are friends and that people have agreed to be abducted. I am here to tell you not to believe that for a second! These are very disturbed beings. They are here to take over the planet for their own selfish purposes. They look at humans with an attitude that is similar to the way the unconscious mass of society looks at animals.

The Grays from Zeta Reticulum appear to be divided into two different groups, one that appears to be a little more tolerant toward human beings and another that is interested in the colonization and conquest of Planet Earth.

The tall Grays have one base near the Aleutian Islands. They seem to have influence over the Grays from Zeta Reticulum and the Beeletrax Grays. These Grays have no stomachs and digest their food by absorption through the skin or under the tongue. They have been cloning themselves instead of practicing reproduction. Each time they reclone, however, the genetic copy becomes weaker, which is part of their problem. Their attitude toward humans is one of tolerance of inferiors. They are technologically superior, but spiritually and socially backward.

For the information in this chapter, I would like to acknowledge Lyssa Royal's *The Prism of Lyra* and also an amazing set of books called *Matrix I, Matrix II,* and *Matrix III* by Valdimar Valerian.

16

The Reptilian Race

The Reptilian race is the other group of extraterrestrials that is particularly negative, destructive, and evil in intent. They are human in shape, but they have reptilian faces. They also have scales, which makes their skin waterproof. They have three fingers and an opposing thumb. Their mouths are like slits. They average from six to seven feet in height.

They are well suited for space travel because they are able to hibernate. They are cold-blooded, biologically, so must have a balanced environment to maintain body temperature. The members of the soldier class can bury themselves in the ground and wait long periods of time in order to ambush an enemy. Some have special wings, which are like flaps of skin, although the soldier class and the scientists are wingless. In an emergency they can survive on one very large meal every few weeks. These Reptilians have been interacting with Earth for a very long time.

On their home planet they apparently live underground. This Reptilian species apparently directs the efforts of the working class who are only about four feet tall and would be considered another subspecies of the Grays. The command progression in this Reptilian society is as follows: the Draco who are the winged Reptilians are first in command; second are the Draco who are the non-winged Reptilians; third are the Grays. The Reptilians, along with the Grays, pose the greatest danger to Planet Earth at this time.

Protection

The specific aim of the Reptilians and the Grays is to take over Planet Earth through covert mind-control methods, much as the secret government is trying to do. These two groups are intimately connected. Most people think of world takeover as occurring only by military means such as bombs and guns, but those are not necessary if the people and the leaders can be manipulated by mind control, hypnosis, and brain implants.

The key question is, what is to be done to stop this? The government has sold out because of greed for power and world domination and now those involved can't stop what they have started. The first step is for the American people to reclaim their government and force the release of all knowledge about extraterrestrials to Americans and to the world at large. Half the battle would be won if the people of the world knew what they were dealing with. If people knew what was happening, they would not allow themselves to go around on automatic pilot. The only means of protection is through strength of consciousness. If a person is attuned to God and the masters, owns his personal power, and has mastery over his energies, he has nothing to worry about. The people of the world need to wake up spiritually and psychologically and stop being victims. It is this victim consciousness that allows them to be abducted and manipulated.

If ever you sense negative extraterrestrials nearby, just pray, make positive affirmations, and visualize protection for yourself. Your connection with God and the masters will bring you immediate protection. The only true hope for this planet is a mass spiritual awakening which, in truth, is beginning to occur. This spiritual awakening must also lead to political action to remove the secret government, the Illuminati, from power. It is these people who are being controlled, manipulated, implanted, and hypnotized by the negative extraterrestrials.

Part of your strength is to think as an individual. The Grays are a group memory complex and have very little ability to think on their own. It is time now to make people aware of what is really going on. Share the information in this book and others like it with your friends. Do more research on your own. If enough people become aware, the hundredth monkey effect will occur; it is already beginning.

You must now take responsibility as you never have before. You, the readers of this book, are the Lightbearers for the New Age. It will happen only if you create it. The world will change when you change it. This change begins in consciousness, which leads to individual and group action. The secret government and the negative extraterrestrials are more vulnerable now than ever before.

The government and the world as a whole are ripe for an overthrow in the positive sense. There will never be a better opportunity for it than in the next ten to twenty years, considering the spiritual forces that are now at work on this planet. I challenge you to fully reclaim your power and Light and be about the Father's business, this noble mission to your beloved Planet Earth.

Valdimar Valerian's extraordinarily detailed books, *Matrix I*, *Matrix II*, and *Matrix III*, are the sources for the material in this chapter.

17

Procyon

One of the positive extraterrestrial groups is from a solar system that revolves around Procyon, a binary yellowish-white star that rises before Sirius in Canis Minoris, about 11.4 light-years from Earth. They have been nicknamed the Swedes because they are humanoid in appearance and have blond hair.

They have a strongly positive attitude toward the people of Earth but the United States government was not interested in negotiating with them because they would not provide new weapons systems. The Procyonians have apparently crossbred with humans during many stages of evolution for a much more noble purpose than that of the Grays. The Procyonians have a philosophy of service to others rather than service to self and have been involved in trying to protect humanity from the evil activities of the Grays and the Reptilians. They serve the Law of One and are here to help humanity help itself, totally respecting free choice.

They are able to travel in time and between dimensions, frequently using mechanical vehicles even though they are not dependent on them. The word "Procyon" translates into English as "the home of those who travel through time."

18

Cessna

An interesting extraterrestrial contact was reported by a man named Robert Hurlburt of Starke, Florida. He was hiking in the Green Mountains of Vermont when he came across a man sitting beside a stream. To make a long story short, he had a long conversation with this man while they hiked and camped together that day and the following night. The man said that his name was John and that he came from the planet Cessna. According to Ruth Montgomery's book, *Aliens Among Us*:

> John went on to tell me about this planet that he claimed to be from, saying that it was a warm, temperate planet with abundant flora and fauna. The atmosphere had a thick cloud cover that consisted of a high quantity of nitrogen, with oxygen and traces of other gases, some of them familiar to Earth, some not.
>
> He stated that this planet had two moons and traveled in an elliptical orbit around its sun. He said that it was slightly larger than Earth, had two polar caps, and a population of around five hundred million; that population control was strictly adhered to, meaning reproduction was not a haphazard occurrence; that there were seventy major centers of population; that there was no pollution or disease.
>
> He said that the inhabitants had a life expectancy of one hundred and sixty years; that a central committee of seventy representatives controlled the government and each member was elected by one of the seventy major cities by electoral vote of the populace; that there was no crime or famine, and everyone worked in unity to assist one another.
>
> The primary concerns of the people were scientific achievement, research and study of alien cultures, and bringing peace to all cultures. They had begun space exploration over twenty centuries ago. Their space vehicles varied in size and shape, were capable of speeds exceeding the speed of light, and were powered by drawing energy directly from the sun.
>
> He stated that this culture had been sent to Earth to study us and somewhat to share its technology with us, but as yet we were not prepared to handle such power. He referred to us infantile.

The next morning upon awakening, Robert found that John had gone. When he arrived home, Robert contacted a woman John had said he had told his story to. The woman confirmed that she knew him and knew he was not of Earth. Ruth Montgomery's spirit guides also confirmed the truth of John's story.

19

Alpha Centauri

The extraterrestrials from Alpha Centauri resonate with violet light. This civilization has enormous scientific and technical knowledge that is of the highest quality in the universe.

The Alpha Centaurians are very theoretical. Part of their mission on Earth is to help increase humanity's scientific, technical, and theoretical knowledge and to find ways to make this knowledge understandable, since they are so much more advanced than humans. One of the ways they are doing that is by telepathically linking up with some of Earth's most advanced scientists. Because these beings are so incredibly intelligent and are of such a high vibration, they sometimes have a difficult time grounding these ideas on the Earthly plane.

The beings from Sirius, whom I have already mentioned, are good at bridging this gap because they are expert in the practical application of ideas and in making the theories usable in third-dimensional society. The Sirians are the workers and doers of the Earth.

I extend further acknowledgment to Lyssa Royal for the information in *The Prism of Lyra.*

20

Lyra

The extraterrestrials from Lyra, as I previously mentioned, have brought a migratory quality and freedom of spirit to Planet Earth. These beings aren't as attached as most to their home planet. They have been called the chameleons of the universe because of their ability to adapt to new environments on various planets. However, they are a very advanced civilization and are not used to the low vibrations that exist in the Earth's atmosphere.

The Lyrans radiate much Light from their head centers but apparently find it difficult to stay in the heart center while in the Earth's atmosphere. The Lyrans are used to total freedom of expression and movement. They are the independents of the universe. They are almost the opposites of the Arcturians who are very orderly and systematic. They would also be opposites of the Zeta Reticulum civilization in this regard.

The Lyrans are very loving beings and they fluctuate through a wide range of frequencies on the color spectrum. As humankind advances and moves into the Golden Age, there will be even more contact with the Lyran civilization.

The Prism of Lyra, Lyssa Royal's book, is the source of this information.

21

Antares

Antares serves as an interdimensional bridge to Andromeda, which is one of the most highly evolved extraterrestrial civilizations in this entire universe. Apparently some souls pass through the Antares gateway upon physical death to reactivate their soul memories. Antares lies in the constellation of Scorpius. It is a binary star of fiery red and emerald green.

22

Andromeda

In 1972, a world-famous Mexican scientist and university professor was contacted by a group of beings from the planet Inxtria in the star group Andromeda, specifically Beta Andromeda. Professor Hernandez' main contact was with a human-looking woman by the name of Lya who was approximately one thousand years old. The connection continued over a ten-year period and the professor had the opportunity to travel on her ship on four separate occasions.

He was told that they were carrying out a well-ordered plan of collecting data and conducting studies and analyses of Earth and its inhabitants. Lya and her group were part of an investigative team that was studying planets throughout the universe. They seemed to have a stunning ability to predict future events on Earth. A lot of the interaction was very scientifically oriented. They warned Professor Hernandez of the dangers of the nuclear tests being done on Earth and of the adverse effects they were having on the atmosphere. They said much of the extreme weather, cyclones, and hurricanes were being caused by the testing. Above all, they were concerned about the chemical weapons that were being tested. This concern has turned out to be prophetic because, as I mentioned earlier, the AIDS virus that plagues the planet is part of the chemical warfare testing program of the United States government.

The professor was told that around 1990 humanity would discover new sources of energy coming from space itself. They also predicted that by around 2015 humanity would be able to obtain energy from sound. Beings from other worlds go to Inxtria to observe the vibrational effects of sound. Sound can be used to preserve cadavers and to control the climate. They said it can also be used to heat a building without irritating the inhabitants.

The main focus of their work with the professor seemed to focus on how humans are ecologically destroying this planet, and he was given much scientific evidence to substantiate it. They said that the most dangerous weapon humanity faces is the hate among people. A belief in God is essential and is integral to their whole cosmology.

UFO: Contact from Andromeda by Wendelle C. Stevens is the source of the above material.

23

Proxima Centauri

A German man named Herr Horst Fenner was traveling in Bolivia in 1976 and camping in the Amazon jungle when he encountered a disk-shaped metallic craft in a forest clearing. Two handsome, fair-skinned, blond males came out of the craft. Each wore on his belt a language translator the size of a pack of cigarettes. They spoke to Fenner in German, telling him that their home planet orbited a small sun in the star system called Proxima Centauri. They were entirely human in every way and were even able to breathe Earth's atmosphere. One of the men's name was Kahun and the other's Athar. They said that Proxima Centauri was the next closest solar system to Earth, at a distance of fifty million kilometers. They told him that they often came to Earth to observe events here and to consider the development of the species evolving on this planet.

They spoke of other races that come to Earth regularly and that also visit the other planets in this solar system. Some have established surface monitoring stations on these planets.

They warned Fenner of the danger of publicizing his encounter, mentioning Billy Meier in Switzerland, who received death threats after coming out with his information.

24

Ra

A fascinating and highly spiritual extraterrestrial contact came through Carla Rueckert, Don Elkins, and James Allen McCarty. (See *The Ra Material: An Ancient Astronaut Speaks*.) Carla was in telepathic communication with an extraterrestrial race called the Ra who landed on Earth approximately eleven thousand years ago on an extraterrestrial mission to help Earthlings with their mental and spiritual evolution. They focused on the Egyptian and the Mayan civilizations and made some contact in the Holy Land as well, traveling in bell-shaped spacecraft. The Ra refer to themselves as a sixth-density social memory complex, although they still have individual identities. They no longer have physical bodies; they are Lightbeings, but they are able to materialize bodies as they need to. They no longer operate in linear time. They call themselves humble messengers of the Law of One.

The Ra attempted to help in technical ways, in terms of the healing of mind, body, and spirit through the use of crystals. They were also involved in the building of the Great Pyramid of Giza. The pharaoh they contacted was Akhenaton, during the Eighteenth Dynasty, who accepted the teachings of the Law of One, even though his priests gave this teaching only lip service. The pyramids they helped to create were used for spiritual initiation, and in this current day and age they refer to the Great Pyramid as "a piano out of tune."

In their physical manifestation on Earth their physical bodies had a golden luster because of their high vibration. They did not apparently stay too long in Egypt once they realized that what they were teaching was being distorted. They stayed a little bit longer in South America, where they had more success.

They speak of having to go to the Saturnian Council before receiving permission to come to Earth. This council is one of the main guardians of Earth against negative extraterrestrial activity. The Ashtar Command also protects Earth under the guidance of the Saturnian Council. Both groups have said that Earth is under quarantine, but the quarantine is not impregnable, so sometimes certain negative groups do get through.

The Ra group belongs to the interplanetary Confederation of Planets, which comprises over five hundred planets. The Galactic Confederation is comprised of many different confederations, just as the interdimensional Federation of Free Worlds is composed of many galactic federations.

The Ra are working toward becoming seventh-density beings. They no longer have physical contact with Earth; however, they do have spiritual contact through dreams, visions, meditations, and spiritual forms of guidance.

25

Alabram

Ruth Montgomery, in channeling her spirit guides, tells of an extraterrestrial civilization called Alabram that is just beyond the Andromeda Galaxy. The beings on this particular planet have a physical appearance similar to that of humans but they have greatly enlarged diaphragms and lungs because the oxygen on the planet is so minimal that a normal human could not exist there. Their birthing process is different from humans' in that they carry the fetus for a shorter gestation period and then regurgitate it when the time for giving birth has come. At that moment the new baby is extremely small, but it reaches full maturity in only seven years.

The beings of Alabram have extremely large brains and are able to absorb information by osmosis. They are very telepathic. They drink a liquid similar to water and live on foods that are grown in caves and tunnels hollowed out beneath the surface of the planet because the star that serves as their sun is so hot that it would burn any plants on the surface of the planet.

26

Zeta Reticulum

The three- to four-foot tall extraterrestrials from Zeta Reticulum are among the most well-known and frequently seen space visitors, as they are often involved in abductions. They share a group mind and are not as individualistic as humans are. They are mentally developed to a fault, in the sense that their emotional sensitivity is not well developed at all. They are strongly oriented toward science.

The channelings of Lyssa Royal suggest that they come from a planet called Apex in the Lyran system, which was very similar to Earth. Their spiritual growth did not match their technological development and that imbalance finally resulted in a planetary cataclysm. The atomic explosions caused the plant life to deteriorate, which led the civilization to build underground shelters. It was during this underground period of their history that they began reproducing through cloning techniques; reproductive research is connected with their continued abductions of members of the human race.

One of the conclusions they came to was that their emotions had been the cause of the destruction of their planet, so they no longer allowed emotions into their lives. This, from an Earthly perspective, is like "throwing out the baby with the bath water."

According to the channeled information of Lyssa Royal in *Visitors Within*, there is a benign group from Zeta Reticulum as well as a negative group that is power-hungry and that is causing a lot of problems.

She also states that the atomic blasts caused the space-time continuum to fold around the planet which in turn caused the inhabitants to emerge on the other side of a dimensional doorway when they finally came to the surface thousands of years later.

Part of the reason they are abducting humans and animals is that generations of cloning using the same genetic material has caused them to become very inbred and their evolution has stagnated. In truth, the race is actually dying. To revive it, they are creating a hybrid race of both human and Zeta origin.

27

Vega

Vega is a star within the constellation of Lyra. It is one of the first Lyran civilizations to develop a unique and cohesive identity which led to the later seeding and colonization of Altair, Centauri, Sirius, and Orion. The beings from Vega manifested a psychology that was opposite from the beliefs and actions of the Lyrans. This caused many conflicts and wars between the Lyran and Vegan races.

28

The Ataien

Dorothy Roeder channels an extraterrestrial being whose name is Ranoash of the Ataien. Dorothy is an exceptional channel and has brought forth some fascinating information from the Ataien in a book called *The Next Dimension is Love.*

This civilization, which is far in advance of Earthly civilization on both spiritual and material levels, has made physical contact with the Earth in the past. Often it has met with disaster, mostly because they don't have the same kind of physical appearance that humans have. They look like gigantic praying mantises. The term "mantis" actually means "divine," and the Greeks as well as the Bushman tribe of Africa consider the praying mantis to have supernatural powers, but that does not preclude a shocked reaction on the part of most human beings. Ranoash says that the belief stems from a race memory of a time when the Ataien physically intervened on behalf of Earth to avert a catastrophe that had to do with Earth's being invaded by aliens from another universe in the very distant past, before humanity was physically incarnated. The Ataien used their advanced mind powers to immobilize the evil aliens.

Although the Ataien look like insects, they do not prey on other life forms as insects on Earth do. It is interesting that in Lyssa Royal's book *The Prism of Lyra*, the beings she called "the founders," who were the creators of all other beings, were also insect-like in appearance. Again, it is important to avoid an egoistical frame of reference and realize that humans probably look as ugly to them as they do to humans.

For a long time, the Ataien lived on plant juices. They have evolved now to the point where they can live directly off the energy of light. They still enjoy eating but it is no longer necessary for their survival. The Ataien have wings, even though they don't need them to travel; however, they do fly for enjoyment and as meditation. They are over six feet tall. Their coloring ranges from light gray to gold. They become more and more gold as they age. They die only if they choose to die.

The Ataien have a strong group consciousness, but they are most definitely capable of individual thought, as well. They have learned to create together a flow of thought and feeling that results in harmony for the whole race consciousness. In this regard they are different from humans whose individualism results in separation and negative ego. However, on the positive side, humans have great diversity and creativity, and that intrigues the Ataien since they have chosen the path of group consciousness. The positive side of their path is the sharing, love, and attunement to the source on a collective level. The negative side is that they miss a little bit of the diversity that humans have. In this respect, the two civilizations can learn from each other.

The Ataien have developed the ability to soul travel in other dimensions. They say that they do not travel forward or backward in time but laterally. This has been one of their main interests as a culture over the past one thousand years.

They have computers that are actually biological in nature. They can record information into the computers with a type of mental telepathy. The computers, in a sense, have become extensions of their own consciousnesses. To say that their computers are more advanced than Earthly computers is a vast understatement.

Although interested in human diversity, they definitely feel that they have chosen the right path by seeking group cohesion — in truth, that is spiritual consciousness. As everyone on the spiritual path knows, there are no separate individuals; that is an illusion. There is only one being in the infinite universe, and that is God. Now that the Ataien have achieved that ideal of group consciousness, they can, in harmony with the Divine Plan, explore the creative diversity of individualism.

The Ataien are wide open to sharing their experiences and their knowledge of how to achieve the world harmony which Earth needs so badly. Humanity has begun to move in that direction but is still very far from the ideal. There is still too much separative consciousness. The Ataien can be great teachers for humans in this regard. They can also help humans to let go of their deep attachment to the Adam Kadmon form of physical body and to recognize that all beings throughout God's infinite universe, regardless of their physical body types, are brothers and sisters in God.

29

The Essassani

Bashar is an extraterrestrial being from a civilization known as the Essassani. He is channeled by Darryl Anka who has actually seen Bashar's spacecraft in broad daylight over Los Angeles. Bashar is not his real name — in his society, he is a commander — but the word means "messenger" in Armenian.

The word "Essassani" means "place of living light." Darryl Anka has described the physical looks of the Essassani as being Eurasian, but with enlarged eyes. They are about five feet tall with whitish-gray skin. The females have white hair, and the males have no hair.

The Essassani civilization is approximately five hundred light-years in the direction of the Orion constellation, but it is not physical as that word is normally understood. They live on a higher vibration, so the star system they are from is not visible. Bashar communicates to us from what would be considered to be the future. If you ever have the opportunity to experience Darryl Anka channeling Bashar, it would be well worth your effort; it is quite a high-energy experience.

30

Implants

It is important to be aware of the issue of extraterrestrial implants. Most people think of them as being only of a mechanical nature, but there are many types of implants that have been placed in peoples' astral, mental, and etheric bodies, also.

Many people feel frightened when this subject comes up; there is no need for fear. I have been told, by sources of knowledge whom I highly respect, that just about every person on Planet Earth has implants, and that has been going on for the past ten million years. People have been functioning with them and living their lives and being successful for eons and will continue to do so.

That does not mean, however, that they are helpful to you on your spiritual path. These implants can be removed by a very simple process that takes less than an hour. Many people do this work. You can contact me for guidance on how to have implants removed.

Implants come in many sizes and shapes. They also have many different functions. One is to suck your Light and energy. Some are used for telepathic control. Some block you from your spiritual goals. They can be found in the chakras, in the glands and organs, above the head – all over the body.

They are usually implanted during childhood or at times of physical, mental, or emotional crisis or illness. Even though everyone has them and can still function quite well, they do prevent you from operating at your full potential. I highly recommend having them removed.

The goal of the spiritual path is refinement and purification on all levels. You want to purify your physical body of toxins, your emotional body of negative feelings, your mental body of impure thoughts, and your etheric body of impure energies. So for total God-realization and optimum performance, at some point in your spiritual progression you will want to remove your extraterrestrial implants, as they can subtly block your clarity, vitality, and prosperity. This is a subject that very few people are even aware of because very few people can see them, except for the physical, mechanical ones. As humanity moves toward full realization of the New Age, the subject of implants is going to be coming into the foreground of people's awareness.

31

The Association of Worlds

In *The Prism of Lyra*, which I highly recommend, Lyssa Royal has described the Association of Worlds in the following manner:

> The association is a group of physical and nonphysical beings from many realms who come together for a number of purposes. Some have called them a Galactic Confederation or Federation. There is no hierarchical structure of authority inherent in the association. The primary purposes for their interactions with Earth are:
>
> 1. To gently nudge humanity toward a greater awareness of itself and its place within the association.
>
> 2. To prevent a critical number of nuclear explosions on Earth, which can cause a rip in the fabric of space/time, affecting the galactic neighborhood.

32

Star People

*The term "starborn" refers to
the feeling and knowingness by some people
that they have come to Earth from another
planet or star system.*

Brad Steiger

The terms "star people" and "starborn" were popularized by books of those titles written by the well-known author Brad Steiger and his wife Sherry Hansen Steiger. He mentions that he has borrowed the term "star people" from Native Americans who believe that the stars are the homes of spiritual beings who have a connection with people on Earth. He defines the term "starborn" as "the feeling and knowingness by some people that they have come to Earth from another planet or star system."

Now it is important to understand that everyone on Planet Earth is extraterrestrial in the sense that everyone came from Heaven or God and is just visiting here. Even though this is the case, some people's past lives have been centered in the schoolhouse called Earth, while other people have been attending schools in other parts of the cosmos. One is not better than the other; they are just different pathways back to the Creator.

Many star people have memories of other star systems and of experiences with non-Earth beings. Almost all these people say they are here to be of service to humankind as it moves into the New Age.

Steiger compiled a list of some of the qualities of star people:

1. Their eyes have an extremely compelling quality;
2. They have great magnetism and personal charisma;
3. They are very sensitive to electricity and electromagnetic fields;
4. They have very sharp hearing;

5. A lower-than-normal body temperature;
6. A high percentage have an extra, or transitional, vertebra;
7. At an early age, they had some kind of extraterrestrial, religious, or mystical experience;
8. They feel a tremendous sense of urgency to fulfill their missions;
9. 65% are female and 35% are male;
10. 90% have experienced a sense of oneness with the universe.

In *Starborn*, Steiger has compiled some interesting statistics on star people through the use of questionnaires. I am grateful to Brad Steiger for his interesting and extensive research. In the paired percentages below, the first number indicates the survey responses in 1983; the second, the update taken in 1990.

★ Chronic sinusitis - 83%/94%

★ Extra or transitional vertebrae - 32%/34%

★ Unusual blood types - 28%/26%

★ Lower-than-normal body temperature - 92%/88%

★ Low blood pressure - 75%/70%

★ Hypersensitivity to sound, light, odors, etc. - 97%/70%

★ Swollen or painful joints - 87%/70%

★ Pain in the back of the neck - 93%/73%

★ Adversely affected by high humidity - 84%/70%

★ Have difficulty in expressing or dealing with emotions - 74%/71%

★ Experience a persistent feeling of great urgency to accomplish their mission - 85%/92%

★ 74% report out-of-body experiences.

★ 57% claim the ability to perceive auras.

★ 63% have experienced a white Light during meditation.

★ 50% have accomplished dramatic healings of themselves or others.

★ 38% practice automatic writing.

★ 55% believe that they have received some form of communication from a higher intelligence.

★ 60% have perceived spirit entities.

★ 55% have experienced clairvoyance.

★ 57% have made prophetic statements or experienced prophetic dreams or visions that have come to pass.

★ 38% report the visitation of an angel.

★ 37% reveal the manifestation of a Lightbeing.

★ 35% feel that they have been blessed by the appearance of a holy figure.

★ 50% are convinced that they have a spirit guide or a guardian angel.

★ 40% admit to having had an invisible playmate as a child.

★ 20% state that they once spotted an elf, a "wee person."

★ 14% have witnessed the activities of the fairy folk, the "gentry."

★ 34% are certain that they have encountered alien entities of an extraterrestrial or multidimensional nature.

★ 55% report an intense religious experience.

★ 72% claim an illumination experience.

★ 90% have experienced telepathic communication with another entity, material or nonmaterial, human or alien.

★ 48% are convinced that they have seen a ghost.

★ 42% have perceived the spirit of a departed loved one.

★ 67% accept reincarnation as reality and have experienced prior-life memories.

★ 37% have survived a life-threatening illness.

★ 34% have been involved in a severe accident.

★ 55% have had a near-death experience.

★ And, perhaps most telling, 78% believe that they have lived a prior existence on another planet or in another dimension.

In the fall of 1988 the editors of *Better Homes and Gardens* conducted a survey on religion and spirituality. The survey had nothing to do with the subject of star people, but I thought you might find the results interesting. The magazine reaches thirty-six million readers each month. The most responses they had ever received to a survey in the past had been twenty-five thousand; this survey drew a response from eighty thousand people, and more than ten thousand attached thoughtful letters. The results, as listed in *Starborn*, were as follows. (It must be said that this was not a scientific poll, but it is still clearly significant.)

★ 89% believe in eternal life.

★ 87% envision a heaven, but only 80% expect hell.

★ 86% believe in miracles.

★ 80% accept that prayer and meditation can lead to miraculous cures for diseases.

★ 73% believe that it is possible to receive direct communication from God.

★ 30% perceive an astral realm.

★ 13% accept that it is possible to channel messages from the spirit world.

★ 11% say that they believe in the reality of reincarnation.

Brad Steiger also told of a Gallup Poll conducted around 1990 that was more scientifically accurate in terms of sampling, and the following results were found:

★ 43% claim to have undergone an unusual spiritual experience.

★ 15% have had a near-death experience.

★ 46% accept the possibility of life on other planets.

★ 23% believe in reincarnation.

★ 71% expect life after death.

★ 95% believe in God or a Universal Spirit.

Father Andrew Greeley, who holds a Ph.D. in sociology, together with colleagues at University of Chicago, released the following polling data in the 1987 issue of *American Health*, also as described in Steiger's book:

★ 42% of the adult population in the United States believe that they have been in contact with the dead, usually a deceased spouse or sibling.

★ 29% have visions.

★ 67% have experienced some manifestation of ESP.

★ 73% believe in life after death.

★ 68% perceive the afterlife to be paradise; and

★ 74% expect to be reunited with their loved ones after death.

New Agers and UFO Enthusiasts

In my investigations into the fields of spirituality and UFOs, I have observed a division between the two areas of focus. For some strange reason they seem to be separate in people's minds; many highly evolved spiritual people have no connections with or understanding of the extraterrestrials, and a great many UFO enthusiasts have no connection to the spiritual realities of life. One of my purposes in writing this book is to integrate and blend the two movements for, in truth, they are one.

Some star people represent the Ashtar Command or other extraterrestrial groups, but everyone is a visitor, living on Earth to perform a mission. Because the Piscean Age is ending now, and so are other major planetary and solar cycles, the space commands are increasing their communications and interactions with their incarnated representatives. The channelings suggest that only one-third of these incarnated representatives have truly awakened to their full missions. Part of the purpose of this book is to awaken or more fully awaken people to these connections and to their true missions on Earth.

I would like to acknowledge Brad Steiger's book *Starborn* as the source of the information in this chapter. It is a book that is well worth reading.

33

The Organization of the Physical Universe

*The stationary isle of paradise
is the geographical center of infinity and the
dwelling place of the eternal God.*

The Urantia Book

The Urantia Book is a revelation of God. It is "written" by a commission of universal beings who reside in the capital of the superuniverse and who call Earth Urantia. They have put forth a clear description of the organization of the physical universe:

> Your world, Urantia, is one of many similar inhabited planets which comprise the local universe of Nebadon. This universe together with similar creations make up the superuniverse of Orvonton from whose capital, Uversa, our comission hails. Orvonton is one of the seven evolutionary superuniverses of time and space which circle the never-beginning, never-ending creation of divine perfection — the central universe of Havona. At the heart of this eternal and central universe is the Stationary Isle of Paradise, the geographic center of infinity and the dwelling place of the eternal God.

> The seven evolving superuniverses, in association with the central and divine universe, we commonly refer to as the Grand Universe. These are the now organized and inhabited creations. They are all a part of the Master Universe, which also embraces the uninhabited but mobilizing universes of outer space.

As I contemplated this description, I began to realize that the entire infinite universe is like a gigantic atom. The Stationary Isle of Paradise is the stillpoint in the center of all of creation; thus, it is like the nucleus of the atom. The superuniverses, universes, galaxies, and solar systems are like the electrons. Djwhal Khul once told me that the monad had a nucleus. This makes sense, for the microcosm is like the macrocosm. To consider one of the smallest physical particles in the material universe is to get a glimpse of God on the macrocosmic level.

The Urantia Book also states that the physical universe extends infinitely. The Stationary Isle of Paradise is not a creation in time but an eternal existence, the perfect and timeless nucleus of the Master Universe which also embraces the uninhabited but mobilizing universes of outer space. The regions of outer space are then divided into the first, second, third, and fourth levels. The fifth level is called open space.

The book states that the Grand Universe has an aggregate evolutionary potential of seven trillion inhabited planets and includes everything in the universe but the outer space levels mentioned above. There is a potential for even more inhabited planets if the outer space levels are included. This particular universe of Nebadon is one of the new universes in God's creation. It lies on the outer edge of the Grand Universe, but that, of course, says nothing, from a spiritual standpoint, about being close to God, because time and space are merely illusions.

34

Summary

I have dedicated a great deal of space to extraterrestrial civilizations because I feel that it is time for the people of Earth to expand out of their egocentric reality. It is time to understand that Planet Earth is part of a greater solar system, galaxy, universe, and omniverse of life.

This solar system is just one of thousands upon thousands of inhabited solar systems in this galaxy. This galaxy is just one of infinite numbers of inhabited galaxies in this universe. This universe is just one of infinite numbers of inhabited universes. Many of the life forms are totally different from life as humans know it, yet all are an expression of God and all are evolving back to the Creator as humans are.

It is time for humanity to take its rightful place in the Interdimensional Federation of Free Worlds of this omniverse. For too long, humans have been run by ego, which has led to the absurd conclusion that there is no other life in God's infinite physical universe. Planet Earth is nothing more than one infinitesimally small electron in God's infinite body. It is time for humanity to make this electron a healthy one, not a cancerous one.

If the electron that is Planet Earth can function in harmony, then the solar system that is an atom in God's body can be healthy. If the solar system can function in harmony and in attunement to God, then the Milky Way Galaxy, which is nothing more than a molecule in the body of God, can function in a healthy manner. If the galaxies or molecules can function in harmony then the universe, which might be considered an organ in the body of God, can function in a healthy manner. If the infinite number of universes function in a healthy manner, then God's physical body will be healthy.

It is a fact that a human being is infinitely small in the grand scheme of things; however, each is essential for the Divine Plan to be complete. One electron malfunctioning throws off the electrical and physical balance of the entire atom, molecule, and organ. That is why extraterrestrial civilizations are so eager to help humanity; to do so is also to help themselves for, in truth, all are one. All are God.

Just as there is spiritual interconnectedness, so there is also limitless interconnectedness on the physical, material plane. It is time for the people of Planet Earth to begin by recognizing the oneness among themselves. Only then can they understand the oneness in the solar system, galaxy, universe, and omniverse.

Earth has been isolated from the solar, galactic, and universal confederations and council meetings that interconnect all of physical reality because of humanity's complete and total egocentrism and lack of belief in God and unclear vision of the true purpose for living.

I hope I have helped to expand humanity's consciousness beyond the artificial wall that has been created by ego and by the secret government. When humanity can break out of this stranglehold, Earth will be openly and graciously removed from its cosmic isolation and accepted as a conscious member of the infinite, interconnected physical universe that is one of the seven heavens of God.

Part Two

The Ancient Mystery Schools

35

The Angelic Hierarchy

*I saw them with my bodily eyes
as well as I see you; and when they left me, I
wept; and I fain would have had them
take me with them, too.*

Jeanne d'Arc

Djwhal Khul, in his teachings, has outlined seven great kingdoms that are evolving on Planet Earth:

1. The mineral kingdom
2. The plant kingdom
3. The animal kingdom
4. The kingdom of humanity
5. The kingdom of souls
6. The kingdom of planetary lives
7. The kingdom of solar lives

Each of these kingdoms is, in a sense, an incarnation of God. There is only one being in the infinite universe and that is God; all that exists is an expression of that one being, including the mineral, plant, and animal kingdoms. So far I have been focusing on the kingdoms of humanity, souls, planetary lives and solar lives. In this chapter I would like to focus on two kingdoms of an order different from that of human beings: the kingdoms of the angels and the elohim.

The Elohim

The elohim are the creator gods, the beings God created to help Him create the infinite universe. In some teachings, the elohim are called the thought attributes of God, whereas the angels are called the feelings of God. The term "elohim" means "all that God is." It is plural so it refers to many gods. This is interesting because the term is used over two thousand five hundred times as the name of God in the Old Testament. So God did not create the universe all by Himself; He had helpers — the elohim.

"Elohim" is also one of the power names of God in the Kabbalah, the book of Jewish mysticism. The Kabbalah refers to elohim as the Divine Mother. The term Yod Hay Vod Hay, or Jehovah, refers to the Divine Father.

"Elohim" is one of the most powerful mantras you can say. Paul Solomon, in his channelings of the Universal Mind, was told to have his students use this mantra above all other mantras in their meditations. This is interesting, given that Paul Solomon's early training was as a Southern Baptist minister.

The Greek word for the elohim is "exousiai." Rudolph Steiner, the great German mystic, called the elohim the spirits of form. In the Bible it describes the elohim as saying "we and our image" in which humans are created.

The Keys of Enoch refers to the elohim as those beings who created the world by the will of YHWH (YHWH being the Jewish name for the Godhead). The elohim and angels might be thought of as the left and right hands of God; they are direct extensions of the Creator. Each elohim has a male and female aspect. There are seven great elohim, just as there are seven great rays emanating from the Creator:

1. Hercules and Amazonia
2. Apollo and Lumina
3. Heros and Amora
4. Purity and Astrea
5. Cyclopia and Virginia
6. Peace and Aloha
7. Arcturus and Victoria

The Angels

There is a lot more information available about the angels than there is about the elohim because the angels work very closely with the kingdoms of Earth. The study of angels is a vast subject; I will attempt to provide the basics and a skeletal sketch of their function on this planet and throughout the cosmos.

The first important thing to understand about angels is that they do not have free will as humans have. Angels are direct manifestations of the Creator and have no will separate from that of their source. As I said, they are like God's right hand. When you pray to God, God does not come Himself; He sends His angels.

There is a hierarchy in the angelic kingdom just as there are hierarchies in the human, planetary, and solar kingdoms. Angels are governed by archangels; the archangels are the directors, and the angelic hosts do the work. They do have specific likes and dislikes and individual characteristics, even though they have been created to perform certain tasks.

The Archangels and the Seven Rays				
Ray	**Master**	**Archangel**	**Qualities**	**Natural Service**
First	El Morya	Michael	Protection, Power, Initiative	Rulers, Executives
Second	Kuthumi	Jophiel	Illumination, Wisdom, Perception	Teachers, Students
Third	Paul the Venetian	Chamuel	Love, Tolerance, Gratitude	Arbiters, Peacemakers
Fourth	Serapis Bey	Gabriel	Purity, Resurrection, Artistic Development	Artists, Musicians
Fifth	Hilarion	Raphael	Concentration, Truth, Scientific Development	Doctors, Inventors
Sixth	Jesus	Uriel	Devotional Worship, Ministration, Peace	Priests, Ministers, Healers
Seventh	St. Germain	Zadkiel	Ordered Service, Culture, Refinement, Diplomacy, Invocation	Diplomats, Mystics

The angelic evolution is a parallel to that of human beings. The angels who cooperate with the Spiritual Hierarchy of Earth are focused on the form aspect of the planet; the Hierarchy is focused on the consciousness that lives within the form.

Because angels do not have free will, they are not yet self-conscious as humans are. They evolve through feeling, rather than through the power of conscious thought. Angels seek to feel, whereas human beings seek to know.

It is important to understand that there are angels working in all the dimensions of reality. The angels of the higher planes consciously cooperate with the Hierarchy and are considered equal to all ranks and grades within the Hierarchy.

When people think of angels they are usually thinking of the archangels who sit at the throne of God and perform services for God at the request of humans. This is not a true picture of the whole process. There is a hierarchy of angelic beings, or devas, to use the Hindu term, moving through the dimensions all the way down into matter itself. It is angels who are the mothers of all form.

There are untold numbers of fairies, gnomes, elves, elementals, nymphs, dryads, fauns, nature spirits, salamanders, sylphs, undines, brownies, and satyrs, to name just a few of the other beings that exist. Every plant, forest, meadow, and garden has a hierarchy of devas who are responsible for it. All dense physical form, be it an animal, plant, mineral, or precious stone, is created by these infinitesimal elemental beings under the direction of devas who are each in charge of a particular manifestation.

Later I will describe the kingdom of the nature spirits and elementals in greater detail, but I would first like to give you an overview of the workings of the angels on all the planes of reality.

Angels are genderless, or maybe a better term is androgynous – they have both male and female characteristics. The word angel itself is derived from the Greek word "angelos" which means messenger. They are the heavenly messengers of the universe.

Currently, the third wave of angelic contact is occurring on this planet. The first wave occured in biblical times; the second wave occurred during the medieval era; during this third wave they are reaching out to everyone.

Angels have appeared to individuals throughout history at critical moments. Mohammed, the prophet of Islam, was a channel for Archangel Gabriel. Mary, the mother of Jesus, was told by Archangel Gabriel that she was going to bear the Christ child. Gabriel also came to the prophet Daniel to help him interpret his dreams. Jacob wrestled with an angel.

There are many good books about angels and channeled from angels in recent times. The two I recommend most highly are *Ask Your Angels* by Alma Daniel, which is the best overview of the angelic kingdom I have found, and *The Starseed Transmissions* by Ken Carey, which is a channeling from Archangel Raphael. It is one of the most profound channelings I have ever read. It is also possible to get the book on audio cassette tape with Ken Carey reading, which makes it even more profound than it seems when you read it yourself.

The goal of the devic, or angelic, evolution is to become individualized and then to become human in a future cycle. This occurs for all devas below the rank of solar pitris. ("Pitris" is an esoteric word meaning angel.) Also, on occasion, it is possible for humans to enter into the angelic kingdom. Angels can incarnate into physical bodies and take on human form, so some of the people you know might actually be angels rather than humans. At some point in the far and distant future, it is part of the divine plan that these two evolutions come together. Angels who have not yet achieved individualization and free choice will eventually be pulled back into Source, ceasing to exist when their missions are complete. Some angels actually do have wings.

The Spiritual Hierarchy of the Angelic Kingdom

There are many different kinds of angels. The angels most people are familiar with are called, simply, "angels," but there are many other names for them, as well.

First Sphere	Second Sphere	Third Sphere
Heavenly Counselors	Heavenly Governors	Heavenly Messengers
1. Seraphim	4. Dominions	7. Principalities
2. Cherubim	5. Virtues	8. Archangels
3. Thrones	6. Powers	9. Angels

The Angels

The angels are the beings humans are most familiar with, for they are the ones who work most closely with humanity. The angels who are the worker bees work under the direction of the archangels. Each person has a guardian angel; such beings fall into this category.

There are infinite numbers of angels who work with humans and are available. There are angels of healing, illumination, creativity, nature, music, dance, writing and literature, protection, emotions, politics, science and technology, devotion, purity, information, salvation, environment, transformation, peace, art, relationships, purity, and ceremonial order and magic. All you really have to do is invoke them and they are happy to come and serve.

The Archangels

The archangels have a higher rank than the angels. In some systems of thought they have been called the overlighting angels, since they serve larger areas of human life. It is the archangels whose names you are most likely to be familiar with, especially the archangels who head the seven rays. Each archangel has its feminine counterpart:

Ray 1 . . . . Michael and Faith
Ray 2 . . . . Jophiel and Christine
Ray 3 . . . . Chamuel and Charity

Ray 4 . . . . Gabriel and Hope
Ray 5 . . . . Raphael and Mother Mary
Ray 6 . . . . Uriel and Aurora
Ray 7 . . . . Zadkiel and Amethyst

Another way of understanding the archangels is to see them in relationship to the Kabbalistic Tree of Life. This system presents some archangels you might not be as familiar with.

The Principalities

At even a higher level than the archangels are the angelic beings called the principalities. These beings are the guardians of large groups like cities, nations, and multinational corporations. For example, one of the beings holds in its heart a unified global order for Planet Earth.

The Powers

The lowest-level beings in the second sphere of angels are called the powers. They are the bearers of conscience and the keepers of the collective history of Earth. The angels of death and birth are part of this group. These beings are able to draw down the energy of the Divine Plan for Earth which enables them to bring to humanity a vision of the spiritual interconnectedness of things.

The Virtues

Above the powers is a set of angelic beings called the virtues. The virtues are able to send out massive amounts of divine energy and virtuous qualities to humanity on Earth.

The Dominions

Above the virtues in the angelic hierarchy are the dominions. These angelic beings govern the activities of all the angelic beings and groups that work below them in this second sphere. They might be called the divine bureaucrats. They also help to integrate and blend the material and spiritual worlds. The dominions do not have much contact with individual soul extensions on Earth.

The Thrones

The thrones are the lowest level of the highest sphere of angels. They are the heavenly counselors and companion angels of all the planets.

The Cherubim

The cherubim are the heavenly counselors who work above the thrones in the angelic hierarchy. They are the guardians of the Light throughout the universe. They usually do not have much personal contact with beings on Earth.

The Keys of Enoch says that these beings are also involved with the keeping of the celestial records. *The Urantia Book* speaks of how the cherubim work very intimately with the sanobim. They work as helpers and assistants to the seraphim who are the angels at the next level up in the first sphere of the hierarchical order of angels.

The Urantia Book has divided the cherubim into three categories:

1. In the first are the ascension candidates. These cherubim are the most advanced and have the opportunity and potential to become seraphim.
2. In the second category are the midphase cherubim.
3. In the third category are cherubim *The Urantia Book* refers to as the morontia cherubim. This term is by no means meant in a derogatory way. It is interesting, however, that the word moron, which is so negatively stigmatized in this culture, probably came from this spiritual category of angels who are not as advanced as the ascension candidates. All this means is that they will probably remain in their jobs as cherubim and sanobim.

The midphase cherubim will also probably remain in their present positions, with a few of the more gifted ones achieving limited seraphic service. In all essential endowments the cherubim and sanobim are similar to seraphim; they have the same origin but different destinies. They are very intelligent, efficient, affectionate, and almost humanlike. They usually serve in pairs. The cherubim and sanobim are the faithful and efficient routine workers on planets throughout the universe. They do not serve as attending angels to human beings; that is a seraphic privilege. When assigned to a planet they enter a local course of training that includes a study of the planetary usage of languages. They are continually engaged in efforts toward self-improvement and, most of all, toward the proper service of their missions.

The Seraphim

The highest order of angels in the first sphere is the seraphim. These are great celestial angels that are said to surround the throne of God. They are the regulators of the movements of the heavens and have untold responsibilities in the administration of God's infinite universe.

There are twelve master seraphim who are working with the supervision of Planet Earth:

1. *The epochal angels.* These celestial beings are entrusted with the oversight and direction of the affairs of each generation and root race.

2. *The progress angels.* These seraphim are entrusted with the task of initiating the evolutionary process of the successive social ages. They foster the development of the inherent progressive trend of evolutionary creatures.

3. *The religious guardians.* These are the angels of the churches.

4. *The angels of national life.* These are the angels of the trumpets, the directors of political performance in Earth life. They are also involved in international relations.

5. *The angels of the races.* These angels work for the conservation of the evolutionary races, regardless of political and religious affiliations.

6. *The angels of the future.* These are the angels who forecast and predict the future and are, hence, the architects of future eras.

7. *The angels of enlightenment.* These angels are involved with planetary education, along with mental and moral training as it concerns individuals, families, groups, schools, communities, nations, and whole races.

8. *The angels of health.* This is the angelic healing corps.

9. *The home seraphim.* These angels are dedicated to the preservation and advancement of the home, which is the basic institution of human civilization.

10. *The angels of industry.* This group of angels is involved with fostering industrial development and improving economic conditions for the people of the Earth.

11. *The angels of diversion.* These angels foster the values of play, humor, rest, and human leisure.

12. *The angels of superhuman ministry.* These are the angels of the angels. These beings are assigned to minister to all other superhuman life on Planet Earth.

The Cosmic Seraphim

The Urantia Book is like an encyclopedia – not of Planet Earth but rather of God's infinite physical universe. It is so unbelievable in its scope of information that it is almost impossible to read except in little tidbits and excerpts.

Whether all the information is accurate is hard to say, but what I would say is that it is hard to believe that anyone could make up such vast amounts of super-detailed information about the nature of the organization of the universe. I bring this point up only to share with you what this book says about the cosmic order of the seraphim that extends far beyond the scope of this infinitesimally small planet called Earth.

The Urantia Book has divided the seraphim of the cosmic level into seven groups, each of which has seven subdivisions based on the cosmic hierarchy of seraphic angels administering to planets and star systems throughout the omniverse.

The Cosmic Hierarchy of the Seraphim

1. Supreme Seraphim
   A. Son-spirit ministers
   B. Bestowal attendants
   C. Universe orientation
   D. Teaching counselors
   E. Directors of assignment
   F. Recorders
   G. Unattached ministers
2. Superior Seraphim
   A. Intelligence corps
   B. Voice of mercy
   C. Spirit coordinators
   D. Assistant teachers
   E. Transporters
   F. Recorders
   G. Reserves
3. Supervisor Seraphim
   A. Supervising assistants
   B. Law forecasters
   C. Architects
   D. Ethical sensitizers
   E. Transporters
   F. Recorders
   G. Reserves
4. Administrator Seraphim
   A. Administrative assistants
   B. Justice guides
   C. Interpreters of cosmic citizenship
   D. Quickeners of morality
   E. Transporters
   F. Recorders
   G. Reserves
5. Planetary Helpers
   A. Voices of the garden
   B. Spirits of brotherhood
   C. Souls of peace
   D. Spirits of trust
   E. Transporters

        F.   Recorders
        G. Reserves
  6. Transition Ministers
        A. Seraphic evangels
        B. Racial interpreters
        C. Mind planners
        D. Morontia counselors
        E. Technicians
        F.   Recorder teachers
        G. Ministering reserves
  7. Seraphim of the Future
       (Categories not listed for this group)

Each of these groups of angelic beings serves God's divine plan in some cosmic capacity. I have included this little section to give you a sense of the vastness of God's networking of divine beings throughout His universe.

Because of space limitations, I have not included a deeper explanation of all the specific functions of these beings beyond their titles. If you would like that information, I recommend reading pages 426 to 442 in *The Urantia Book*. This book is channeled from a commission of beings from a planet or star system called Uversa which they say is the capital of Orvonton, one of the seven superuniverses of time and space of which Earth is a part.

The following is a chart from Geoffrey Hodson's book, *The Brotherhood of Angels and Men*. It is a diagram given to him by an angel concerning the organization of the angelic kingdom.

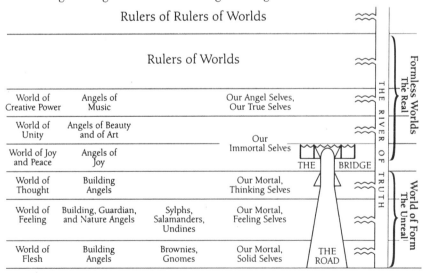

Rulers of Rulers of Worlds					
Rulers of Worlds					Formless Worlds / The Real
World of Creative Power	Angels of Music		Our Angel Selves, Our True Selves		
World of Unity	Angels of Beauty and of Art		Our Immortal Selves		
World of Joy and Peace	Angels of Joy			THE BRIDGE	
World of Thought	Building Angels		Our Mortal, Thinking Selves		World of Form / The Unreal
World of Feeling	Building, Guardian, and Nature Angels	Sylphs, Salamanders, Undines	Our Mortal, Feeling Selves		
World of Flesh	Building Angels	Brownies, Gnomes	Our Mortal, Solid Selves	THE ROAD	

THE RIVER OF TRUTH

Nature Devas

There are many types of devas, both subhuman and superhuman. There are also many different hierarchies of devas that are distinctly different from the human kingdom's hierarchy, although they work in perfect harmony with the other hierarchies.

Djwhal Khul has referred to the greater builders as the solar pitris and the lesser builders as the lunar pitris, which are the nature spirits. Each group of devas has specific work and methods of development whereby they attain their goals and evolve.

The violet devas' path of evolvement lies through feeling, through educating humankind, and through perfecting the physical body. The green devas' path of service is focused in the realm of magnetization of the energies that protect plant and vegetable life and sacred spots on the Earth. The white devas guard individuals in the human family and control the water and air elementals and the fish kingdom.

The evolution of the devas is speeding up now in synchronization with the evolution of the human family. There is another group of devas who have recently arrived from another planetary scheme. They have already passed through the human kingdom and are equal in rank with certain members of the Hierarchy. They have chosen, like bodhisattvas, to stay and work with the Earth plane. Djwhal Khul has said that there are twelve of these angel masters; five work in the violet group, five in the green group, and two in the white group.

There are three subsidiary groups:

Group 1. Here are found all elementals working with the etheric doubles of humankind and all elementals working with the etheric bodies of inanimate objects. The violet devas are on an evolutionary path. The elementals are on the involutionary path, and their goal is to evolve into the deva kingdom with the violet color.

Group 2. In this group are found the fairies and elves who build and color the flowers, the elementals who work with the vegetables, fruits, and all the verdure that covers the Earth's surface. Also connected with this group are the devas of magnetization that are connected to stones, talismans, and the sacred spots of the Earth. There is one last group of devas in this group that are found around the habitations of the masters who live on Earth.

Group 3. Those in this group work with the elementals of the air and sea, the sylphs, the water fairies, and the devas who guard human beings.

The solar pitris are omnipresent superphysical agents of the creative will of the Solar Logos. They are directors of all natural forces, laws, and processes – solar, interplanetary, and planetary. The solar and lunar pitris are all subservient to and expressive of God and God's will. The devas live on all planes of consciousness — etheric, astral, mental, and spiritual.

The following chart is from the Theosophical Society's literature; it shows the evolution of life from mineral life all the way up to the solar spirits and solar pitris.

The tiny individual devas that make up the soul body, or causal body, come from the Sun and hence are also called solar pitris. The lunar pitris make up humans' lower bodies. At some point in the distant future, human evolution and devic evolution will come together.

As humans learn to work more closely with the devic evolution they will learn how to heal and control their etheric bodies to a greater degree. There are also devas with which humanity does not have direct contact but which play a crucial role in transmitting prana, life force, to humankind from the Sun.

The angelic evolution is on the left side and the human on the right side. Note where the level of individualization begins for each separate hierarchy.

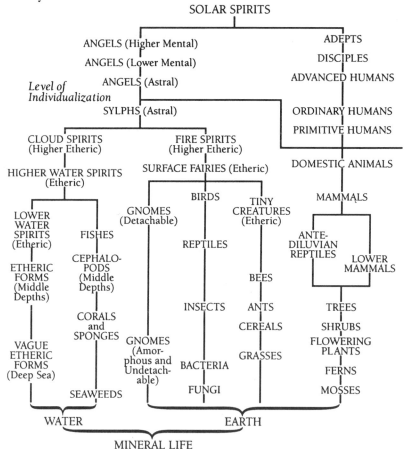

36

Pan and the Nature Spirits

I am a servant of Almighty God,
and I and my subjects are willing to come to the
aid of mankind in nature if he affirms belief in us
and asks for our help.

Pan

Nature spirits and devas are an angelic order. They hold the patterns that underlie all living and growing things on Planet Earth. That includes the mineral, plant, and animal kingdoms along with the four elements of fire, air, earth, and water. Even human bodies are governed by these nature spirits where they are the spiritual equivalent of the cells, organisms, and microorganisms that work together to make the organs, glands, and tissues function properly.

The world of devas and nature spirits is the most wonderful and fascinating reality you can imagine. It is a world filled with fairies, elves, gnomes, sylphs, salamanders, undines, brownies, satyrs, dwarves, goblins, fauns, trolls, elementals, and, last but certainly not least, Pan, who is the god of the nature spirits. It is a world that makes *Alice in Wonderland* look unimaginative.

Devas and nature spirits must be distinguished from each other. Devas are the architects. They are the guiding force that gives form and structure and energy to the plant world. They carry the archetypal patterns for each of the material forms.

The nature spirits have a slightly different function. They actually do the work of building the plants. They channel the etheric forces they receive into physically constructing the particular plant patterns they are receiving from the deva. The nature spirits are like the physical workers who carry out the architects' blueprints. They express great delight and joy in their work. They vary in size from a fraction of an inch to elves who are three to four feet tall. All nature spirits are under the direction of the god Pan. He is a most loving being who serves God by guiding all the nature beings who work under his authority. Pan is half man and half goat in appearance. He has been negatively stigmatized by Western societies, which is unfortunate because all such negativity is based on illusion.

A Glimpse into the World of Nature Spirits

The nature spirits are, for the most part, composed of etheric matter, so very few people on Planet Earth are able to see them in their full glory, variety, and number. Probably the best account of them I have ever found is in the Findhorn material.

Findhorn is a spiritual community in Scotland. It was started by Peter and Eileen Caddy, Dorothy Maclean, and Lena Lamont. Later in the development of the community David Spangler and a man by the name of R. Ogilvie Crombie became involved. The fascinating thing about this group of people was that they each had very specific and unique talents. Eileen Caddy was a channel for God. Dorothy Maclean was a clear channel for the deva kingdom. David Spangler was a channel for a being called Limitless Love and Light. R. Ogilvie Crombie had the gift of being able to clairvoyantly see and talk to the nature spirits. The combined talents of these four individuals covered all the bases of inner guidance into these unseen worlds.

Peter Caddy was not a channel but represented the human worker aspect of the group. Peter was the one who was in charge of the physical work of creating the Findhorn garden.

One day he asked a young man by the name of Dennis to cut back some bushes that were interfering with the growth of several trees in the garden. Gorse flowers that had just bloomed covered a particular bush. Peter boldly ordered Dennis to cut the bush anyway. Dorothy Maclean, the channel for the devas, was almost in tears, saying that Peter was butchering them. Peter was quite stubborn and said, "Oh, don't be so damned silly."

Shortly thereafter, he received an emergency call from Crombie who asked Peter what he was doing to upset all the nature spirits in the garden. Peter said he didn't know. Crombie came to Findhorn and found himself immediately surrounded by a throng of little gorse elves who were all extremely upset. They said to Crombie, "We thought Findhorn was a place where there was cooperation between man and the nature spirits. How in heaven's name could they have done such an awful thing as destroy our homes?" It turned out that the elves lived in the gorse blossoms.

They went on to tell Crombie that they had all left the garden and refused to work there any longer because of this thoughtless destruction. Crombie explained to the elves that it had been unintentional, that this kind of cooperation was new, and that they were all extremely sorry. Later, a little ceremony was held in front of the bushes and Peter apologized profusely. The elves accepted his apology and agreed to return to work.

If this happened to Peter in the Findhorn garden, can you imagine what the nature spirits go through on Planet Earth as a whole? Humans take such a scientific, mechanistic attitude toward nature, allowing for absolutely no relationship to the infinite numbers of tiny beings who are in actuality doing all the work. Crops are grown almost in defiance of nature, with chemical fertilizers and insecticides that banish the fairies from fields and gardens. We perpetuate cruel and wanton destruction upon nature. It is a wonder these beautiful little beings are willing to help us at all!

On the other side of the coin, fairies will draw close to those who love them and who love to grow things. They are obviously very forgiving beings, a trait humans would do well to absorb from them. Some of these nature spirits will evolve into a higher level of the angelic kingdom.

Have you ever stopped to think what causes a flower to bloom or to be a certain color or to have a particular fragrance? It is the tiny etheric beings who work ceaselessly to manifest these qualities. Behind all of nature are beings large and small, working under the direction and control of an angel on one of the seven great rays. These nature spirits are carrying the life force that they receive to beautify the form, color, and fragrance of flowers and plants.

You might not be aware that the plant kingdom on Planet Earth is one of the most advanced in this entire Milky Way Galaxy. It would behoove humans to enjoy the wonderful work the nature spirits are doing even though humans have lived like parasites instead of caretakers of the environment.

The fairy spirits working in gardens usually do not take much notice of humans; however, they do respond to harmonious and loving thoughts. Even stones are inhabited by tiny etheric beings. They are also connected to the jewels you wear, and they respond if you love and treat them kindly.

R. Ogilvie Crombie

Crombie tells a fascinating story about his first encounter with the nature kingdom. His story actually began when he was four years old. One day he dropped a penny into a wishing well and prayed that he would be able to see fairies and talk to them. Little did he know that sixty-three years later, God and the nature kingdom would grant his wish.

His first experience occurred one day when he was walking in the botanical gardens of Edinburgh. He was sitting under a tree when all of a sudden a figure appeared, dancing around a tree about twenty-five yards away. It was three feet tall and he realized it was a faun, a being that is half human and half animal. It had shaggy legs ending in cloven hooves, pointed ears and chin, and two little horns on its forehead. The faun danced around the tree three times and then sat down crosslegged in front of Crombie, having no idea that Crombie was actually able to see him. When Crombie said, "Hello," he leaped into the air with a start.

To make a long story short, he told Crombie that his work was to help the trees. He also said that the nature spirits have lost interest in the human race since they have been made to feel that they are neither believed in nor wanted. He went on to tell Crombie that his name was Kurmos. He wanted to know why human beings wrap themselves up in such strange coverings. Crombie and Kurmos had a long talk, and Kurmos even went back with Crombie to his apartment. He ended by saying that he would come if Crombie called to him in the gardens again. Kurmos was true to his word.

About a month later Crombie had an even more extraordinary experience. He was walking along beside the National Gallery when he became aware of a figure walking beside him that was taller than he was. It was a faun radiating a tremendous power. A conversation ensued and he became aware that it was Pan, the god of all nature.

Approximately a month later, Crombie was walking in a natural area when he saw a large figure lying on the ground. It was a monk in a brown habit with the hood pulled over his head. As the being stood up, it became apparent that it was Pan. He was over twenty-five feet tall. Pan smiled and said, "I am a servant of Almighty God, and I and my subjects are willing to come to the aid of mankind in nature if he affirms belief in us and asks for our help." This was the beginning of a reconciliation between Pan and the nature spirits, and humanity.

About four months after that, Crombie was out walking again when all of a sudden Pan appeared at his side. Pan quickly stepped behind Crombie and then walked into him so that they became one. Crombie could then see the world through Pan's eyes. The moment this happened the woods became alive with a myriad of beings. He saw elementals, nymphs, dryads, fauns, elves, gnomes, fairies, and other beings too numerous to categorize. He saw two beautiful elfin creatures three or four feet tall. He saw tiny little beings not more than a fraction of an inch tall swarming around a toadstool. Many of the nature spirits danced around Crombie in a ring. All of them were welcoming and full of joy and love. Crombie felt as though he were outside of time and space — which he was.

As he walked he was aware of holding panpipes and having shaggy legs with cloven hoofs. Crombie "himself" began to dance down the path. Then Pan withdrew his presence and Crombie walked home in silence.

The Elemental Kingdom

The four basic elements of nature are fire, air, earth, and water. Within each of the four elements are nature spirits that are the spiritual essence of the element. The nature spirits of earth are called gnomes. The nature spirits of water are called undines. The nature spirits of fire are called salamanders. The nature spirits of air are called sylphs.

These beings are made up of an etheric substance that is unique and specific to their particular element. They are living entities oftentimes resembling humans in shape but inhabiting worlds of their own. They have the power to change their size and appearance almost at will. They cannot, however, change elements. Gnomes' work is specific to the earth, and they cannot change into fire, air, or water elementals.

The elementals take their orders from the devas. They do remain individualized, as humans are. These tiny beings are animated by the thought power of the lower angels and so are thought forms of sorts. In reality, however, everything in God's universe is created from thought.

These beings may be etheric thought forms, but they have etheric flesh, blood, and bones. They live, propagate offspring, eat, talk, act, and sleep. They cannot be destroyed by grosser material elements such as fire, air, earth and water because they are etheric in nature.

They are not immortal, however; when their work is finished, they are absorbed back into the ocean of spirit. But they do live until a great age. The gnomes of the earth have the shortest age of the four, their average age ranging from three hundred to one thousand years. The following chart gives a list of some of the beings that make up each group.

Gnomes	Undines	Salamanders	Sylphs
Pygmies	Oceanids	Fire spirits	Air spirits
Sylvestres	Oreads		
Satyrs	Nereids		
Dryads	Limoniades		
Hamadryads	Naiads		
Durdalis	Water spirits		
Elves	Sea maids		
Brownies	Mermaids		
Earth spirits	Potamides		
Pans	Water spirits		

There are many kinds of gnomes. These beings have great power over the rocks and mineral elements of the earth and also over the mineral elements in the animal and human kingdoms. The pygmies work with stones, gems, and metals and are guardians of hidden treasures. There might be some association here with the leprechauns. The pygmies are also involved in the cutting of crystals and the developing of veins of ore.

The gnomes build their houses out of substances that resemble alabaster, marble, and cement. Gnomes marry and have families. They are said to have insatiable appetites and they earn their food by their diligent and conscientious work. Some gnome families gather and live in large communities indigenous to the substance in which they work. The female gnome is called a gnomides.

The type of gnome most frequently seen looks like a dwarf and is twelve to eighteen inches tall. These beings are called brownies or elves. They usually look rather old and have white beards. They can be seen scampering out of holes in the stumps of trees and sometimes vanishing into the tree itself. The gnomes meet at certain times of the year in great conclaves where they discuss the beauty and harmony of nature and the prospects of a bountiful harvest. The king of the gnomes is called Gob, hence his subjects are often called goblins. There is also a queen, but I don't know her name.

The gnomes have dwellings, clothing, manners, customs, languages, and governments of their own. They often live inside the Earth. They usually wear caps on their heads, long, tight leg coverings, and tunics with a band around the waist.

The gnomes are kind and friendly to humans, although they are repelled by humans who are selfish and misuse their power. They respond well to love, as do all the elementals and nature spirits. The food they eat is composed of their own element and is not anything like the food humans eat. When humans develop their etheric vision, they will be able to see these wonderful beings.

Undines

The undines are the elemental beings that compose water. They are able to control, to a great degree, the course and function of the water element. Etheric in nature, they exist within the water itself and that is why they can't be seen with normal physical vision. These beings are beautiful to look at and are very graceful. They are often seen riding the waves of the ocean. They can also be found in rocky pools and in marshlands. They are clothed in a shimmery substance looking like water but shining with all the colors of the sea, with green predominating. The concept of the mermaid is connected with these elemental beings.

The undines also work with the plants that grow under the water and with the motion of water. Some undines inhabit waterfalls, others live in rivers and lakes. Every fountain has its nymph. Every ocean has its oceanids. The undines closely resemble humans in appearance and size, except for those inhabiting smaller streams and ponds. The undines often live in coral caves under the ocean or on the shores of lakes or banks of rivers. Smaller undines live under lily pads.

The undines work with the vital essences and liquids of plants, animals, and human beings. They are present in everything containing water. There are many families of undines, as the chart indicates. The ruler of the undines is a being called Necksa. The undines love, serve, and honor her unceasingly. They are emotional beings, very friendly and open to being of service to human beings.

The smaller undines are often seen as winged beings that people have mistakenly called fairies. These winged beings are seen near flowers that grow in watery areas. They have gossamer wings and gossamer clothing.

Salamanders

The salamanders are the spirits of fire. Without these beings, fire cannot exist. You cannot light a match without a salamander's being present. There are many families of salamanders, differing in size, appearance, and dignity. Some people have seen them as small balls of light, but most commonly they are perceived as being lizard-like in shape and about a foot or more in length.

The salamanders are considered the strongest and most powerful of all the elementals. Their ruler is a magnificent flaming being called Djin. Those who have seen him say that he is terrible, yet awe-inspiring in appearance.

Salamanders have the ability to extend their size or diminish it, as needed. If you ever need to light a campfire in the wilderness, call to the salamanders and they will help you.

It has also been said that salamanders (and the other elemental beings) can be mischievous at times. For example, a fiery temper and inharmonious conditions in a person's home can cause these beings to make trouble. They are like children in that they don't fully understand the results of their actions. They are greatly affected, as are all nature spirits, by humankind's thinking.

Sylphs

The sylphs are the air spirits. Their element has the highest vibratory rate of the four. They live hundreds of years, often reaching one thousand and never seeming to get old. They are said to live on the tops of mountains. The leader of the sylphs is a being called Paralda who is said to dwell on the highest mountain of Earth.

Sylphs often assume human form but only for short periods of time. They vary in size from being as large as a human to being much smaller. They are volatile and changeable. The winds are their particular vehicle. They work through the gasses and ethers of the Earth and are kindly toward humans. They are usually seen with wings, looking like cherubs or fairies. Because of their connection to air, which is associated with the mental aspect, one of their functions is to help humans receive inspiration. The sylphs are drawn to those who use their minds, particularly those in the creative arts.

Other Types of Elementals

There is another type of elemental being that is different from the spirits of the four elements I have just mentioned. These beings are called elementals also but are created by thought from elemental essence. They are one of the reasons it is so important for humans to control their thoughts. Even the elementals of the fire, air, earth, and water are greatly affected by our thoughts, for good or bad. Negative thoughts such as violence, depression, and fear actually create these little beings which are called astral elementals. Edgar Cayce, in his Universal Mind readings, always used to say that "thoughts are things." As long as you strive for mastery of your three lower bodies (physical, astral, mental) and serve your soul and the ideal of love, you will not be troubled or hurt to any degree by these elemental entities.

One way to create negative elementals is to drink too much alcohol and fall into a drunken stupor. You might then see very unpleasant creatures that are not hallucinations but in reality are elemental forms created from the thinking of the lower self, which is out of control. People who give free reign to their anger and violent passions might see kinds of elemental beings that look like an army of devils. They are fiery red creatures about twelve to eighteen inches in height, with horns and tails. These can actually be seen by psychics. Depression creates elementals of a more clinging nature.

On the other side of the coin, it is also possible to create elementals of a happy and service-oriented nature. All thought that is repeated over and over again draws to it elemental substance. One example could be found in the thoughts of the mother of a son or daughter who has been sent to a battlefield. The love of the mother that goes forth, day after day, surrounding her beloved child with prayers and visualizations of protection, creates an actual thought form which is then ensouled by an elemental. The elemental's task is to carry out the wishes of the person who created it, in this case the mother, so it becomes a shield of protection surrounding the child, as the elemental being strives to carry out the pattern of the thought.

Djwhal Khul has stated that it is important that a human refrain from manipulation of these elemental forces until he has unfolded the consciousness of the soul and attained a certain degree of self-mastery. Just as the astral elementals can cause problems for a person who lives in victim consciousness, so can the devas of the astral plane. If a person is victim of his physical body, feelings, emotions, desires, and thoughts, he can also be controlled by devic life of a lower order.

All dense physical form, be it mineral, plant, animal, or human body, is created by elemental beings under the direction of a deva who is under the direction of a higher deva who ultimately is under the Divine Architect, God Himself.

The Findhorn Garden

Dorothy Maclean was the woman in Findhorn who could communicate with the deva kingdom. During the first year the community of Findhorn was in operation, they grew sixty-five different vegetables, twenty-one different fruits, and forty-two different herbs. That was quite amazing, since none of the people involved had ever done any gardening before. Dorothy would contact the individual deva of each plant, welcome it to the garden, and ask it for guidance. Aside from receiving guidance about the physical components needed for the soil, the most important thing they could do, according to the landscape deva, was to radiate a sense of love and appreciation to the plants.

By the end of a year of following the directions of the devas, they had produced forty-two-pound cabbages and a broccoli that fed three families for several weeks. This was all done in sandy ground that had barely an inch or two of soil. In one of the channelings, the devas said to Dorothy, "At this we rejoice and are glad, for the connections between us are greater than you realize, and it seems strange to us that you should be so unconscious of so much of your own being. We see you rather like an iceberg with seven-eighths of your consciousness submerged and only an eighth alive. . . . We are in a line of consciousness from the One Great Whole to the smallest unit of life, and therefore we perform the miracles which you see in the growth of the seed. . . ."

More about the Devas

The devas are differentiated from the nature spirits and elemental beings in that they hold the archetypal patterns for all physical forms on Earth and direct the energy that is needed for their materialization. Most people think of the growth of plants and animals as occurring through natural law; in truth, it is the devas or angels that carry out this law, and they do their work ceaselessly and joyously.

There is an individual deva for, let's say, a carrot plant, and there is an overlighting deva who is in charge of all the carrot plants in the whole world. The devas are the architects, and the nature spirits and elementals are the craftspeople who do the work, receiving not only the blueprint but also the energy to physicalize the plan.

The devas have no particular form; the word "deva" actually means "shining one." They take on form as needed, and the forms they take when appearing to humans are often correspondent with the thought forms humans hold of them, such as the assumptions that angels have wings and dwarves carry pickaxes. The numbers and kinds of devas are infinite because of the enormous variety of physical substances present on Planet Earth which, according to Vywamus, has a very highly evolved plant kingdom. There are devas of all the flowers, plants, landscapes, lakes, rivers, soils, gardens, manures, rains, winds, elements, and trees, to name just a few. Each change in the structure and color of a flower, for example, requires another group of builders. When the actual flower itself blossoms, the fairies appear.

Most people just plant their gardens. From the devas' point of view, a garden must be sown both physically and spiritually. The nature devas and elementals are so used to being invisible and ignored that it brings them great delight to be able to work with humans who are aware of them and willing to work with them and who treat them as equals, appreciating the wonderful work they do. They are very appreciative of human admiration.

It must be understood that the minerals, plants, and animals are not here just to serve humans, but that humans are here to be of service to them, too. In Buddhism these kingdoms are looked at as being completely equal with humankind, which is as it should be. Each is here to express itself and glorify God perfectly.

When flowers are cut, the fairy builders might accompany the bloom for some time. Every garden has not only a beautiful appearance and aroma, but also a beautiful sound. When a flower blooms perfectly it creates a full chord that is the keynote of that flower. That chord can be heard in a meditative state.

Clairvoyant Sightings of Nature Spirits

There is a book I recommend highly: *Fairies* by Edward Gardener. In it are five actual photographs of nature spirits. They were made famous by Sir Arthur Conan Doyle (of Sherlock Holmes fame) in the early 1900s. These pictures might well be the only actual photographs of nature spirits ever recorded, and they are beautiful and absolutely breathtaking. I have copied and enlarged them at the print shop and have them hanging in my office. If you are not clairvoyant but have wanted to see fairies and gnomes, then look for this book. It also describes what the two young ladies and Geoffrey Hodson, who were all clairvoyant, saw in the glen where these pictures were taken. I have included a number of the clairvoyant sightings and descriptions from this book.

Water Nymph: "I saw a water sprite. It was an entirely nude female figure with long fair hair, which it appeared to be combing or passing through its fingers. Its form was a dazzling rosy whiteness and its face very beautiful. The arms were long and graceful and moved with a wave-like motion. It sometimes appeared to be singing."

Wood Nymph: "Two tiny wood elves came racing over the ground past us as we sat on a fallen tree trunk. Seeing us, they pulled up short about five feet away and stood regarding us with considerable amusement but no fear. They appeared as if completely covered in a tight-fitting one-piece skin which shone slightly as if wet. They had hands and feet large and out of proportion to their bodies. Their legs were somewhat thin; ears large and almost pear-shaped, pointed upwards."

Brownie: "He is rather taller than the normal, say eight inches, dressed entirely in brown with facings of a darker shade, big-shaped cap, almost conical knee breeches, stockings, and has thin ankles and large pointed feet like gnomes' feet. He stands facing us, in no way afraid, perfectly friendly and much interested."

Fairies: "Frances sees tiny fairies dancing in a circle, the figures gradually expanding in size till they reach eighteen inches, the ring widening in proportion. Elsie sees a vertical circle of dancing fairies flying slowly round. The fairies who are dancing have long skirts through which their limbs can be seen.

"Viewed astrally, the circle is bathed in golden-yellow light, with the outer edges of many hues, violet predominating. There is a tinkling music accompanying all this. It appears to have more of the aspect of a ceremony than a game. Frances sees two fairy figures performing as if on the stage, one with wings, one without.

"Elsie sees a big beautiful fairy quite near. It is nude, with golden hair, and is kneeling in the grass looking this way, with hands on knees, smiling at us. It has a very beautiful face and is concentrating its gaze on me. This figure came within five feet of us, and after being described, faded away."

Fairy Band: "There has suddenly arrived in the field a fairy director with a band of fairy people. Their arrival causes a bright radiance to shine in the field, visible to us sixty yards away. The director is very autocratic and definite in her orders and is holding unquestioned command. The band spread themselves out into a gradually widening circle around her, and as they do, a soft glow spreads over the grass. They are actually vivifying and stimulating the growth in the field. Each member of the band is linked to the leader by a thin stream of light."

Golden Fairy: "One especially beautiful fairy has a body clothed in transparent, shimmering golden light. She has tall wings, each of which is almost divided into upper and lower portions."

Gnomes and Fairies: "The gnomes are like little old men, with little green caps, and their clothes are generally neutral green. The fairies themselves are in light draperies. I have also seen them in the conservatory of my house, floating about among the flowers and plants. The fairies appear to be perpetually playing, excepting when they go to rest on the turf or in a tree, and I once saw a group of gnomes standing on each others' shoulders like gymnasts on the stage. . . . They always look happy, as if they were having a real good time."

Findhorn and Perelandra

If you are interested in learning more about the devas and nature spirits and the elemental kingdom, the two best sources of information are *The Findhorn Garden* by the Findhorn community and a book about Perelandra called *Behaving as if the God in all Life Mattered* by Machaelle Small Wright.

Machaelle is able to see and hear the invisible forces of nature much as Dorothy Maclean was able to do at Findhorn. Machaelle started a twenty-acre farm in Virginia dedicated to a co-equal relationship with the devas and nature spirits. She is an extraordinary woman, and I can't recommend her book highly enough. It is one of the most interesting books I have ever read about the nature kingdom, and I would like to relate some of her insights.

Machaelle gives a very interesting description of how a plant is actually grown. She describes the archetype, or pattern, of each plant a deva is in charge of as a package of energy. The deva very gradually brings this package down through the dimensions of reality. Once the package reaches the etheric level, it is then the job of the nature spirits to take over.

Nature spirits, like devas, are bodies of Light energy, but the nature spirits are slightly denser in vibration because of their closer proximity to Earth. If you wanted to change the color of a vegetable or flower you would have to talk to the devas in charge and they would help to change the package. If you were concerned about how to care for the package once it was grounded into the etheric and physical planes, then you would have to communicate with the nature spirits and elementals.

Every garden needs to have a special place where humans are not allowed to go. This was communicated to Dorothy at Findhorn and to

Machaelle at Perelandra. The space doesn't have to be right in your immediate garden, but it should be close by. It is also important to realize that the creation of a garden is a cocreatorship between the devas and nature spirits and the human kingdom. Most humans pay no attention to the devas and nature spirits, but on the other hand, Machaelle tells how she went to the other extreme for a while and exhausted herself doing every little thing the devas and nature spirits wanted her to do. She was finally told that this was not the proper attitude. The devas and nature spirits just want an equal relationship, not to be totally in charge.

She was also told by the nature spirits that the best time to transplant was in the evening around ten o'clock, because that is when the energy of a plant is in its roots rather than in its stems and leaves, as it is during the day.

Manifestation

One of the subjects the devas and nature spirits insisted that Machaelle work with was the understanding of manifestation. This is an extraordinary sequence of events. She was told to decide what she wanted to manifest and then to contact the deva directly involved with that item. She began initially with the desire to manifest hay for the garden. She contacted the hay deva and made the request, very clearly, specifically, and concisely for what she needed. Two days later, someone called spontaneously and guided her to the exact amount of hay she needed – for free.

Machaelle's next more profound and accelerated lesson in manifestation came when she decided she needed one cubic foot of manure. She connected with the devas connected with the manure and clearly visualized her exact need.

The following is a quote from Machaelle that describes what she experienced upon connecting with this deva:

> As soon as I connected, I felt myself lift (vibrationally) to a very familiar level – the level where astral traveling is done. There we waited until suddenly I felt a third energy enter my awareness. We had been joined by the energy of the manure. With great care, we all three moved down in vibration more slowly than I had ever experienced in meditation – or perhaps it was simply more clearly than I had ever experienced. As we moved from one level to the next, I could feel the shift in the manure energy. Eventually, I felt the manure take on a sense of physicalness. I sensed atoms, then molecules, then cells. I sensed form within the manure energy. Eventually, even smell. At the moment I touched down from my own meditative state, I opened my eyes, and there before me was the cubic foot of manure.

This is extraordinary! I know Sai Baba can do it, but he is the Cosmic Christ. Here is a woman who with simple attunement to God and the devas and nature spirits is able to manifest physical objects. The principle is quite similar to the way the devas and nature spirits manifest a plant. The deva visualizes the archetypal pattern and package in the spiritual dimensions. Once the image is set, the energy is called forth and slowly made to descend downward through the dimensions of reality. Upon reaching the etheric plane the nature spirits begin using their energy to physicalize the pattern in the form of the visualization of the devas. Do you see that Machaelle just uses the same principle? The only difference is that she visualizes the archetypal pattern herself and the devas work with that.

In Machaelle's next meditation she manifested a squash seed that appeared right in front of her. Her next experience was to manifest tools. There are actually devas of garden tools. She describes the almost instant manifestation of tools: she would go into meditation and enter the void. On the level just outside of the void she would make herself become a hammer, for example. With the help of the devas she would then descend downward through the levels until she reached the etheric level where the nature spirits would jump in and do their work. When she opened her eyes, there was the hammer.

She speaks of the experiences with great humility, knowing they could not occur without the help of the nature kingdom. They can't help eliciting profound respect for the powers of the devas.

Most of the gardens and farms around the world are now without nature spirits. They have been so mistreated, abused, unappreciated, and raped that they have retreated from humanity. Without their help, the amount of energy that actually grounds into the physical form is at its bare minimum. The result is empty food with no energy or Light in it. The nature spirits end up going to forested areas humans don't frequent. The Findhorn and Perelandra gardens produced such large and wonderful produce because the devas and nature spirits were invited to help and to work with humans as copartners.

A story that emphasizes the interrelatedness of all things has to do with an early phase of the Perelandra garden. Machaelle was preparing to visit Findhorn and had tons of other responsibilities as well. She changed her attitude toward the garden, beginning to consider it a drill sergeant. She stopped enjoying the garden and became goal-oriented instead of finding a balance between goal and process.

Shortly after falling into this attitude, she found that the Brussels sprouts had been attacked by hordes of bugs. She immediately attuned to the deva of the Brussels sprouts and it said, "When you look at the garden now, you see a half-empty glass. You focus on the negative. You deal only with the work to be done. You no longer see the beauty and what is being accomplished here. Your attitude has unbalanced the energy of the garden, leaving it vulnerable to being overpowered and destroyed by insects. Since you have altered the balance, it is important for you to reestablish the balance. You must understand the power contained in thoughts and attitudes and the integral part they play in the balance of the whole."

Most gardeners look at balance only in terms of soil composition, water, and sunlight. These physical components are only one part of the true balance that needs to be sought in a garden. Machaelle's negative attitude alone caused the garden to be attacked by insects.

Closing Down a Garden for the Winter

Machaelle thought the closing of the garden would take one day, but it ended up taking seven days. Just as it is important for the death experience to be handled properly for humans, so is the same true for a garden. Machaelle tuned in to each plant that had become part of the garden, thanked it for its presence, and released it from the garden. Even though many of the plants were already dead because of frost, the energy, or consciousness, of the plants was still in the garden. You could say metaphorically that the soul had not yet left. The nature spirits that had worked in the garden had moved to the elemental annex, the special spot in the garden just for devas and nature spirits. This process allowed for the proper "bardo" experience for each and every plant in the garden. It was quite a powerful experience, as I am sure you can imagine.

Other Interesting Information

Some spiritual people who are involved with gardening have gone to the extreme of thinking that if they deal with the devas and nature spirits they don't have to concern themselves with the physical needs of the plants like bone meal, manure, nitrogen, lime, and water. That would be like saying that humans don't require healthful food because they are spiritual.

Another interesting point is how devas and nature spirits feel about the eating of plants by humans. Machaelle was told that this was part of the plant kingdom's service to humanity. The nature kingdom celebrates this special relationship and just wishes humans would appreciate and honor it in a nonselfish manner.

37

Evolution and Ecology

*What I would tell you is that as we forge ahead,
never deviating from our course for one
moment's thought, feeling, or action, so could
you. Humans generally seem not to know where
they are going or why. If they did, what a
powerhouse they would be!*

Pea Deva
though Dorothy Maclean
of Findhorn

The Animal Kingdom

The main difference between humans and animals lies in the kinds of consciousnesses they embody. Human beings have self-consciousness and an individual soul, whereas animals are guided mainly by instinct rather than by a reasoning mind, and they are connected to a group soul.

It is possible for more highly evolved animals, usually those that have a domesticated nature, to evolve eventually into the human kingdom. This doorway was open prior to Atlantis but it was closed at that time except for special cases. Sai Baba has said that his pet elephant, Sai Bita, will be a human in his next lifetime. If more people realized that animals can evolve into humans, they might treat animals with more respect. The treatment of animals in this society is atrocious. They are not looked at as the equals they truly are. Every animal is God visiting you in physical form. Eventually, over eons of time, the entire animal kingdom will move up to the lower levels of the human kingdom. Since animals have group souls, individualization is the portal of entry into the human kingdom. An animal can experience life as an individual in a pack of animals or as a loner but it is usually through the interaction with humans as a domesticated animal that the goal of fully expressing as an individual is achieved.

Animals do reincarnate. In one of the Cayce readings a woman asked if she had known her cat in a past life. The Universal Mind said, through Cayce, that her cat had been with her in an incarnation in Egypt as a pet lion.

The animal kingdom can be an emotional buffer for humankind. Animals are very sensitive to emotions. I'm sure you have seen how dogs will growl at certain people and not at others, depending on the vibration the human is radiating. Animals are able to absorb and, to a certain degree, transmute negative human emotions and imbalances. Wild animals are apparently able to take in the imbalance of massive group action such as war, famine, poverty, and mass death. The animals who serve as pets do the same thing for their individual human caretakers. Dogs and cats might defuse an argument by asking for love and attention. Other times the companion animal reflects human emotions of a negative nature in its own behavior.

Recently my sister went through an intense emotional crisis, and a week later her cat stopped eating for four days and almost died of thyroid failure. A spiritual teacher told her that her cat was running the crisis energy through her little body and it was much too powerful for her. As soon as my sister disconnected emotionally from her cat in regard to the matter, her cat recovered and was fine.

Findhorn and the Animal Kingdom

There is a wonderful story about the animal kingdom concerning an occurrence during the first year at Findhorn. Because of all the compost that was being spread around, there were a great many earthworms. Earthworms are the favorite food of moles, and moles attacked the garden, building tunnels everywhere.

Dorothy Maclean decided to meditate on the situation and she tuned into a rather scary-looking great king mole with a crown on his head, sitting in an underground cavern. She proceeded to explain the situation to him and promised not to hurt his moles. She also suggested that he go to a neighboring area close by that was not used for gardening. Lo and behold, the moles left the garden! Several years later, when Findhorn was given the neighboring plot of land, there were the moles, exactly where she had asked them to go.

Perelandra and the Animal Kingdom

There are a number of fascinating stories of a similar nature that occurred at Perelandra. As part of Machaelle's desire for good soil, she put out a call for earthworms. Sure enough, when planting season came there were earthworms everywhere. The problem was that it was impossible to till the soil without killing the worms in the process.

Machaelle got very frustrated and declared out loud that she was going to have a fifteen-minute tea break and when she returned she wanted the earthworms out of a particular area. When she returned, the earthworms were gone. Once she was finished working, she said, "You can come back now," and they did.

Machaelle also had a problem with moles. She spoke with the mole deva, and thirty minutes later she looked up and saw a whole band of over one hundred moles heading toward the open field, exactly where she had asked them to go.

She tried this one more time with cabbage worms. They had infested all her vegetables. She connected with the deva of the cabbage worms and requested that they leave all her vegetables except four special ones that were being planted specifically for their purposes. When she woke up in the morning all the worms were gone except for the one plant at the end of each row that was specifically designated for them.

Can you imagine what it would be like if all the farmers and gardeners of the world communicated with their plants? There would be no need for insecticides or pesticides. This applies even to homes. You can communicate with the deva of the ants or cockroaches or fleas and ask them not to enter the house.

One interesting story on this subject: Sai Baba was asked if it was ever permissible to kill insects invading a house. Sai Baba said it was permissible and no karma would be incurred if the insects were invading the house, but karma would be incurred if they were killed outside. An even better method, however, would be to just tune in and ask them to leave. Why not? An ant, a flea, or a cockroach is God incarnate. Everything has its place in nature, and all kingdoms resound to the call of God.

In the future, those people choosing to eat meat will receive their meat from cattlemen who put out a call to the overlighting deva of cattle and draw to themselves those cows that wish to serve humanity in this capacity. Eventually humankind will evolve beyond the eating of meat, but humanity is not at that level of evolution yet. Certain animals are willing to serve in this capacity as a service to humankind if it is part of the divine plan. The above-mentioned example would be an ideal way to facilitate the situation.

The Wonderful Pig Story

One of my favorite stories of all time comes from a set of tapes made by John Robbins who wrote *Diet for a New America*, a wonderful book I highly recommend. He tells a story about a pig farmer he visited while doing research for his book. He was invited to dinner but did not let on who he was. The pig farmer was running what might be called a pig concentration camp in which the pigs were in small cages stacked one on top of the other in the most horrendous of conditions imaginable.

Toward the end of dinner, the pig farmer intuitively picked up on who John Robbins was and slammed his fist on the table in anger. John Robbins was rather frightened. However, the man calmed down and then proceeded to talk. He explained that he was just trying to make a living by competing successfully with other pig farmers. He told how, as a young child, he had had a pet pig who was super smart. If I am not mistaken, the pig even saved him from drowning in a lake. One day the pig farmer's father told his son that they were going to have the pig for dinner. The boy was crushed. The father made him choose between the pig and himself. It was after that that the boy started to shut down emotionally.

John Robbins sent a copy of his book to the pig farmer who was so disgusted by the book that he actually threw it into the toilet. Meanwhile, he had been getting severe migraine headaches on a regular basis. Finally, his wife fished the book out of the toilet, dried it out, and said maybe if he read the whole book, his headaches would go away. He followed her advice, and some time after reading the book, the farmer decided to sell his pig farm. The headaches immediately stopped.

John Robbins received this information in a letter but then didn't hear from the farmer for quite a while. About a year later he received a letter saying that not only had the farmer sold his pig concentration camp, but he had bought a new farm and opened a pig-petting zoo where children from all over could learn about how smart pigs were and could pet them and play with them. The pigs had become his pets and were no longer locked up in cages. Needless to say, the pig farmer had never been happier or more at peace with himself.

Some Final Comments on Animals

Animals are the young brothers and sisters of humans. As the older siblings, humans can help them to evolve and become more spiritual. A domestic animal usually takes on the personality of its master: a vicious dog comes from a vicious owner; a dog owner who trains his animal to hunt and kill and be an attack dog is degrading the animal spiritually. Just the opposite should be occurring. People should be teaching animals to be of the Christ consciousness and to realize their Godly nature to the fullest. For example, an unevolved dog might be rabid and biting everyone. A more highly evolved dog is happy and loves and serves his master to the best of his abilities.

In truth, every encounter with an animal is a holy encounter – God meeting God. It is time for humankind to be of service to the mineral, plant, and animal kingdoms instead of looking upon those kingdoms as nothing more than objects of service to self.

Native Americans and Nature Spirits

Native Americans have the best relationship with and understanding of nature. They love the flowers and they talk to their brother trees and to the running water. They talk to the spirit of mountain and even to blades of grass, for everything is alive with the Light of God. The Great Spirit lives within every creature, plant, and stone.

The American Indian would pray over an animal after it had to be killed and thank it for its service. This is nothing like the white man who would kill the buffalo just for sport. The Native American walks softly on Mother Earth; there is much the rest of humanity could learn from his example.

Devas, Humans, and the Earth Mother

The nature spirits work under the directorship of the devas. In the Findhorn community it was Dorothy Maclean who had the gift of communicating with the devas. In her first experience at the very start of the community, before it had even gotten off the ground, she made an attempt to speak with the garden pea and got an immediate response from the deva of the garden pea.

The garden pea deva said, "I can speak to you, human. I am entirely directed by my work which is set out and molded and which I merely bring to fruition, yet you have come straight to my awareness. My work is clear before me: to bring the force fields into manifestation regardless of obstacles, and there are many in this man-infested world. While the vegetable kingdom holds no grudges against those it feeds, man takes what he can as a matter of course, giving no thanks. This makes us strangely hostile. What I would tell you is that as we forge ahead, never deviating from our course for one moment's thought, feeling, or action, so could you. Humans generally seem not to know where they are going or why. If they did, what a powerhouse they would be! If they were on the straight course of what is to be done we could cooperate with them. I have put across my meaning and bid you farewell."

This is quite a message from a little pea deva! Its message is so very true – humankind as a whole has been totally unappreciative of the work the devas and nature spirits do. Science has turned nature into a cold, mechanistic process completely devoid of spirituality. Science has become a nightmare of the soul and spirit of all things. The motto of science is that nothing exists except what you can see with your physical eyes and sense with your other physical senses; nothing could be farther from the truth.

The pea deva called the world "man-infested." That reminds me of a movie called *Emerald Forest,* about a rain forest in South America. The Indian tribe living there called white people "the termite people" because of the way they were destroying the forests.

Humankind has lived upon the Earth as a parasite, destroying the forests and polluting the air, the rivers, the lakes, and the oceans. He is destroying the ozone layer, and the fossil fuels are causing a greenhouse effect. He is using up the natural resources. He is junking up space with satellites and the Earth with nuclear waste he doesn't know what to do with. Man has been a cancer to the Earth Mother. His selfishness, greed, and self-centeredness will lead to his destruction if he doesn't change his ways.

Besides the violence he has perpetrated upon the Earth Mother, Pan, the devas, and the nature spirits, there has been a complete and total lack of appreciation for all these beings have done for humanity. Vywamus has said that the Earth Mother herself has actually had to pull away from humanity because of the injuries she has suffered. There has been a long-standing pattern of lack of integration and cooperation among the seven kingdoms.

As the human kingdom awakens to the kingdom of souls, its members will also awaken to the beautiful kingdoms of minerals, plants, and animals and will cease the atrocities now perpetrated on animals in the name of science, luxury, sport, and greed, realizing that anything done to an animal is done to God, for an animal is God.

The planet's surface is the skin of the Earth Mother, but is has been covered up with cement so that the Earth can't breath. The destroying of the rain forests is causing an oxygen imbalance across the entire planet. The planet has been scarred by strip-mining and ripped by the explosion of nuclear bombs beneath her surface. Djwhal Khul has said that every time a nuclear bomb is detonated beneath the surface, an earthquake occurs somewhere on the globe. All I can say is that the Earth Mother, Pan, the devas, and the nature spirits must be very forgiving and loving beings to carry on as valiantly as they have for the past ten million years even though they have been physically, emotionally, and mentally violated.

The United States finally has a Vice President, Al Gore, and a President, Bill Clinton, who are advocates of the environment. Vywamus has said that on July 1, 1986, a new communicative link was set up among the five kingdoms — mineral, plant, animal, human, and soul. The human kingdom began to move beyond its first steps. It is interesting that around that time Earth Day was instituted and the ozone layer, greenhouse effect, and rain forest controversies came to the public awareness. The Harmonic

Convergence and Hands Across America occurred. It does seem that a small shift has taken place.

The Secret Life of Trees

In my research for this chapter I came across a wonderful little book called *Secrets from the Lives of Trees,* by Jeffrey Goelitz. Jeffrey developed a spiritual relationship with trees that allowed him to communicate with them and with the nature spirits that work with them. I would like to quote a section of his book about the role trees play on Earth that is the channeling of a spirit called Good Friend who often helped in the research.

> Their main purpose on the planet is to help all beings evolve to a higher consciousness. Trees have a non-threatening energy for humans to pick up on, as are many things in nature, like plants, flowers, and meadows. They bring to the world peace and tranquillity. Wood, food, and beauty are then extras within the subpurpose of a tree. The energy they give out goes indiscriminately toward everyone. Trees do not have what you would call a learning or growing pattern of right or wrong. They are more in harmony with the planet and would not be able to take a left-hand turn, as humans can.

> Trees provide essence levels of energy for the planet to use. . . . There is also a wisdom band in trees because they have been on the planet much longer than humans. They hold a higher vibration of the truth. Through-out the ages trees have been used as spots for higher teachings. Buddha, Jesus, and many others held their classrooms in a grove of trees. . . . A tree puts out a higher, clearer vibration which enables people to receive more clarity. Even in the other worlds, there are what you would call etheric trees that many teachings are given under.

The following is a very short quote from the same book on the role of nature spirits: "Because trees are extremely important to the planet, there are a lot of spirits working with them. Just as trees have Light coming from their essence band on the other side, the nature spirits have a different band of energy sent down to them, which they put through their system and adapt for the tree's use. They supplement the tree's energies that Earth's negativity would otherwise alter. In a city, devas help the trees tremendously, let's say in a city park, by putting out positive energy. As devas work with trees, plants, or whatever job they have, they evolve."

The Mineral Kingdom

Everything in the universe is in a state of evolution, including the mineral kingdom. Again, the gnomes are the elemental beings who work specifically with the mineral kingdom. The following chart, indicating the hierarchy of minerals and gemstones, was channeled by Vywamus through The Tibetan Foundation.

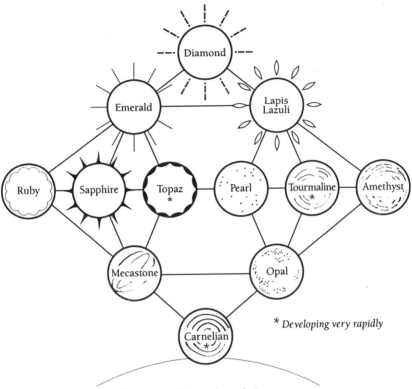

Hierarchy of Minerals and Gemstones

People have a hard time realizing that minerals are alive. The signature of life in the mineral kingdom is the crystalline formation the gnomes have created. Moreover, there are also dead minerals. When a stone is quarried from its source, its vital life force is cut off; the gemstone is still evolving and growing while it is in its natural rock formation. That is not to say that a rock should never be cut from a quarry, but, like a cut flower, it is no longer a living rock. Fairies sometimes accompany a freshly cut flower to its new home, and the same is true of gemstones. Sometimes nature spirits will accompany the gemstone you wear on your hand.

In reality, the mineral kingdom might be the most important to life of all the kingdoms. It makes up the crust of the Earth upon which humans and animals live. The mineral kingdom also provides the basic source of nutrients for the three higher kingdoms, in that plants are rooted in mineral soil, and plants then nourish the physical bodies of both human and animal life, animals then being a food source for the human kingdom as well. Without the mineral kingdom, the other three kingdoms could not survive on Earth. In the evolutionary process, each kingdom acts as the mother from which the succeeding ones are born. The offspring thus depend upon and draw life and sustenance from the preceding kingdom from which it has sprung. The mineral kingdom is spirit at its densest form of vibration.

Minerals and crystals have a profoundly healing effect on the human body and on a garden, too, for that matter. It is time to appreciate the great service the mineral kingdom renders humanity.

The Gemstone Guardians

The best book I have ever read regarding the missions, purposes, effects, and therapeutic applications of gemstones is a wonderful book called *Gifts of the Gemstone Guardians* by Ginny Katz. In a state of meditation one night, she was taken to meet a group of beings known as the Gemstone Guardians. Each Gemstone Guardian's duty is to fulfill the purpose of the particular gemstone it has charge over and to maintain its effects. In recent times these Gemstone Guardians have been given a new responsibility and duty: to teach humans the correct way to use gemstones for therapeutic purposes.

Ginny and her husband, Michael, had been working with gemstones for more than ten years in their business and had studied their healing properties extensively. Since the existing knowledge available on Earth concerning gemstones was limited and very general in nature, Ginny was given the spiritual assignment at the first meeting with the Gemstone Guardians in meditation to interview each of them and bring forth the new information on gemstones straight from the horse's mouth, so to speak. For example, who would know more about the therapeutic uses of an emerald than the actual Emerald Gemstone Guardian?

Michael was put in charge of asking questions of the Gemstone Guardians. They said stones were divided into three groups: the gemstones; the guardians of the Earth stones; the guardians of the ocean stones. The first interview was with the Gemstone Guardian of Quartz. When she first saw him he was wrapped in a white cape that radiated a soft Light. He proceeded to unwrap his arms and open his cape to reveal his body which was made of clear quartz crystal. Ginny blinked her eyes and his body changed into that of a human about thirty years old with blond hair. He was dressed in soft white pants and a shirt. Thus the first interview began.

In the book she tells of her experiences in interviewing the Gemstone Guardians of quartz, lavender, aventurine, emerald, rose quartz, ruby, rhodochrosite, amethyst, purple rainbow fluorite, sapphire, indigo, carnelian, citrine, aquamarine, green tourmaline, rubellite, sodalite, leopardskin jasper, poppy jasper, bloodstone, ivorite, opal (light), riverstone, rhodonite, malachite, lapis lazuli, onyx, mother of pearl, pearl, and coral.

At the end of all the interviews she met with the overseer of the Gemstone Guardians. The overseer stressed the importance of using only the finest quality gemstones for therapeutic purposes. She explained that the average commercial quality gemstones commonly available would not have the powerful effects described by the guardians. Ginny and Michael Katz do sell therapeutic quality gemstones which can be obtained by writing them.

After reading Ginny's book I was extremely impressed. I am not going to describe the qualities of each gemstone, for Ginny has done this far better than I could. My purpose is to introduce you to the Gemstone Guardians and guide you to this wonderful book. The Gemstone Guardians will work with you personally in your own self-healing work if they are called in any sincere manner.

38

The Huna Teachings

*The Huna teachings are the clearest form of
psychology and religion on the planet.*

The Universal Mind
through Paul Solomon

I was first exposed to the Huna teachings by Paul Solomon who is a
channel for the Universal Mind and whom people call the next Edgar
Cayce. In Paul's channelings, the Universal Mind has said that the clearest
form of psychology and religion on the planet are the Huna teachings of
Hawaii. I immediately went out and bought everything I could find about
the Huna teachings. The following is the essence of Huna. An astonishing
point I became aware of in my research for this book is that the Egyptian
teachings involved in becoming initiated into the Order of Melchizedek
during the Third Dynasty were almost word for word the same as the Huna
teachings of Hawaii.

The Psychology and Teachings of Huna

The Huna teachings are an ancient secret science that has come to the
West through the work of Max Freedom Long. Long initially learned about
the teachings of Huna from William Tufts Brigham who had spent forty
years living in Hawaii, trying to understand the secret of the Huna
teachings. He had been able to obtain much information, but he had never
been able to get to the core of the teachings. Long had heard of Brigham's
interest in Huna and searched him out. Mr. Brigham knew after a short
chat that at the age of eighty-two, he had found the man who would carry
on his study and his search for the substance of the Huna teachings that he
had been unable to find.

Max Freedom Long studied the work of Brigham and did carry on his work but he came across the same stumbling block that Brigham had encountered. The Huna teachings were an ancient tradition that had been passed on by word of mouth. Every time Max Freedom Long made an effort to understand Huna, he was shunned. The few kahunas left in Hawaii would not speak to him. For many years he was stuck at this impasse.

Then in 1935 he had a breakthrough. Upon waking from sleep, he had the insight to make a fresh translation of the recorded chants and prayers based on the root words. (The Hawaiian language consists of long words built from short root words.) The new translation was the key that unlocked the secret of how the kahunas performed their seemingly magical feats.

Max Freedom Long spent the next forty years studying and working with the Huna teachings, until his death in 1971. It was at that time that the apprenticeship passed to Dr. E. Otha Wingo. It is Mr. Wingo who is head of the Huna Research Associates and who is the author of the Twelve-Lesson Huna Correspondence Course. The Correspondence Course teaches the practical application of the Huna teachings, and I have found it to be quite helpful.

The following presentation, then, is based on the teachings of Huna as understood by Max Freedom Long and Dr. E. Otha Wingo. It is their interpretations I will refer to in this chapter as the Huna teachings.

The essence of the Huna teachings is that the human being is made up of three selves, or minds. They can most easily be called the subconscious mind, the conscious mind, and the superconscious mind. The kahunas call the conscious mind the "uhane," or middle self. This middle self is the part of a human that is conscious of its own existence and has the ability to reason. It has also been given free will to create as it pleases, along with the low self.

The subconscious mind is called the "unihipili," or low self. It is the part of the human that presents the unconscious material to the conscious mind so it may reason for or against it. The low self is the storehouse of all memory and the seat of the emotions. Its form of mentation is considered to be that of animal-level reasoning. The term "low" has no reference to rank or importance, only to the fact that it is below the level of consciousness of the middle self and to the fact that its bodily center is in the solar plexus rather than in the head.

The third part is the high self, called the "aumakua" by the kahunas. The high self is the "older, utterly trustworthy parental self of spirit." This higher self lives at a higher plane of consciousness outside of the physical body. It will not intervene in the affairs of life unless asked to do so. This is understood to be a cosmic law the high self must adhere to.

The high self has a higher form of mentation than the middle and low selves have. It is the part that directs dreams, intuitions, and premonitions through the subconscious self. Huna teaches that it is the high self that constructs your future from the thoughts, hopes, and fears of the middle and low selves.

The high self is supposed to be able to see into the future as far as your thoughts have been crystallized. As thoughts change daily in the lives of the middle and low selves, so does the future change, according to Huna teachings. Huna also teaches that communication with the high self occurs quite naturally during sleep. It is in that contact that most of the thoughts of the day are supposedly averaged by the high self and used, by some mysterious mechanism, to materialize conditions in the future.

In the Huna teachings, each of the three selves has its proper role to perform in the life of each individual. Life, health, and happiness have to do with the integration, blending, and harmonizing of these three selves.

The other basic teaching of Huna is that people are made up of ten basic elements. To understand this concept it is necessary to understand the triad of mind-force-matter. I have already mentioned the three levels of mind — subconscious, conscious, and superconscious. It is also believed that the basic vital force, or energy, in a person's body is divided into three voltages. The lowest voltage is that of the lower, or subconscious, self; this same vital force, when used by the middle self, or conscious mind, is thought to be raised to a higher voltage; in the same way, when the vital force is raised to the level of consciousness of the high self, it is raised again to an even higher voltage. The basic vital force of a person changes according to which self is using that energy.

The last element of this triad is that of matter. Huna teaches that each of the three selves has a shadow body, or etheric body. The shadow bodies are metaphysical bodies that are thought to be exact duplicates of everything that exists in the physical world. It is these energetic molds that hold all physical form together. Everything that has ever been created has a shadow body.

The shadow body of the low self is said to be a mold of every tissue of the physical body. The low self's shadow body, hence, looks exactly like the physical body except that it is metaphysical in form. Huna teaches that all memory is stored in this shadow body of the low self. The shadow body of the middle self is an energy body in the region of the physical head. The low and middle selves, hence, interpenetrate the physical body with their shadow bodies.

The high self has a shadow body also, but it does not interpenetrate the physical body. The high self is connected to the low self by an energy cord. This energy cord has been called the silver cord in other mystical teachings.

I have so far mentioned nine elements. The tenth element is the physical body, which is the vehicle, or instrument, in which the low self and middle self operate and live.

Huna teaches that the high self expresses all the divine qualities — compassion, patience, love, forgiveness. It is the ideal to which the middle self is to aspire. It is a step advanced in the mental powers and creative abilities. The high self is also considered to be a combined community of spirits. High selves are considered to be individual in identity and yet one with all other high selves at the same time. The high self is also considered to be a perfect blending of masculine and feminine, an androgynous self.

The shadow bodies of the three selves are made of a substance called "aka." Aka has a sticky and elastic quality to it and can stretch without breaking. This substance is also a perfect carrier and conductor of vital force. According to Huna teachings, the lower self's shadow body is capable of changing shapes temporarily or permanently to form a connecting thread between the middle self and the high self. If you have a good relationship and a strong rapport with your low and high selves, you have developed these aka threads into aka cords. It is upon these aka threads and cords that vital force and thought forms travel.

Every time you contact your low self, your high self, any object, or any person in the world you are sending out aka threads. When contact is made between two persons, a long sticky thread is drawn between them. Further contact adds other aka threads, and they become braided together into an aka cord. An aka cord results in a strong rapport between the two individuals.

Telepathic communication, according to Huna, has to do with the traveling of vital force and thought forms along aka cords. This telepathic sending of thought forms and vital force can occur among the middle, low, and high selves and between two people who have a strong aka cord connection.

Every thought you think has a shadow body around it, also. As a thought is formed it is fastened by a thread of aka to the thought threads that came before it. This concept is the explanation for the association of ideas which is acknowledged by modern psychology. In other words, a given thought attracts the threads of all similar thoughts.

Another extremely important aspect of the Huna teachings is the importance of mana, or vital force. Mana is the basic energy in all things. Huna teaches that mana is taken from food and air by the low self and stored in the low self's shadow body. This vital force in the lower self's shadow body can be used for anything the middle self wants. When used by the middle self the mana is raised from the shadow body of the lower self to the physical head region of the middle self and in the process of being raised is changed in some subtle way. This force, when raised, is called the will by modern psychology. When the middle self does not use this will power as it should, the lower self acts out and flits from one activity to another without carrying out any suggestion or command effectively.

The low, or subconscious, self is thought to be like a child. It needs to be loved, and it needs to be treated firmly and in a disciplined manner. A real physical child, if spoiled and not given any discipline, will act out. It is the same with the lower self. That is why it is essential that the middle self raise the mana for use as will power. The middle self is the reasoning mind which is like the parent of the low self, just as the high self is the parent of the middle self. The three selves are gradations of consciousness.

The kahunas believe that everything in the universe is in a state of evolution, including the elements, plants, insects, animals, low selves, middle selves, and high selves. They see the entire universe in gradations of consciousness.

The kahunas believe that God is a triune being, just as people are triune beings. They believe that God is a trinity of levels of spirit; they term these three levels Ku, Kane, and Kanaloa. This concept of God correlates with that of other religions such as Christianity (Father, Son, and Holy Spirit) and Hinduism (Brahma, Vishnu, and Shiva). The kahunas believe that the process of evolution is one of moving through these levels of consciousness back to eventual at-one-ment with God the Creator, or Ku.

Making prayers to the high self is similar to the process that is used between the low self and middle self. Once the middle self has raised the vital force from the shadow body of the low self to use as will, it can do whatever it wants to do with that energy. Such will can be used for physical exercise or controlling the lower self or thinking or praying or anything else. The process of prayer to the high self involves raising the vital force, or mana, up from the middle self to the next voltage.

The aspect that is unique to the Huna teachings is that it is the low self that takes the prayer to the high self. If the low self has a complex of sin, guilt, unworthiness, or doubt, it will not deliver the prayer. The low self uses the mana the middle self has raised and sends that vital force up the aka cord with the prayer.

Huna teaches that the high self cannot manifest a prayer unless it receives the needed mana from the middle and low selves. Thus, it is essential, according to Huna teaching, to accumulate a surcharge of vital force before beginning to pray to the high self. A great deal of emphasis is given in the Huna teachings to how this is done. As I mentioned before, a certain amount of vital force is created from the food you eat and the air you breathe. Huna teaches a number of other ways to accumulate extra energy:

1. Asking and commanding the low self to build up a surcharge of vital force for use in prayer;
2. Physical exercise;
3. Deep breathing, which causes more blood sugar to be burned (the main method);
4. Postures;
5. Nutritious food;
6. Visualizing vital force rising like a fountain of water from the base of the spine up through the top of the head;
7. Holding a mental attitude of gaining personal power and strength, such as the attitude you would maintain when preparing for a race;
8. Proper sleep and rest;
9. Affirmations spoken out loud, such as "The Universal life force is flowing into me now. I feel it."

In addition to the need for a surcharge of mana, there is the need for "the Clearing of the Path." Clearing the path means removing all thought forms that could sabotage the prayer. Such thought forms can occur in the conscious or the subconscious mind. For example, if you make a prayer for healing and then say you don't think it's going to work, then you are obviously sabotaging your efforts with antithetical thought forms. It can also happen that your conscious mind is behind the prayer, but your subconscious mind is not. The low self might deliver the prayer but ruin it with thought forms of doubt or fear. Another possibility is that the low self will refuse to deliver the prayer at all because of its fixations on guilt and unworthiness. The relationship between the middle self and the low self is, hence, essential before you can even get the high self effectively involved.

Huna teaches that the only sin that exists is that of hurting another person. It is not possible to sin against God or the high self. To clear the path, you must make amends, or balance out the hurts that were inflicted upon another. This can be done in an infinite number of ways as long as the low self is convinced, along with the middle self, that amends have been made. Some kind of physical act or stimulus is usually most convincing to the low self. Any act that is perceived as a sacrifice or a service to others can help to balance out guilt complexes and feelings of unworthiness.

The middle self and low self must also be trained to know what truly is sinful as opposed to what is considered sinful by the dogma of traditional religion. Once the clearing of the path has been achieved, the low self can send the accumulated mana and thought form prayers right up the aka cord (the antakarana, in Hindu terminology) to the high self.

The last step in the process is to create a proper thought form prayer. Huna teaches that thoughts are like seeds. In some strange and unknown way, the high self uses the thoughts you think to create your future. The action of prayer is a way of sending new thought forms to the high self in order to materialize a desired outcome on the Earth plane.

In making prayers, the kahunas stress the importance of preparing very carefully the thought form seeds you wish to create. The one rule is that what you ask for not hurt others and that it be a reasonable request for something that is sincerely needed for yourself or for others. It is suggested that the exact wording of the prayer be written out on paper so a precise picture of what is desired can be visualized. It is also essential that the prayer be worded in positive rather than negative language.

Huna teaches that a prayer for healing should be worded in a way that describes the desired result as opposed to mentioning the ailment. For example, a poor prayer, according to Huna, would be "Heal my injured leg." Mentioning the injured leg is presenting a negative thought form. A better way to phrase the prayer is "I ask that my leg be healed so that I may run and jump and walk to my heart's content, with perfect ease and balance and comfort." In this example the thought form does not mention the injury but, rather, visualizes the healed result. The visualization of the desired thought form is a way of strengthening the seed thoughts that are sent to the high self.

In summary, the Huna prayer method begins with clearing the path, removing any negative thought forms in the middle and low selves that would prevent the low self from taking the thought form prayer to the high self.

Step two is the creation of the exact thought form prayer, including writing it out on paper and developing a strong visualization of the result.

Step three is the building up of an accumulation of vital force in the shadow body of the lower self for the use of the middle self when the prayer action begins.

When these three steps have been accomplished, the prayer is formed by saying it aloud three times over, using your will to impress the prayer on your low self and to build strong thought form clusters. Once it has been stated in this way, the prayer is held in mind, and the low self is ordered to reach out and take it to the high self (the soul). When an answering electric tingle is felt, the prayer is recalled or spoken aloud again so that it can be sent to the high self with the extra supply of vital force needed to materialize the thought forms of the prayer into the present or the future.

The closing portion of the prayer should be made definite; otherwise there is the danger of mixing a jumble of contaminated thoughts into the prepared thought form. The kahunas end their prayers with these words:

"The prayer takes flight. Let the rain of blessings fall." This is an important statement since the high self will manifest only what it is asked to manifest; "Let the rain of blessings fall" is the request that the prayer be answered.

The formal ending of a prayer can be delayed fifteen seconds to a minute to allow the low self to do its work of sending the vital force and thought form prayer up the aka cord. During this time it is essential that the middle self relax so as to avoid calling the low self immediately back to begin another task.

Once the prayer has been completed, it should be released to the keeping of the high self. All that is needed then on the part of the middle and low selves is faith and trust that the prayer will be answered. Any thought other than this would sabotage the prayer procedure. How the prayer will be answered should be left to the workings of the high self.

It is extremely important at that point, according to Huna teachings, for the middle self, you, the conscious personality who has made the request, to do everything humanly possible to help manifest the prayer. Just because a prayer has been made doesn't mean you can just go sit in your room and wait for the results to manifest. The middle and low selves must continue to do their part to manifest the prayer, while avoiding negative thinking.

It is also important that you not speak about the prayer with anyone who would suggest any doubt or negativity about the manifestation of the prayer.

Huna teaches that if a prayer is made for the healing of another, that individual must be cleansed of all negative complexes as a preliminary act; otherwise his low self will prevent the healing.

The last point in this discussion of the Huna prayer method is that you must be prepared to make the prayer action in the exact same manner daily until the desired result is accomplished.

The phenomenon of instant healing by the high self, according to Huna, involves the shadow, or etheric, body of the low self. As stated before, the shadow body of the low self is a perfect metaphysical mold of the physical body. A bone can break in the physical body, but the blueprint, or perfect mold, in the etheric will not be affected.

In the process of instant healing, the mold is emptied of broken or diseased tissues and is refilled with basic substances that conform to the uninjured mold. This is done by the high self in some unknown manner, once it has been asked for, the path has been cleared, and the needed vital force to make the change has been provided.

Huna teaches that the same process is what accounts for the phenomenon of apports. This usually refers to the moving of physical objects over long distances by discarnate spirits. The explanation the Huna teaching gives is that the discarnate spirit somehow obtains an accumulation of extra vital force and uses it to dematerialize the physical object into its etheric, or shadow, form, then moving the object to the desired place and materializing it back into physicality.

Huna teaches that it is also possible for the high self to control such things as the weather, animals, insects, plant life — indeed, anything on this third-dimensional plane of reality.

The presence of spirits at a seance is thought to occur because the spirit uses the vital force of the medium and of the group to form itself into denser matter.

There is an interesting note about vital force and its uses by kahunas that has to do with times of war in Hawaii. A kahuna would take a stick and fill it full of vital force. When he threw the stick at the oncoming enemy, the person it hit would be knocked immediately unconscious.

The process of psychometry, according to Huna, involves ordering the low self to follow the aka threads of an object back to its owner. The owner can be on the other side of the world or on the astral plane; it apparently does not matter to the low self. The thoughts and memories and appearances of the person are noted and then brought back and given to the middle self.

Since the low self's shadow body is a duplicate of the physical body, the low self, hence, has five inner senses, just as the physical body has five outer senses. The low self can be trained to go and get information that it would be impossible for the middle self to get. The phenomenon of astral travel occurs when the low self or the low self and the middle self leave the physical body for a period of time and travel in the astral frequency. The Hunas taught that all people do this every night in their sleep even though they don't remember it when they wake up.

It was believed that after physical death, a person would create a thought form world, or "purgatory," in which he would experience, as in a dream, all events and occurrences he needed to live out.

The last point I would like to discuss in relationship to Huna is the concept of normal living. The integration of the three selves was the goal, but the kahunas believed that each living thing was in its intended stage of evolution and that there was sufficient time for all to grow upward. They believed that family life was good and that all normal living was good. They did not preach a doctrine of asceticism or self-denial. They believed that the low self was just as important in the workings of life as was the high self. They believed that God could not be reached by going straight up but rather by living properly, normally, and in brotherhood on the Earth.

39

The Egyptian Mysteries

As within, so without;
as above, so below.

Hermes

This chapter tells one of the most fascinating true stories in the history of humankind. Archeologists have been trying to figure out for centuries what really went on in ancient Egypt. However, because they approach the subject only with their left brains and are not open to information from the right brain, their hypotheses (with no judgment intended) have been very inaccurate.

It is possible to know exactly what went on in ancient Egypt and to know exactly how the pyramids were built by looking at the information provided by the great prophets and mystics who are able to read the Akashic Records, the storehouse of all knowledge.

In researching this chapter I have studied the Edgar Cayce files, the profound channelings and lucid past-life memories of Earlyne Chaney, the transcripts of The Tibetan Foundation, the totally recalled past-life memories of Elizabeth Haich in *Initiations*, the Paul Solomon channelings on the great pyramid, the past-life memories from the Akashic Records of Joan Grant in *The Winged Pharaoh*, and Manly P. Hall's material on ancient Egypt. The mind-boggling conclusion I have come to is that they all tell basically the same story. What follows are the true secrets of ancient Egypt as read from the Akashic Records.

To understand what really went on in Egypt you must go back in time to the continent of Atlantis, just before its destruction. The great prophets and masters of Atlantis who served the Law of One could see the final destruction of Atlantis coming and they began to guide the spiritual community to leave. The story of Noah's ark is the biblical version of this event.

The Atlanteans traveled in all directions and settled in various parts of the world, but many of them went to Egypt. One of the great teachers in that group was Thoth-Hermes. Thoth was an incarnation of the Buddha and a spiritual master of the highest order. He began to help the Egyptians to develop spiritually.

Thoth had brought with him from Atlantis many great spiritual teachers, and he was closely connected with positive extraterrestrials from Sirius and the Pleiades and with the Great White Brotherhood. Both of these groups helped Thoth in his efforts. Needless to say, they were very successful and Egypt became one of the greatest civilizations ever to exist on this planet.

This great nucleus of teachers and spiritual masters over a long period of time helped to build the pyramids and temples throughout Egypt.

It must be understood that before the coming of the Atlanteans and other groups, the Egyptian civilization had been in operation for over one hundred thousand years, according to Tibetan Foundation channelings. Humanity had been on Earth for over 10.5 million years, but no real advance in consciousness had occurred before the Atlanteans' high level of spirituality and technology, most of which they had received from extraterrestrials visiting Atlantis.

The existing Egyptian civilization had a hard time assimilating the great number of Atlanteans. Thoth and his group were highly respected, even looked at as gods; however, not all the Atlanteans were at the spiritual level of Thoth. This difficulty in assimilation went on for many generations.

When the great flood was about to occur, many of the Atlanteans utilized the tunnels that existed underneath the pyramids to go and live in the inner Earth. They left for two reasons — to escape the flood that might overtake Egypt and because they weren't being accepted by the existing Egyptian civilization.

This vast network of tunnels was built with the use of the ark of the covenant and smaller versions of the ark that utilized a staff with an ankh on it. These instruments could cut through stone like a knife through butter. They could, in essence, dematerialize any object instantly, so it was only the highest initiates who were able to use them. The people of the hollow Earth are, hence, descendants of the Atlanteans and Egyptians.

The extraterrestrial-Atlanteans and the Egyptians interbred and brought forth many children. These children were quite advanced, for the physical structure of a child does affect the consciousness.

It was the extraterrestrials in conjunction with the Great White Brotherhood who brought forth the plans for the building of the Great Pyramid, many of the smaller pyramids, and the Sphinx. The step pyramid of Zoser is the oldest. This initial pyramid was designed to rest upon the ley lines, or electrical grid points, of the planet. The Great Pyramid of Giza is actually in the geographic center of the Earth. Some of the later pyramids were simply burial tombs.

Many of the great pyramids of the Mayan and Incan civilizations were built around the same time, for Atlanteans and extraterrestrials traveled to Central and South America, too, and they also went to India and Tibet. They did have flying machines in Atlantis.

The Anunnaki and the Arks of the Covenant

The Anunnaki were the extraterrestrials who came from Sirius. They first visited Atlantis, taking with them the ark of the covenant which looked much like the ark in the movie *Raiders of the Lost Ark*. It was a device that transmitted high-frequency energies. This device, in conjunction with mini-arks of the covenant which could be worn around an initiate's neck or placed on a staff, could be used as laser beams. The pyramids were built with the use of these devices obtained from the Anunnaki. The rays from the device could cause the nullification of gravity: ten-thousand-pound stones could be levitated into the air; a one-pound rock could be made to weigh ten thousand pounds. This was how the Great Pyramid of Giza was constructed. It had nothing to do with the millions of slaves and pulleys that archeologists fantasize about.

The children of the Anunnaki were called the Annu. At some point the Anunnaki left Atlantis to return to their own world and they left the Earth in hands of the Annu. It was the misuse of the arks of the covenant in relationship to the great crystal that destroyed Atlantis when the Sons of Belial, or the lords of materialism, had gained too much power.

The arks and the smaller ankhs could also be used for healing. In times of danger they could be used as weapons of war and would kill instantly. At the time of the Great Flood, the Egyptian Annu took many of the arks and ankhs with them into the inner Earth which they entered beneath the Great Pyramid. They then sealed the entrance to the underground cities with their arks so they could not be followed and so the flood waters could not enter. This colony of Annu have remained in the inner Earth ever since, following the Order of Melchizedek. This occurred around 12,000 B.C.

The Great Pyramid

The Great Pyramid is, in reality, a large antenna. It was originally encased in white limestone which caused it to glow and sparkle. According to Earlyne Chaney in *Revelations of Things to Come*, floating in suspension at the top of the pyramid was a mammoth crystal. Around the crystal was a border of pure gold. The capstone actually floated in space slightly above the pyramid because of the tremendous currents of energy that were flowing up from the center of the Earth.

There is a shaft that goes down deep into the Earth right in the center of the pyramid. In this shaft were microwave generators. In the heart of the capstone was an ark of the covenant. Occasionally the capstone would be changed to a copper one or one made of lapis lazuli.

Now it is important to understand that the arks of the covenant had to be charged by the use of mental powers. Once they were charged, they functioned on their own, but a great spiritual initiate and master had to charge them initially. The Great Pyramid, in conjunction with the capstone that had the ark of the covenant inside of it, distributed light and energy throughout Egypt. One of the great masters, who might also have been present in the physical at the building of the pyramid, was Osiris. He was assigned to bring the teachings of the Order of Melchizedek to Earth, that Order being the large cosmic branch of the Great White Brotherhood. Djwhal Khul has told me that Osiris, Isis, and Thoth were all actual people, not mythological beings as modern historians assume.

Each of the pyramids acted as a generator of force, especially if it housed an ark of the covenant. An ark was like a psychotronic generator or a miniature nuclear reactor but without the adverse radiation of modern-day nuclear power plants. The Great Pyramid was actually a receiving device for cosmic energy and also a transmitting device for the Earth's own planetary kundalini. The Great Pyramid was created in such a way as to be perfectly aligned with the cosmic current of this solar system and the Great Central Sun itself.

The golden crystal capstone acted as the third eye of the entire planet, according to Earlyne Chaney. It also served as a universal communication device that allowed the voice of God and the Spiritual Hierarchy to be heard more easily. The pyramid was built to be a place of initiation for the Great White Brotherhood.

The Great Pyramid has a square base and is constructed of huge blocks of yellow limestone weighing as much as fifty-four tons each. The cutting of the stones is so precise that the joints are hardly discernible. Each of the four sides of the pyramid is a perfect equilateral triangle that slants inward and upward from the base in the proportion of ten to nine, meeting at the apex.

The Sphinx is a stone figure with a human head and a lion's body. It is carved from a single block of stone and is one hundred eighty-nine feet long. I think it is within the Sphinx that the Hall of Records lies. It contains all of the records of the Atlantean civilization. John of Penial, who is the incarnation of John the Beloved (Kuthumi), is to open the hall in this century. Edgar Cayce said that the Great Pyramid and the Sphinx were built around 10,000 B.C. and took about one hundred years to complete.

The ark of the covenant contained within it a pulsating crystal infused with a living Light. Today the ark of the covenant and the capstone of the pyramid have been removed. The pyramid, or house of Light, has lost much of its former power, but it is still considered the greatest house of Light on Earth. It was the shape of the pyramid that allowed it to withstand the massive amounts of white Light that ran through it at its peak.

The pyramid symbolizes the spiritualization of matter. The Annunaki came to accelerate this process for humankind and then left. Besides its function as a temple for initiation, the Great Pyramid was also an observatory for use in charting the heavens. It also served as an insulation chamber for the ark, so that the general population would not be endangered by the incredible spiritual force it generated. Each part of the pyramid also had a chakra, according to Earlyne Chaney's book, *Initiation in the Great Pyramid*. The heart chakra was the King's Chamber. The third eye was the capstone. The Chamber of Rebirth and the Well of Life were other chakras.

The Story of Ra-Ta

This section is an absolutely fascinating bird's-eye glimpse into ancient Egypt through the eyes of the Universal Mind as channeled by Edgar Cayce. A great many readings that were done concerned ancient Egypt because Edgar Cayce had an important past life at the time of the building of the Great Pyramid. His name then was Ra-Ta, and he was one of the great prophets and spiritual masters of his time. It was because of his great works in that lifetime, according to the Universal Mind, that he was able to do what he did in his life as Edgar Cayce.

This intriguing story begins in the year 11,016 B.C., or three hundred years before the massive Earth changes in Atlantis. There lived, in the Caucasus Mountains of eastern Europe, a group of people of the white race. Their ruler's name was Arart. Arart was greatly influenced by a young godly priest by the name of Ra-Ta, who prophesied that the tribe of Zu would march on Egypt and rejuvenate the culture for the betterment of both races and that Egypt would then become the leading nation of the day. Arart appointed his son, Araaraat, to rule in Egypt and to quell the political turmoil. The former king of Egypt, King Raai, married one of the beautiful daughters of the invaders, which helped to calm the political unrest. Emigrants were coming to Egypt from India, Mongolia, and Atlantis in great numbers. The social order of Egypt was much less advanced than that of Atlantis. Some Atlanteans brought with them their slaves and their "things," unfortunate half animal, half human creatures that were products of genetic manipulation.

Ra-Ta became the high priest of Egypt. He was interested in both the physical and the spiritual evolution of the people. He taught the law of the one God as opposed to the worship of the Sun which was very prevalent at that time. Ra-Ta made many trips to Atlantis and other places, enhancing his knowledge and stature, and he gained in popularity and influence. He and his associates began setting up social codes to conform with the worship of the one God. They helped to create civil laws, penal codes, and moral ideals for the people.

In one of Ra-Ta's trips to Atlantis he met Hept-Supht in the city of Alta. Hept-Supht was the custodian of the records of spiritual and religious secrets that had been handed down from generation to generation. Hept-Supht was very much interested in having the laws of the Children of One be preserved in Egypt.

Upon Ra-Ta's return home to Egypt, he built the Temple of Sacrifice and the Temple Beautiful. The Temple of Sacrifice was a hospital and health care center; the Temple Beautiful was a school of higher learning and vocational training. Men and women in flowing robes worked in the temples on an equal footing.

The Temple of Sacrifice was both a physical and a spiritual hospital. It was there that they corrected the deformities of the "things" on a physical as well as a spiritual level. They used surgery, medicines, electrical therapy, massage, spinal adjustments, diet, music, colors, dancing, song, chanting, and meditation as healing modalities. The idea was to clear the carnal desires and the mental and physical defects. They also used the flames of the altar fires for purification. It often took as long as six and a half years to make the complete change in these individuals.

When work in the Temple of Sacrifice was complete, the patient graduated to the Temple Beautiful and to courses in vocational and spiritual training. Music was used in healing and in the raising of vibrations. Instruments such as flute, lyre, harp, and viola were played.

Ra-Ta was very successful in this endeavor, for the "mixtures," or "things," began to disappear altogether from the face of the Earth. Ra-Ta spent much time traveling and much time in prayer and meditation, which greatly enhanced his psychic abilities. After returning from one of his protracted journeys he found that a group of priests who were more attuned to the Sons of Belial (negative ego and materialism) had incorporated into the religious practices carnal sexual practices, blood sacrifice, and drug use in the form of strong drinks. It was the same problem that had occurred in Atlantis – disagreement between members of the Law of One and members of the Sons of Belial.

The small but powerful group of priests plotted to get rid of Ra-Ta. Their plan was to use one of the temple dancers who worked in the Temple Beautiful. She was regarded throughout the land as the most beautiful woman in all of Egypt. Her name was Isris, which was later changed to Isis. She was tricked by the evil priests into convincing Ra-Ta to have a child with her which would produce one of the most perfect physical and spiritual babies in all of Egypt. Unfortunately, she did not realize their evil intention.

Ra-Ta gave in to the idea for many reasons, even though there was a law in Egypt which he himself had written that said that a person could have only one companion or spouse. She gave birth to a daughter she named Iso. Upon the birth of the child, the evil priests cried for Ra-ta's banishment. The King Araaraat was in great conflict, but he finally agreed to banish Ra-Ta for breaking his own law. So Ra-ta traveled with two hundred thirty-two of his most devout followers, including Isis and Hept-Supht, to Abyssinia, south of Egypt. The king kept the child Iso as a hostage; she died at the age of four.

Then great conflict and fighting occurred in Egypt. The evil priests and the Sons of Belial wanted to keep the "things and mixtures" as slaves and maintain their carnal sexual practices and blasphemies in the temple. Meanwhile, in his nine years in Abyssinia, Ra-Ta had helped to bring peace and prosperity to the people living there. Hept-Supht (who had migrated to Egypt from Atlantis) returned to Egypt to help create a reconciliation between Ra-Ta's group and the king. Things were in such turmoil in Egypt that Ra-Ta was invited back. He was one hundred years old.

The announcement of his return caused rejoicing throughout Egypt. From that time onward Ra-Ta was known as Ra, which is a name for God in the Egyptian language. Isis became influential in working for the rights of women. Years later she came to be worshiped as a goddess. Upon Ra's return, the Temple of Sacrifice and the Temple Beautiful were cleansed of all profane practices, and a period of social and spiritual rebuilding began.

By that time word had spread around the world of the wonders taking place in Egypt. Learned men and priests came from all over the world — from China, Mongolia, India, Norway, and Peru — to see Egypt's spiritual and material accomplishments, and Egypt became a leader among the nations of the world.

The records Hept-Supht had brought from Atlantis proved invaluable. The site selected for the safekeeping of those records, the esoteric content of the law, was the fertile plain of Giza because the area was determined to be the mathematical center of the Earth and also was safe from earthquakes and floods.

The Sphinx was also constructed at this time. In the right forepaw of the Sphinx a passage was built leading to the entrance of the record chamber. It was to remain undiscovered and protected by a mystical code until humankind as a whole had overcome the negative ego and lower self. It was then that the great initiate would come to open these records for the glory of humanity and God.

The exact dates of the construction of the Great Pyramid, according to Edgar Cayce, were 10,490 to 10,390 B.C. According to Cayce, the actual construction and engineering were worked out by Hermes, a descendant of Hermes Trismegistus, also known as Thoth. Djwhal Khul told me that Thoth did help from the spiritual plane in the pyramid's construction. Metatron, the archangel, also helped in its building and in energizing it with cosmic Light. Cayce's readings confirm exactly what Earlyne Chaney's readings said about its construction.

The Great Pyramid is a record in stone of the history and development of humankind from the time of Ra and King Araaraat to the year 1998. The records and prophecies of the pyramid are written in the language of mathematics, geometry, and astronomy. The pyramid accurately predicted the birth and death of Jesus Christ, to the year, day, and hour. The year 1936 was prophesied as a year of disturbances, turmoils, storms, war, and land upheavals. After 1956 a time of adjustment was to follow. The pyramid prophecies end in 1998, the time of the coming of the "Master." The accuracy of the pyramid prophecies is quite extraordinary, for the master it speaks of is here and his name is Lord Maitreya, the Planetary Christ. This was predicted twelve thousand four hundred years ago.

I would like to end this section with a quote by Edgar Cayce noted in a fabulous little book called *The Origin and Destiny of Man* by Lytle Robinson: "Then with Hermes and Ra . . . there began the building of that now called Gizeh . . . that was to be the Hall of the Initiates of that sometimes referred to as the White Brotherhood. . . ."

Much of the information in this section was researched from Robinson's book, and I highly recommend it.

Earlyne Chaney's Past Life as a High Priestess

Earlyne Chaney went through all seven levels of initiation in the Great Pyramid during the Third Dynasty, at the time of King Zoser. King Zoser was a God-realized pharaoh and a ptah, Supreme Master of the Lodge of Light and the Order of Melchizedek, who is now an ascended master spirit guide for Earlyne Chaney, along with Kuthumi and the Virgin Mary. In that life, Earlyne's name was Nefre-Tah-Khet. From the moment of her birth she was destined to become a high priestess within the temple, for both her mother and father were seventh degree initiates in the Order of Melchizedek. It was the Melchizedeks who were the ptahs and high priests of the Great Pyramid. Only those initiates who passed through all seven levels of initiation in this Great House of Light were called Melchizedeks, and they were revered almost as gods at that time.

One day, two spaceships arrived in Memphis, one from Peru and the other from a remnant island of Atlantis. Shortly thereafter, a third and enormous craft arrived from outer space. The presence of these spacecraft transformed Egypt. One particular being who arrived was called Imhotep. It was under his guidance and through his friendship with King Zoser that Egyptian civilization made great progress. Upper and lower Egypt were united, and great advances in culture, art, and architecture were achieved. Zoser and Imhotep constructed the step pyramid at Saqqara.

These beings brought with them a new ark of the covenant. The priests and high priests were ecstatic with joy. The original ark of the covenant had been brought around the year 13,000 B.C. Nefre-Tah-Khet's father had told her that the Great Pyramid had been built three thousand years earlier. It was explained to Earlyne that the major Earth changes that had taken place had caused the planet to be thrown out of alignment; thus, the Great Pyramid was out of alignment with the great cosmic current which prevented the kundalini energy of the Earth from rising as it once had.

Earlyne's Training for Initiation

As a child in that life, Earlyne trained at the school in Heliopolis. (I bring this up because the Edgar Cayce readings say that Jesus and John the Baptist trained at the same school three thousand years later.) During her early years she studied the teachings of Hermes-Thoth. She was placed on a strict vegetarian diet consisting of vegetables, fruits, nuts, seeds, grains, plant proteins, and milk and cheese from sacred cows and goats. She was also given special herbal concoctions and was taught body movements, asanas, mudras, breath control, and meditation.

The essence of her training was to unite her conscious and subconscious minds with her superconscious mind, or soul. (In Egypt, the soul was referred to as the aumakua, precisely the same word used in the Hawaiian Huna teachings.) Part of her training was to work with the subconscious by using a pendulum. She was taught to chant and listen to the sacred sound of Aum. She was taught psychic development and channeling. She developed the ability to speak to her higher self and spirit guides. She became proficient in telepathy and in the ability to control the weather and communicate with the nature spirits. She learned about astronomy, astrology, and alchemy. She had to learn to get rid of negative tendencies such as anger, pride, envy, and impatience. She was trained in the language of symbology, dreams, hieroglyphic writings. She studied magic and learned to control the genies that protected the sacred tombs. (The genies were angel-like beings that actually do exist; I confirmed it with Djwhal Khul.) She learned how to use the words of power and to use amulets, gemstones, and talismans.

The greater mysteries were taught only to the temple initiates, while the lesser mysteries were taught to the general public. She had to work with daily affirmations and prayers to reprogram her subconscious mind.

Over time her clairvoyance, clairsentience, and clairaudience developed. She was trained in the sacred science of geometry. She had to learn the sacred signs, grips, and passwords needed to gain admission to the lodge. She had to learn to use the power in her eyes as a type of ray to hypnotize animals. She was trained in moral and spiritual development and in the refinement of her character.

She was taught the importance of raising the sexual energies into the higher chakras and not be overtaken with carnal desire. She was trained in the art of raising the kundalini in a safe, gradual manner as she progressively went through the seven levels of initiation.

She was taught to clear her negative emotions and rise above the animal nature. Her physical body was being gradually trained to build the power in her nervous system to withstand the gradually increasing vibrations of each initiation. She was taught how to commune with the angels. She was trained in a sacred form of dance that put her in tune with the spiritual world.

She was taught the cosmology of the universe. She was trained in the science of how to unite her ego with her spirit. She was taught to face and overcome her own dweller on the threshold. She became proficient at psychometry and inner smelling. She was trained in the science of soul travel. She was trained to merge with clear Light of God, as most people attempt to do during death and the subsequent bardo experience.

Elizabeth Haich's Training

Elizabeth Haich went through training similar to that of Earlyne Chaney (see her book, *Initiation*), but Elizabeth was also trained to create emotions at will. The final result of those exercises was that the initiate could keep her emotional composure and imperturbability at all times and under all circumstances — hence the transcendence of duality and all attachment.

She was taught to balance the twelve sets of opposite characteristics:

> Keeping silent versus talking,
> Receptivity versus resistance to influence,
> Obeying versus ruling,
> Humility versus self-confidence,

> Lightning speed versus circumspection,
> Accepting everything versus being able to differentiate,
> Fighting versus maintaining peace,
> Caution versus courage,
> Possessing nothing versus commanding everything,
> Having no ties versus being loyal,
> Contempt for death versus regard for life,
> Indifference versus love.

She was trained in the importance of keeping silent. She was trained in psychic abilities and concentration and taught to give expression only to the divine and not to the satanic, while remaining in absolute mastery of physical, emotional, and mental forces. She was trained in detachment and observance of the lower bodies and, most of all, to identify herself with the soul and Eternal Self.

She was taught how to control all her physical organs — for example, how to slow her heartbeat. She was trained to differentiate the divine self from the personal I-self, or ego. She was taught the seven octaves of vibration:

> Physical . . . . . . Mineral and Plant
> Emotion . . . . . . Animal
> Mental . . . . . . Average person
> Intuitive . . . . . . Genius
> Atmic . . . . Prophet
> Monadic . . . . . . Divine Wisdom and Universal Love
> Logoic . . . . . . God-Being

She was trained to use the ark of the covenant staff for healing. She was trained in sacred geometry. She was taught to control her lower self and carnal nature. She was taught to not fear death or be attached to people or things. She was taught to put union with her soul and spirit above even the highest form of human love. She was taught to overcome the pull of desire and the physical appetites. She was trained to put others before self.

Summation

It is clear that an initiate had to go through training that was both comprehensive and profound in order to be accepted and to be able to pass the seven levels of initiation.

Once again, I would like to acknowledge Earlyne Chaney, Elizabeth Haich, Levi, Joan Grant, Edgar Cayce, and The Tibetan Foundation as sources for the material in this chapter. The titles of their books can be found in the bibliography.

40

Initiation in the Great Pyramid

The all is mind: the universe is mental.

Hermes

I find the subject of initiation one of the most interesting of all subjects. Initiation deals with specific requirements, procedures, and rituals that take place in the process of achieving ascension and union with God.

This chapter will be concerned with the seven levels of initiation as practiced by the spiritual masters and ptahs of ancient Egypt. As I describe the initiations, I recommend that you look within yourself to see if you have passed these tests in your own consciousness and life on your path to union with God. In my opinion, all these initiations are still applicable. In a sense, the reading of this chapter can be used as a path of initiation and self-examination and as a springboard to a more finely focused commitment to your own spiritual path.

Initiation

To begin with, I would like to talk about initiation as it was experienced by the ancient Egyptian ptahs, priests, high priestesses, and hierophants.

The initiations were divided into seven graded levels. The exact procedure varied with the period of history. I will describe three different experiences of initiation as read from the Akashic Records. They were very different in their procedures but the essence of their teachings was the same.

During the higher initiations, if you were an initiate, you were usually placed in a sarcophagus. You were put into an altered state of consciousness to undergo the test of meeting yourself. For example, if in your subconscious mind there were a fear of snakes, then in the altered state of consciousness – which seemed absolutely real to you – you would have to overcome that fear. The overcoming, in part, had to do with the realization that what you were facing was your own dweller on the threshold, your own fear. As soon as you came to that realization and overcame the fear, which is just a state of mind, then the snakes would immediately disappear.

Initiations in the Great Pyramid were in actuality very similar to the three-day bardo experience you face upon the death of your physical body. The experiences you will have will seem totally real, even though you are merely meeting your own dream pictures.

The Egyptian spiritual masters set up a way to accelerate spiritual growth by allowing a disciple to experience the process before having to die physically. The goal of the bardo experience is to merge with the Light; the same is true in the Egyptian initiations. The idea is, no matter what you go through, to put union with God first. In essence, the initiations are tests to see if you, the disciple, will succumb to other temptations in the seven octaves of your being.

The Egyptians believed that the dream pictures lying latent in the subconscious mind would, with absolutely certainty, become real events on Earth if you, the disciple, didn't experience them during the initiation process. Initiation allowed you the opportunity to resolve your issues and your relationship to your dweller on the threshold (glamour, illusion, maya, and ego) in meditation rather than in your current Earthly life or in future physical incarnations. In essence, you would experience your own personal karma from the beginning of your first incarnation. Instead of letting it arise in your future, you had the opportunity to experience it in dreams that seemed real. Initiation, hence, was the process of going down into the depths of your soul to confront all that was not of God.

In a sense, you go through a similar process every night when you go to sleep. In your dreams you are experiencing the return of that which you set in motion through your thoughts, words, and deeds during the previous day. The only difference is that you usually are not conscious enough in your dreams to be able to change them while they are happening, even though such lucid dreaming is possible. The process of initiation in ancient Egypt was similar to lucid dreaming. By experiencing your karma in the dream state, you had met the law and did not have to experience it in physical reality in a future lifetime – if you could pass the test.

One of the things that happened in the higher stages of initiation in the Great Pyramid was that many initiates didn't pass the test and physically died in the sarcophagus, passing on to the spiritual world. They gained spiritually by all they had gone through, however, even though they hadn't completed the whole process.

The personal odyssey of Elizabeth Haich during her life in Egypt is an example of this. She didn't physically die but she didn't complete her training either, because of failing to pass a particular spiritual test. I will get to her story in just a bit, but before I do, I would like to speak a little more about the process of initiation in general.

During the process of initiation, the candidate's body was subjected to high frequencies of energy, the specific frequency being determined by the level of initiation the candidate was taking. With the influx of that energy the candidate would become conscious on a higher level. During the final – the seventh – level of initiation, the currents of all seven levels of consciousness were conducted through the body, gradually increasing from the lowest to the highest. The initiate, hence, was given the opportunity to become aware on all seven levels of consciousness.

A candidate who had not been prepared properly within his nervous system and consciousness by having gone through the preceeding initiations would actually burn up, or spontaneously combust, because of the high frequency of the energy at that highest seventh level.

During the initiation process all unconscious portions of the soul and unconscious mind become conscious. Passing the initiation involves experiencing all this material as it comes up at each graded level of initiation and mastering it through your consciousness and spiritual gifts.

In Elizabeth Haich's experience of initiation, as related in her book, *Initiation*, she prepared for a long period of time to take her initiations and then took them all at once while lying in the sarcophagus. Earlyne Chaney took her initiations one at a time and lay in the sarcophagus only for her seventh initiation, the other six initiations having been tests of another sort that had been set up by the ptah and the hierophant.

If you are a God-realized being you manifest and control all seven levels of creation, but you identify yourself only with the seventh level. You use the other levels but identify with the highest plane. If the initiation was not passed, then those dream pictures had to be experienced as real events in outer reality either in that life or in a future one. Each level seemed real, so in a sense you went through seven different deaths and rebirths. The passing of all seven levels of initiation allowed you to become a high priest or priestess, a Melchizedek.

The Initiations of Elizabeth Haich

After going through a vast amount of training, Elizabeth was permitted by the ptah to take her initiation. Her experience began with three days of prayer, meditation, fasting, and introspection. When she decided she was ready, her spiritual master, Ptahhotep, guided her to get into the sarcophagus and lie down. To make a long story short, she began to experience an awful monster that was the personification of evil itself. That energy took over her consciousness and blended its energies with hers. Horrified, she finally came to her wits and began to disidentify with the energy and to affirm her identity as the Eternal Self, free from fear and evil. At last the monster disappeared. She had passed her first initiation. It was only after the monster had left that she realized she had had a horrible dream. During the experience it had seemed so real.

Her second initiation began when she found herself in a room with soft reddish light. Pleasant, well-mannered people began offering her wonderful food and drinks in golden vessels. She was tempted with the most wonderful delicacies you can imagine. However, she affirmed to herself that she desired God above the pleasures of the palate and refused politely. She had passed her second initiation. The dream image faded away, even though it had seemed totally real.

At the third initiation she found herself in a room with attractive men and women dancing together and lounging on couches in heated sexual passion. An attractive man began to talk with her and tried to come on to her in a romantic and sexual manner. Elizabeth, having lived in the temple since childhood, had almost no experience with relationships so in a sense she was protected, since she was not tempted in the slightest. She lectured the man about the debasing, exceedingly degrading way all the people in the room were letting their lower selves and carnal passions completely take over their consciousnesses. She proceeded to describe love between two people in Godly terms rather than carnal terms. The man turned into a flaming spirit and tried to possess her, forcing himself upon her. She remained strong and affirmed, "I Am That I Am," and the vision passed.

A side note to the story is that Elizabeth's lack of experience in romantic relationships proved to be her downfall later in life. Ptahhotep had warned her as a young child not to ask to be initiated because of her lack of experience in that area. She was adamant, however, and three different times came to Ptahhotep asking to be initiated even though he had previously refused, saying she was not ready. Upon the third request he had to give in, for it was written in their laws that if a candidate asked three times to be initiated and was refused each time but continued to ask, the request had to be granted, even if going through with it was ill-advised. His prophecy turned out to be correct, for even though Elizabeth passed this initiation and her later ones during the initiation process, during the probationary period when she was learning to stabilize the energies from the sixth to the seventh level, she succumbed to the temptations of this initiation and the one following it.

Upon passing the third initiation, Elizabeth moved to the fourth initiation. There she was confronted with her twin flame, or twin soul. That experience did not contain the carnal sexual energy of the previous one; it was much sweeter and more loving in a spiritual sense. But Elizabeth remained firm in her commitment to putting her union with her own soul and spirit above even her soulmate, so she passed this test.

Elizabeth's fifth initiation was a lengthy experience of a future life during World War I or World War II when her children and husband were her closest friends and spiritual comrades from her life in Egypt. Although they didn't know that, she did, and she felt great love for her family. She was confronted with deaths of her son, husband, family, and self. It was a spiritual test of attitude toward death to see if she would put her total faith and trust in God. It also had to do with the lesson of attachment.

Elizabeth passed this test by seeing the Eternal Self in her entire family and not seeing them as merely physical bodies and personalities whom she loved. She also affirmed her faith and trust in God in the face of other tests during this long, drawn-out experience in what seemed to be war-torn Europe. She passed because she surrendered all into God's hands and put God even before death itself. These images then faded, even though they had seemed to be occurrences that were actually happening while she was going through them.

This brought Elizabeth to the sixth initiation. She found herself under a crystal-clear blue sky, confronted with seven steps that she had to climb. The first step had to do with mastery of the physical body. The second step had to do with mastery of the vital forces within the physical body. The third step had to do with mastery of the emotional body. The fourth step had to do with mastery of the mental body and all self-doubts.

With each step she climbed she found she had grown taller physically, but the steps were getting higher at an even faster rate so that at the fifth step she had to pull herself up as though she were climbing a mountain. It took great effort, but upon finally succeeding, she realized that she no longer had a physical body but was in her spiritual body.

The sixth step could be climbed only by the demonstration of universal love. She found another person reaching the step at the same time she did. He begged her to help him climb to the seventh step. Elizabeth forgot about her own journey and proceeded to help the person reach the seventh step. Upon doing so she found herself upon the seventh step also, for by forgetting about herself in the service of another, she realized God. She had transcended her self-centered desire for initiation only for herself.

Summation

These are all tests that each one must pass, even today, to achieve ascension and full self-realization. Please read Elizabeth Haich's *Initiation* to fully appreciate the details of her experience.

The Initiations of Jesus Christ in the Great Pyramid of Giza

Edgar Cayce, as well as Levi, in his book *The Aquarian Gospel of Jesus the Christ*, tells of Jesus' experiences of initiation in the Great Pyramid of Giza. Edgar Cayce says John the Baptist was also initiated there, as was Plato.

Levi provides a short narration of the initiation and spiritual tests Jesus went through in the Great Pyramid. The first initiation Jesus passed was the test of sincerity. The second test was that of justice. The third test was that of faith. The fourth test and initiation was that of philanthropy. The fifth test was that of heroism. The sixth test and initiation was that of divine love. In passing the seventh, the brotherhood test he received the highest degree, which is that of the Christ.

The Initiations of Earlyne Chaney

Earlyne Chaney's initiations in the Great Pyramid were quite different in some respects from Elizabeth Haich's experiences. From the time she was born she was being prepared to become a high priestess in the Order of Melchizedek. Her actual training began at the age of three, although it wasn't until she was twelve that she was allowed to take her first initiation. It was only at the final initiation, or seventh degree, that she was to lie in the sarcophagus as Elizabeth Haich had. In some ways, without judging the two experiences, Earlyne's seems more powerful because of the great amount of time, training, and preparation required for her to be allowed to take each initiation. All of Earlyne's initiations were quite complex and long-lasting so I am going to give only the briefest account of them. For the full explanation, please do read her book, *Initiation in the Great Pyramid*.

The First Initiation

Her first initiation began with a three-day fast that included vegetable and fruit juices and special herbal concoctions. Then she was blindfolded and her wrists were tied together with a manacle. She was spun around several times and told to move toward the light. She was in total darkness. All of a sudden she was engulfed by a tremendous storm with hail and lightning and thunder. The water rose to her waist. Without the use of her hands, she kept losing her balance and falling into the water. Earlyne then opened her crown chakra and her spirit guide began to guide her to where she needed to go. Upon passing this part of the test her blindfold and manacle were removed.

Suddenly a gigantic man came toward her and put a dagger to her throat. She vowed to not give away the secrets of the lodge and the man took the knife from her throat. She then realized that forty-nine judges, or high priests, were present, watching her. She was given instruction and then baptized three times which symbolized the purification of the different aspects of her nature.

The experiences she went through were symbolic. The blindfold had to do with the blindness of the human race, reminding her that she could not find the inner Light with physical eyes but only with the eye of the soul. The dagger at the throat symbolized the sword of the karma that would occur if she became disobedient to God's laws upon taking the initiations. The battle against the elements tested her courage and perseverance.

Earlyne was then led to a place between two columns where stood a ladder of seven steps. At the top of the ladder were thirteen gates of different dimensions. The next part of her initiation was to climb the seven steps and choose which gate she would go through to pass her future initiations. Her inner guidance told her that only one of these gates would allow her to take any future initiations. If she chose wrongly no further initiations would be allowed.

With the help of her inner guidance she chose the right door. She was then given a new cream-colored robe and a lambskin apron of pure white. Her white apron was to symbolize the need to purify and control the passions of the physical form. (At each initiation the initiate was given a new robe and apron. Each new apron symbolized control over another one of the seven bodies.)

She also received the first of seven ankhs, the pewter tau cross of the first degree initiate. She learned the secret sign of the first degree and was given the secret word of the first degree, which meant discrimination. It also meant to turn away from the attractions of the outer world. She was also given a bracelet of pewter with a signet of the first degree and a ring with a crystal in it. She was told that the ring would reflect her future progress as her Light unfolded. The ring also served to protect her from negative vibrations. It was a charmed talisman. When they spoke to her they referred to her as a child to reduce the outer ego into a state of humility. Earlyne had passed initiation number one.

The Second Initiation

After seven more years of intensive training Earlyne was given permission to take the second initiation. It began again with three days of fasting, prayer, and meditation. She had to memorize the signs, grips, and passwords to gain admission to the lodge.

The initiation began when one of the priests ran toward her and tossed a live serpent directly at her. Earlyne threw it to the ground and hypnotized it with the power of her eyes as she had been trained to do. She also talked to the serpent as the incarnation of God that it was. She was congratulated by the assembly for passing the first part of the initiation.

In the next part she was led to a strange creature called a griffin that was twirling a wheel containing four spokes. Her test was to give the meaning of the symbol. The griffin had the body of a lion with the wings and talons of an eagle. Her inner guidance told her that the griffin symbolized physical man with spiritual attributes that would allow him to fly into the heavenly spheres and thus to control the wheel of the four seasons and the elements of nature. She had passed the test.

She was given a new secret word that had to do with the negative nature of matter of which she was to learn the secrets. She receive a new apron and ankh. She was given five years to prepare for her next initiation and was told what she needed to study and master, which included self-mastery of her mind and psychic faculties.

The live serpent symbolized escaping the illusions of the astral plane and demonstrating mastery over that plane and over the animal kingdom in a loving way. Her father explained to her that the griffin on the wheel also symbolized humankind's being caught in the wheel of reincarnation and the need for humankind to overcome their lower nature and lower selves. Control of the serpent also had to do with the raising of the kundalini. The directive of the second degree initiate was "To know, to will, to dare, and to keep silent."

The Third Initiation

The third initiation began when Earlyne passed through an entrance above which were the words Gate of Death. As Earlyne walked through the area she came upon a sarcophagus in which lay the body of one of the great ptahs, or high priests, who had just been assassinated. Swarms of officials came running toward Earlyne, wanting to know if she was responsible. She was roughly dragged into the hall of the high priest.

The hierophant apologize for her mistreatment and as a recompense offered her a golden crown that would help her in her future trials. She was about to grab it when her inner guidance warned her that it was a test. She then threw the golden crown to the floor with disdain and the hierophant proceeded to strike her with a forceful blow.

She was wrapped in mummy bandages that left only her face exposed and taken through a gate labeled Sanctuary of Spirits. She was taken downward in a boat to the judge of the dead. The bandages were then removed. She was given instruction and told that she was going to have to stay in the underground sanctuary of the dead until the judges could determine whether she had mastered the sciences of the soul, magic, and alchemy. She was told she would spend a good portion of the rest of her life in these pits until she passed the tests.

The symbolism so far dealt with the question of whether she had had anything to do with the assassination of her own higher self, or soul. The golden crown she had been offered tested the temptation of placing worldly power and wealth above God. Being wrapped in bandages symbolized the soul's being bound by ignorance, superstition, and fear. The removal of the bandages in the lower cavern symbolized the shedding of the physical body at death. The probationary period in the sanctuary of the dead symbolized a time of temporary imprisonment in the lower astral realms after death to impress upon the incarnated personality that he or she must live in a way that doesn't cause imprisonment in these lower astral worlds after death.

Earlyne was then tested by the tribunal on her psychic, intuitive, and magical skills and passed her test. She was given a new robe and apron and ankh.

The Fourth Initiation

The fourth initiation began when Earlyne and her priest guide were attacked by figures wearing hideous masks and brandishing weapons. The priest sprang to her defense, pleading with her to run and make her escape. Earlyne refused to run. She fought but was soon overpowered.

They were blindfolded and a cable tow was placed around their necks. They were physically bruised but not seriously injured. Upon the removal of the blindfold they found themselves in front of an assembly of priests and she was complimented for not running to save her own life but fighting to help the priest. The attackers represented the animalistic nature, negative emotions, and temptations every initiate must overcome.

Earlyne was then given a bitter potion to drink. Her physical fatigue and aches lifted and she was then given a sword of righteousness. She was told to strike off the head of the foe that she would meet in the valley below.

She traveled to the valley to meet her foe, but to her surprise her twin soul, or soulmate, whom she recognized, came toward her. She sprang forward to meet him but her inner guidance warned her that this was a test. Her psychic senses told her that this being who looked real was more like a hologram and not a living being at all. She proceeded to chop off his head. This was obviously a test about not succumbing to romantic love over union with God. She was told that she would one day meet her twin flame but only when the time was right. The chopped-off head symbolized victory over human carnality and temptation, the death of the base desires of the negative ego and lower self. Only by slaying the lower nature could the initiate hope to merge with the higher self, soul, and spirit.

The passing of the fourth initiation allowed her to attend all the sacred meetings. She was given a new robe, apron, and ankh. Part of her training for the next initiation had to do with learning to soul travel and gaining mastery of the elements of nature.

The Fifth Initiation

For the fifth initiation, Earlyne was told that she was to watch a theatrical drama in which members of the Order of Melchizedek would take part. She would be a spectator and not take part.

The drama depicted the battle between the divine Horus and the hideous monster Set. Set had a hundred serpent heads and was like a dragon. The divine Horus overcame the dragon with his superior spiritual and physical strength. The symbolism was that of the battle all initiates go through on the physical plane. All must be like spiritual warriors and remain detached from the temptations and desires of the lower self and negative ego. Earlyne's watching but not participating symbolized this need for detachment and objectivity. The destruction of Set symbolized the victory of good over evil and the removal from the consciousness of the initiate of all negative emotions, desires, fears, and separation.

The dragon, Set, symbolized the kundalini power turned downward instead of upward which resulted in lust, greed, hate, jealousy, and anger. The divine Horus represented the upturned kundalini leading toward soul and spiritual merger and liberation from the wheel of rebirth.

Earlyne received her new robe, ankh, apron, and secret word. The secret word had to do with chemistry, the alchemy of changing lead into gold. On the human level it meant changing the base human nature into the divine spiritual nature.

The Sixth Initiation

The sixth initiation began with her being taken in a small boat onto a large lake where she was blindfolded. She was towed into the middle of the lake where there was no sight of land in any direction. Her blindfold was removed and her companions left in another boat and rowed off into the mists. A gigantic storm was approaching. It hit with tremendous ferocity, frequently threatening to capsize her boat. There were no stars, no moon, no light of any kind, just blackness and the storm. Earlyne was extremely fearful. Then her inner guidance told her to use her spiritual powers to communicate with the nature spirits of the storm and ask them to stop and help her. She called aloud to the undines (water spirits) and the sylphs (wind spirits) and they immediately came to her aid and stopped the storm. She then used her knowledge of astronomy to guide her boat in the right direction. Earlyne had passed her sixth initiation.

Earlyne's Seventh and Final Initiation

The seventh initiation could be taken only with the permission of the pharaoh and the master ptah. In this initiation the divine self was to forever unite itself with the soul and spirit. The initiate would become a Melchizedek priest or high priestess. Each initiate was also called a prophet or an opened eye. This initiation took place in the great sarcophagus. The soul would leave the body, much as in the death experience, and the kundalini would rise. The initiate would have the opportunity to merge with the clear Light of God just as in the bardo experience. That would lead to merger with God and complete liberation from the bondage of matter. The God-being would then have mastery over the seven octaves of vibration as the little ego merged with the divine ego.

As a preparation for the final initiation Earlyne spent three days alone in the Sphinx temple. As Elizabeth Haich did, Earlyne would have to confront her own dweller on the threshold. She would have to meet and conquer the thought forms of a lower nature that had not yet been destroyed but remained in the deepest recesses of her subconscious mind. They had to be brought into her conscious awareness; otherwise, they would have to be made manifest physically in this or a future incarnation. Only when the dweller on the threshold (glamour, illusion, maya, negative ego) has been confronted fully and subjugated can the initiate truly see God. The base metals must be changed into gold. The initiate's frequency must match that of the clear Light of God. If that does not happen, only a partial awakening can occur.

Some initiates who took this initiation didn't emerge alive, for their bodies could not handle the high voltage of the clear Light frequencies. Hence, they passed on to the spiritual world without achieving the initiation.

The initiation began with Earlyne's drinking what has been called Amrita which is an ambrosial nectar of the gods. As she drank, her spiritual faculties began to awaken and expand. She traveled to a subterranean chamber called the Pit of the Fiery Ordeal. The dwellers of the threshold began to appear! Vile insects, crawling reptiles, crocodiles, swarming bats, stinging asps, and ghosts began to surround her. They looked totally real; however, her inner guidance reminded her that they only represented thought forms she had created during her incarnations on Earth.

Earlyne had thought her mind was already purified, but on the deepest subconscious level it was not. She was experiencing not only her current life but all her lifetimes. The clear Light of God could not enter a consciousness filled with pride, judgment, fears, and other lower-self qualities. She was guided to use the power of the ankh around her neck as a sort of ark of the covenant, and she proceeded to de-energize the creatures. She then began to chant words of power and the creatures evaporated.

Then a being that was half human, half dragon attacked her. She wondered to herself what she could have done in a past life to create such a monster. She prayed. To her astonishment, her twin flame appeared and they proceeded to fight this monster with "thought power and rays." Using these rays in conjunction with a crystal, they were able to kill the beast. She embraced her knight and twin flame and they were immersed in love energy.

But her inner guidance said, "Beware the womb door." Channeling that energy sexually could cause the need for incarnation in a future life. She affirmed to herself that this was not the time to meld in love with her knight and twin flame, even though he had helped to save her life. She had passed the first part of her initiation.

The divine Ptah, whom she referred to as Thoth, took her to a deep cavern within the Great Pyramid called the Well of Life. There she was wrapped in an animal skin and placed on the ground. She was then taken in her soul body up the shaft of the Well of Life to the Chamber of New Birth, also known as the Queen's Chamber. In this chamber her soul was "born again." She was merged with her divine senses of clairvoyance, clairaudience, and psychometric touching, smelling, and tasting. This new birth was taking place in her soul body not in her physical body. It was then she felt her male and female aspects merge and become united.

She was given a choice between remaining on the spiritual planes and returning to her Earthly physical body. Earlyne chose to return to her physical body and began her descent downward. She felt herself take on the different envelopes, sheaths, and bodies as she descended back to her physical body, and she realized that it was much like a soul extension's journey into incarnation.

She had to go through the Hall of Judgment. She passed before each of the forty-nine judges and then came to the scales that weighed the seed atom (the recording device of all past karma that resides within the heart) against all her good deeds and good karma. The seed atom with all the bad karma was placed on the scale first and it tipped far down to the left. Thoth then placed on the scale a white feather, the symbol of her good karma. With the white feather came a gleaming white stone. The scale tipped strongly to the other side and the heart's seed atom merged with the white stone. Earlyne stood victorious! The four Lords of Karma replied, "Go thou forth! We obliterate thy faults. We annihilate thy sins. We have weighed thy heart and it has not been found wanting."

The passing of this phase of her initiation allowed her to then go to the "great sarcophagus" for the final stage of her seventh initiation. She lay down in the sarcophagus and the priests began to chant the Om mantra. Thoth performed a blessing over her head and intoned, "Thou art crowned in the Hall of Death that hereafter, thou mayest wear a Crown of Life that fadeth not away."

Earlyne was then given a golden ankh with a radiant crystal which was placed about her neck. He then pointed his staff directly at her third eye and as the voltage entered she began to leave her body. Thoth prayed, "Almighty and Everlasting Architect of the Universe, into Thy keeping we commend her spirit." Earlyne was being given the opportunity to merge with the clear Light of God. As she rose she could see the etheric pyramid of Light that was superimposed upon the physical pyramid. Approaching now from far away was a resplendent Light like that of a thousand suns. Earlyne merged into the heart of the Light.

As she merged into the Light she encountered the spirit guide of all her incarnations who suddenly transformed into her twin flame. They were one and the same being. Then Isis appeared. The Lady of Light unrolled a scroll from which Earlyne was to absorb the prayer and password "for the food and drink of the dweller's house," which was the writing that confers perfection.

She was told that she was clothed in the power and crowned by Light. She then had to traverse the scenes of her former weakness. Isis took her by the hand and they soul-traveled to the star Sirius. It was there that she saw a glorious temple carved of crystal diamond. Upon reaching the temple they were asked by whose name they sought admission. Isis said, "In the name of the Anaki, the Mighty Ones, Sons of Melchizedek the Just, the Grand Carpenters of the universe of worlds and men, by whom all things are made." They mounted seven steps and stood in the midst of the white Light.

It was there that the initiate officially became the Melchizedek, the ascended master. There Earlyne was crucified. The Rod of Power ignited at the base of her spine which charged the kundalini with the force of resurrection. Every cell of her being was filled with Light and she was fully resurrected. Complete merger of the soul extension with the soul and spirit occurred. The personal ego had merged with the divine ego.

Earlyne was a free spirit, completely liberated. In the final stage of the initiation she went before Osiris and received his blessing. The entire initiation took three full days.

Summation

First let me say that in no way have I done justice to Earlyne's experiences. I have drawn only an essence of her experience from her book *Initiation in the Great Pyramid*, so you would have a sense of what it was like to be initiated in ancient Egypt.

For some of you, this material might have triggered past-life memories of your own initiations. For others it might serve as an inspiration for similar initiations you will be taking in the future. I strongly recommend that you get Earlyne's book and read the whole story. I hope my small endeavor here has sparked your interest in learning more.

There is an interesting addendum to this story. During the final stages of Earlyne's initiation Isis told Earlyne, "When the signs of Heaven point to the dawn of the Age of Aquarius and a rebirth of the mysteries, you will come again, my last-born Isis. You will come again to hold the torch high. And you will remember the days of your anointing and the ankh cross with the crystal eye. And you will wear again the new symbol of the mysteries and Melchizedek. The symbol of the new dispensation . . . the seven-pointed star with the unfolded lotus in its heart. A host of the liberated little ones will come teaching the inner way, and you will be among the host."

This, of course, was a prophecy of Earlyne's future mission to be reborn in this century. Earlyne, with her husband, has created a mystery school called Astara which has been in existence for forty years. It is interesting that two of the greatest prophets of these times, Earlyne Chaney and Edgar Cayce (Ra-Ta) were both seventh degree initiates in the Great Pyramid. It is because of this that they have been able to bring through so much incredible information.

My feeling is that close study of this material with a reverent and committed attitude could allow you to go through these initiations yourself in meditation.

41

The Science of Soul Travel

*In my Father's house
there are many mansions.*

Master Jesus

The science of soul travel is something that has intrigued seekers on the spiritual path since the beginning of time. Soul travel is something that every person on Planet Earth does every night during sleep: the emotional, mental, and spiritual bodies travel to their respective planes of consciousness.

I am an advocate of soul travel as opposed to astral travel. In soul travel you separate from your physical body and travel to the higher dimensions of God's universe. In astral travel you separate from your physical body and travel to the astral plane; traveling in your astral body means the only plane you can travel to is the astral plane which is the plane of glamour, illusion, and maya. If you travel in your soul body you can travel through the astral to the mental and up into the soul plane itself.

It is also possible to travel in your mental body. (In truth, you can travel in all seven bodies; when you become an ascended master, you will travel in your glorified Lightbody.) You travel in your mental body all the time, even if you don't realize it. When you are intensely thinking about someone, perhaps wondering what he is doing, you are projecting your mental body to him and trying to attune it to him. If you are on the spiritual path, when you are sleeping, you go in your soul body to the inner-plane ashram of the master with whom you are associated.

The big question is, if all this is going on how come you aren't aware of it? The answer is that sometimes you do have faint recollections when you wake up in the morning. You might remember attending classes or receiving some important information or guidance. You might remember a dream of flying which is usually a sign that you have been astral traveling. Sometimes you recall visiting someone while in one of your other bodies. Other times you might have a lucid dream in which you are totally conscious while dreaming. This is definitely a form of soul travel, for it means you are awake in your dream body. If you have a lucid dream, use your awareness to create the dream reality you want.

The real science of soul travel is learning to leave your body and travel while conscious and to be able to do it at will. For most people on this planet, that is not easy to do.

You have had the experience to a certain extent when meditating or when doing a guided meditation to other places or to the spiritual world. Most often a fragment of yourself goes or your mental body goes, but it is not a complete out-of-body experience. In this chapter I have included some tools and techniques that will make a full out-of-body soul traveling experience more likely to happen.

Why Soul Travel?

Soul travel allows you to have a direct experience of God. It gives you an absolute knowingness that you are not your physical body. Soul travel allows you to travel to seven dimensions of reality and explore. It allows you to meet with the masters while in your other bodies, receive their guidance, and bring that information back to Earth.

Rudolph Steiner, who was a past president of the Theosophical Society, broke away and started his own society based on knowledge he gained by soul traveling for long periods of time. He brought back vast amounts of advanced and esoteric scientific knowledge.

One of the greatest soul travelers of all time was the poet-saint Kabir (a past life of Sai Baba) who never read books but received all his knowledge directly from God through soul travel.

When you soul travel, it is usually best to call for your spiritual teacher so you have a guide to the inner worlds, just as when you travel to a strange country on the Earth plane you often hire a trustworthy guide to show you the best spots and teach you about the country.

When you travel in your soul body, you travel with the power of your mind. If you want to go to Saturn all you have to do is think Saturn and you are instantly there; no time or space exists once you leave your body. You know that energy follows thought and that thoughts create feelings, actions, and experience. Soul travel is based on the same principle.

I remember my first out-of-body experience. It came as a result of going on a short fast. I had not eaten all day, as I had spent the day counseling clients. I got home very late and didn't want to eat right before bed so I just called it a couple of skipped meals. As I lay in bed I experienced a feeling of wind blowing through me. I closed my eyes and was enjoying it. The next thing I knew, I was out of my body, floating up toward the ceiling. I was aware that I could determine where I was going with my mind. The experience was totally different from partially leaving my body during a guided meditation. I was definitely out of my body – I saw it lying on the bed. Next thing I knew, I was up in space. It was beautiful. The only problem was that I got scared that I was going to fall, and the second I gave into the fear, I began to fall. I prayed to God for help and the next thing I knew, I was back in my physical body and my heart was pounding a mile a minute.

I have many friends who can soul travel or astral travel at will and have proven it to me. I am not as proficient at it as they are so I have studied it extensively to learn everything there is to know about traveling and how to facilitate it for myself and for others.

There are a number of spiritual organizations that specialize in the science of soul travel. The most well-known is probably Eckancar, which was founded by Paul Twitchell. Two other well-known spiritual teachers who were part of Eckancar and left to start their own spiritual organizations were Darwin Gross and John Roger. Darwin Gross was actually the head of Eckancar after Paul Twitchell's death, I believe, but after a time there was some kind of division in the organization and he stepped down and formed his own group.

The following chart is a conglomeration of all three of these groups. Since I am so closely affiliated with Djwhal Khul's ashram, I personally don't use their system or format. Every spiritual teacher seems to have different names for the different dimensions of reality. Even though this is the case, I do find their cosmology quite fascinating.

The Science of Soul Travel Mantras

Dimension	Mantra/chant	Ruler	Sound	Color
Physical	Alayi (senses)	Elam	Thunder	Brown to Green
Astral	Kala (emotion)	Jot Niranjan	Roar of the Sea	Pink to Red
Causal	Mana (memory)	Ramkar	Tinkling of Bells	Orange
Mental	Aum (mind)	Omkar	Running of Water	Blue
Etheric	Baju (intuition)	So Hang	Buzzing of Bees	Violet

Dimension	Mantra/chant	Ruler	Sound	Color
Atma Lok	Sugmad	Sat Nam	Single Note of Flute	Gold to White
Alakh Lok	Shanti	Alakh Purusha	Wind	Yellow to White
Alaya Lok	Hum	Alaya Purusha	Humming	White
Hukikat Lok	Aluk	Hukikat Purusha	Thousand Violins	White
Agam Lok	Huk	Agam Purusha	Music of Woodwinds	(unknown)
Animi Lok	Hu	Animi Purusha	Sound of Whirlpool	(unknown)
Sugmad Lok	Unspoken	Submad Purusha	Music of the Spheres	(unknown)
Sugmad	Unspoken word	Sugmad	Music of God	(unknown)

Notice particularly the column listing the sounds associated with each plane. Even though I don't relate to this cosmology in terms of its description of the dimensions of reality, I know the sounds of the various planes are accurate. They match the sounds I have learned about in studying the Eastern paths, in particular Sabda or Nada Yoga, and even Paramahansa Yogananda has described the exact same sounds for each of the dimensions.

You will also see a mantra associated with each of the different dimensions of reality. One of the secrets of soul travel is to chant these mantras or others that you already know of; the sound will actually carry you to the dimension of reality with which it is associated. This is something I recommend that you experiment with if it is all right with your inner guidance. For example, according to this chart, the mantra "Aum" is associated with the mental plane. I checked this out with Djwhal Khul and he told me that it was true. I particularly recommend the "hu" mantra, which Djwhal Khul has associated with the third eye chakra in his teachings through The Tibetan Foundation. He also told me a fascinating bit of information:

Amen is the sound associated with the Lemurian root race;

Aum is the sound associated with the Atlantean root race;

Om is the sound associated with the Aryan root race;

Ong is the sound associated with the new Meruvian root race which is just coming in now.

All three of the organizations that specialize in the science of soul travel are very much concerned with the light and sound of God. Thus, a color is attributed to each dimension. Also listed is the cosmic being who is said to govern each dimension. The Sikhs use the mantra "Sat Nam" which they got from Guru Nanak or maybe even from Kabir; Sat Nam turns out to be the cosmic being who governs the soul plane. Paramahansa Yogananda teaches the mantra "Hong Sau," which means "I Am the Self." He says it is actually the sound that occurs as humans breathe. It is closely associated with the So Ham mantra. Interesting enough, Sohang is the name of the cosmic being who governs the etheric plane in this system. God is called Sugmad, a name I had never heard before studying Eckancar.

Another interesting point concerns the cosmic being Omkar, on the mental plane. In Sai Baba's ashram, the morning practice of chanting Aum twenty-one times to start the day is called Omkar. These synchronicities are definitely enough to get your attention.

The great spiritual master who guided Paul Twitchell was Rebazar Tarz. Of the spiritual masters associated with these three groups, I, personally, had the best feeling about him. I think there are certain masters who specialize in the soul-traveling experience and he is one I definitely trust.

Another person who tells a fantastic story of his soul-traveling experience is J.J. Hurtak in the introduction to his book, *The Book of Knowledge: The Keys of Enoch*. He tells of being taken out of his body and guided by Enoch and Metatron into the highest spiritual planes where the sixty-four keys of Enoch were implanted into his third eye. On his return to Earth he recorded all he had been shown in this book, which can only be described as a revelation from God.

The nice thing about learning to soul travel is that you can shed your physical, etheric, astral, and mental bodies and travel to the highest planes. The practice of soul travel is really an early stage in learning to bilocate. The first step is to go somewhere in your soul body. The next step is to travel to a distant location and take your physical body with you. If you can take your soul body, why can't you take all your bodies?

According to Paul Twitchell, once you have learned to travel in your soul body, you can travel to the highest spiritual planes without limitation, whereas each of the bodies below the soul level is limited to the plane with which it is associated.

Another advantage of soul travel is that there is much service work that can be done on the inner planes. C. W. Leadbeater of the Theosophical Society learned to travel out of his body at night while maintaining total recall. Every night, he would take disciples to El Morya, Kuthumi, and Lord Maitreya in the Himalaya Mountains. His students often would not remember very much of the teachings, but he would remember the information, as well as what went on at the various initiations.

Guru Nanak, the founder of the Sikh order, was also an expert in soul travel. He followed right along in the footsteps of Kabir.

An additional advantage of learning to soul travel is that when you physically die you can leave your body consciously and at will. In India this is called mahasamadhi. Paramahansa Yogananda demonstrated it at his death; he gave a lecture and then left his body. Even Pythagoras taught his disciples to go out through their crown chakras and to gain control of their bodies and environments from a distance.

One of the most important practices concerning soul travel is learning total control over your mental and emotional bodies. It is your attitude, attention, and state of consciousness that determine where you go. Soul travel is not for you if you are not in control of your energies. Indulge in negative emotions and you will end up on the lower astral plane.

Just as in death, your soul can leave your body through any one of the chakras. I would recommend always leaving from the crown, if possible, or at least from the third eye.

The three keys to soul travel are the use of thought, light, and sound. As you begin to soul travel, you will find your sensitivity to and awareness of light and sound will greatly increase. The practitioner can even travel on beams of light and sound.

Guru Nanak tells in his writings of being taken by angels to the fifth plane where he stood before the Sat Nam, the cosmic being governing that plane. Appolonius of Tyanna (Master Jesus in his subsequent incarnation when he was a fifth degree initiate) had the ability to be in two places at once. Master Sai Baba is another striking example of a being who has this remarkable ability. Zoroaster (formerly Buddha) was taken in his soul body to the higher realms where he appeared before the Supreme Being and was given his mission in the material universe. He was to have many such experiences during his lifetime, and they are recorded in his writings.

Mohammed had similar experiences of traveling to the seven heavens, and he too recorded his experiences. Hermes (another incarnation of the Buddha) was reported to have traveled in his soul body to the higher worlds where he met Osiris who took him to the highest spiritual worlds. This was all recorded in his book, *The Vision of Hermes*.

It is clear that the potentials that lie in learning to soul travel are unfathomable.

Potential Dangers

In considering the subject of possible dangers involved in traveling while out of your body, a couple of thoughts come to mind. The first is, again, to try to travel in your soul body rather than in your astral body, so as to avoid being limited to the astral plane. The second safeguard is to travel with your spiritual teacher all the time until you become skilled at it. Don't be a big shot and go exploring on your own when you are a beginner.

Then there is the issue of what happens if you do run into trouble during an out-of-body experience. This can happen, especially on the astral plane. If you run into trouble, start praying for help. Immediately project yourself back into your physical body.

Paul Solomon told a story of trying to get into an inner plane mystery school without being invited. He was surrounded by all sorts of dark figures. He has recommended saying your own name, which is the mantra of your particular physical body.

I met a women who astral traveled all the time. Once, after she had been traveling for about forty-five minutes, when she returned to her body she couldn't get back in. Her fear attracted all kinds of dark astral figures that started to glom onto her. She was screaming at the top of her "astral lungs" when Sai Baba appeared and yelled, "Silence!" He got rid of the lower astral beings and told her that the reason she couldn't get back into her body was that she had somersaulted out of it, and the law states that if you somersault out, you have to somersault back in. Sai Baba then picked her up and somersaulted her back into her body.

Stories such as this must be taken as a warning that out-of-body experiences are not something to play with lightly. You need a trustworthy guide. Pray for the protection and help of your spiritual teacher and the ascended masters before you start the exercises I have included. As long as you are under the care and guidance of the ascended masters, you will be fine. People run into trouble when they innocently or unconsciously fail to ask for this help.

Soul travel, in actuality, becomes a very normal and natural activity, once you learn how to do it. Eventually, it will take no effort at all, which is true of any new habit. I do not mean for the warnings to scare you but rather to help you keep the whole process in the proper perspective.

Techniques for Soul Travel

In this section you will find a variety of tools and techniques. You can experiment with them and use your intuitive guidance to discover which ones work most successfully for you. Begin all these techniques with a prayer of protection and ask for help from your soul, monad, spiritual teacher, and the ascended masters.

1. Choose a time when you will not be interrupted by a ringing phone or anything else. Lie down on your bed, get comfortable, and place your attention on your third eye. Visualize a blank screen. Then visualize your

destination. It can be a place in this world or a location in a higher dimension. In the beginning it could be a friend's house or another room in your own house, if you feel more comfortable starting off nearby.

The idea is to imagine your destination using all five senses. See it, hear it, smell it, taste it, touch it. Make it so real it is as though you are actually there, not just imagining yourself there. Remember the law: wherever your thought goes, your body must follow.

2. The second method is the same as the first except that it involves thinking about being at your chosen destination rather than visualizing it. Some people visualize better than others; both methods are equally effective. Ideally, you can use both of these methods simultaneously. In the experience of soul travel you will suddenly find yourself in the place you were thinking about and visualizing.

3. One of the ways to condition yourself for out-of-body experiences is to read about them. This serves as a suggestion to your subconscious mind and to your soul to create the experience. Add to that prayers to your soul, monad, spiritual teacher, and the masters for their help in achieving soul travel.

Be patient. It might take some perseverance at first. Some people can do it quite easily, while others have to practice. We all have different strengths and weaknesses.

4. Go to bed at night deeply concentrating on a place you want to go. Make the desire super strong. Your destination can be in this dimension or on one of the higher spiritual planes. Allow yourself to fall asleep with that place being the last thought in your conscious mind. This technique is based on the law stated in the *Bhagavad-Gita* by Krishna: where you go when you die is determined by the last thought in your mind. The same is true of going to sleep. If you go to sleep watching the news, you might end up in Somalia or Bosnia.

This technique is from Paul Twitchell's book, *Eckankar, the Key to Secret Worlds*. He suggests that trying this method often allows you to wake up out of your body and float above yourself. If this does happen, then immediately think of your destination again and you will find yourself instantly there.

5. This technique is also from Paul Twitchell's book, but I am varying it slightly. As you are falling asleep just say to yourself, over and over again, "I am leaving my body. I am going to _____!"

6. Another method is to say a mantra over and over again, either silently or out loud. And allow your consciousness to ride the sound current to its destination on the inner planes. See yourself metaphysically surfing, riding the wave of sound — or a wave of light, if you are more visually oriented.

7. Go through your entire body and give it suggestions to relax. You might want to use a self-hypnosis or relaxation tape. When your physical, emotional, and mental bodies are totally relaxed then give yourself the suggestion that you are leaving your body from the top of your head through your crown chakra. Clearly visualize yourself doing so.

8. Go to your local metaphysical bookstore and buy guided meditation tapes that help you to travel out of your body.

9. Imagine a cone on the top of your head. Imagine rising up through it and popping out of the top of it.

10. Imagine a rope coming down from your monad and soul. See yourself holding on to it while your soul and monad pull you right out of the top of your head. Actually ask your soul, your monad, and the ascended masters to pull on the rope.

11. Visualize yourself in your merkabah vehicle (looking like a double-terminated crystal) and see yourself spinning like a top inside your body in a clockwise motion. Spin faster and faster until you spin right out of your crown chakra.

12. Try any one of these techniques after fasting for a day. Food tends to ground you in your body.

13. Imagine that you are looking at yourself in a mirror. Then transfer yourself into the mirror image and look back at yourself.

14. Stare at a candle in a darkened room for fifteen minutes or until you are in a deep hypnotic state. Then give yourself the suggestion that you are leaving your body. Experts suggest that the more relaxed you are, the more easily it happens. People often say, also, that they hear a crackling or popping sound as they leave.

15. A technique from Scott Rogo's book, *Leaving the Body*, is to imagine yourself as steam rising from a hot rag or from a kettle on the stove. See the steam just rising up right though your crown chakra.

16. Scott Rogo also suggests concentrating on a space a yard or two in front of your body and then trying to step into it.

17. Concentrate on a spot above your head and try to rise up into it.

18. Visualize a horizontal bar above your head. With your spiritual arms, pull yourself up out of your body and give your spiritual body a command as to where you want it to go.

19. Just imagining or pretending you are soul traveling might be the best method of all. If you pretend hard enough and often enough, pretty soon you will find yourself doing it. Fake it till you make it. This will give a super-powerful message to your subconscious mind.

20. Write out on a piece of paper "I am leaving my body tonight and traveling to _____!" Put this piece of paper under your pillow or under your mattress. The subconscious mind often needs a physical

stimulus to be convinced.

21. Write in your journal before going to bed that you are going to leave your body tonight. Write this twenty-one times right before sleeping and then put the notebook under your pillow. This will definitely get the suggestion into your subconscious mind.

22. Before going to sleep each night, imagine that you are flying, like superman, to various destinations.

23. Visualize a spot in the corner of your bedroom. In your mind, project yourself there and look back at your body. Make it as real as possible. See every detail. Hold this image until you leave your body or fall asleep. This too will be a powerful suggestion to your subconscious mind.

24. Say to yourself one hundred times during the day, "I am going to leave my body while I sleep tonight and remain lucid." Part of what makes it happen is super-intense desire. Make up your mind that you are going to have this experience if it is the last thing you ever do.

Pray to God three times a day without exception for the next six months for His help in making it happen. Paul Solomon made a statement about healing that is relevant. He said that if you were willing to give your entire life to caring for and healing another person, in total and complete selfless service, then you would attain in an instant the ability to heal others.

The correlation is that if you are willing to practice and work with these tools all the time, building up an enormous amount of desire and intention, then, in reality, you could soul travel at any moment you desire to do so. You are God, and energy in all its various forms follows thought. If you make up your mind 100% that you are going to travel out of your body, and if you are willing to practice and pray and do the exercises, then you will do it, because you are God! You have been conditioned through many other lifetimes, as well as during this one, to identify with your physical body at all costs; that is the nature of the ego. But you can change that conditioning.

25. You can work on training your subconscious mind as you fall into the hypnagogic state, that state between wakefulness and sleep. It is a state of hypersuggestibility and deep meditation. You can give yourself suggestions right before falling asleep at night, as you are just waking up in the morning, and also in the middle of the night when you wake up and turn over. Give yourself the suggestion and command, "I am leaving my body and going to _____." If you want to, add the suggestion that you will be "conscious, aware, and lucid" during this experience.

26. Visualize yourself standing next to your own physical body and inspecting it.

27. An unusual technique is to squeeze an object as hard as you can for as long as you can until you are exhausted and the object falls out of

your hands. Then give yourself the suggestion to project out of your body.

28. One avenue for learning soul travel is to approach it through lucid dreaming. If you can become aware while you are dreaming, you can give yourself the suggestion while traveling in your dream body. One technique might be to say to yourself as you are falling asleep, "I am lucid in my dreams." Say this over and over again as you are falling asleep, or write it in your journal.

A technique from Stephen Laberge's book, *Lucid Dreaming*, which I highly recommend, is to count backwards from one hundred down to zero. At each count say, "I'm dreaming." The intent to be lucid during your dreams will make it start to happen.

Another excellent technique from Laberge's book goes as follows. When you awake from a dream, go over it in your mind until you have memorized it. Then go back to sleep, giving yourself the suggestion, "Next time I'm dreaming, I want to recognize that I am dreaming." Then visualize yourself being back in the dream as you memorized it, only this time see yourself realizing that you are in the dream. Give yourself this suggestion and do the visualization a number of times before falling back to sleep. This particular technique is extremely effective for inducing a lucid dream.

29. Lie in bed and visualize yourself hovering above your bed, looking down at yourself. Visualize this super clearly. Then do a reversal and become the other you that is looking at your physical body lying on the bed.

30. I found this method in a book called *Have an Out-of-body Experience in 30 Days* by Keith Harary and Pamela Weintraub. I am shortening their method for these purposes.

Choose a place outdoors such as a park, for example. Then choose an indoor location other than your bedroom. Go to the outdoor place, close your eyes, and imagine you are having an out-of-body experience. Open your eyes and look around the park, pretending you are out of your body. Then go to your indoor spot and do the same thing. Don't fiddle around with physical things, because you would not be able to do that if you were out of your body. Make it totally real. Go to your bedroom, lie down, and imagine that you are back in the outdoor spot, as you remembered it when you were imagining being out of your body. Do the same for the indoor spot. Then imagine you are floating above your body as you fall asleep. If you awake and are out of your body, immediately give yourself the suggestion to go to your outdoor spot and then to your indoor spot.

31. Lie in bed and rotate your soul body as though you were rolling over, although your physical body remains in the same position. In a sense, you are separating from your physical body by twisting out of it. Once you are separated, then leave through your crown chakra.

42

Healing with Color and Sound

Aum is the arrow,
Brahman is the target.

Sathya Sai Baba

Everything in life is made up of energy. Becoming a master has to do with your ability to change energy from one form to another which can be done through prayer, affirmation, visualization, breathing, physical activity, and many other methods too numerous to mention.

Two of the most powerful methods of transforming energy involve the use of color and sound. These have been dealt with somewhat in two chapters in *The Complete Ascension Manual*: Esoteric Psychology and the Science of the Twelve Rays and Mantras, Names of God, and Words of Power. In this chapter I will discuss some of the other methods that can be used to transform energy.

The following chart was given to me in a class I attended on this subject. I don't know where the teacher of the class extracted it from, but it serves as a helpful chart for understanding some of the basic colors and the effects they have on the human body.

Each color, of course, relates to one of the chakras. Each color in the chart also relates to a certain musical note. The chart delineates the color's effects and the problems that may be treated with that particular color.

The Spiritual Meaning of Color

The following information on the spiritual meaning of color has been extracted from a book called *Aha! The Realization Book* by Janet McClure, founder of The Tibetan Foundation. This information has been channeled from Vywamus, the higher aspect of Earth's Planetary Logos. Although there are many books on color, this information is from one of the highest spiritual beings currently working with the Earth. He has brought through some information that goes far beyond the standard knowledge about color.

Red: the dynamic energy associated many times with thrusting into new/unknown areas; your association with the male polarity, whether you are in a male or female body; your association with the evolutionary process and, for many of you, with the evolving Source.

Orange: the mental body, in both its logical and conceptual form; your association with structure or organization; your ability to see the whole picture in any situation and your life in regard to the whole; your ability to use the fifth dimension. For many of you, this color links you into a crystalline association with the mineral kingdom on the Earth. For about 50% of you there is a link here into the overall energy grid system associated with the Earth.

Yellow: clear thinking, intelligence, and the means to freeing misperceptions through a magnification process; has third-dimension transformational qualities; has healing associations, especially when the healing moves through the Earth and back into the individual; helps focus or gather energy together, thus helping the mental qualities to be more focused; addresses scattering and the memory area; connects directly with the physical aspects of Sanat Kumara and thus forms a chain or linkage system to the Solar Logos, Helios. In this connection, also see the color gold.

Green: associated with healing; associated with growth and evolution; associated with harmony and tranquillity; associated with a clear use of the emotional body; has a specific connection to the fourth dimension; has a connection to artistic development, including painting, music, and dance; is able to draw from the Source level itself a perspective of wholeness, thus addressing the area of allowing unlimitedness.

Blue: helps to balance the polarity area through the association of love and wisdom; is an opener and a carrier of the electrical or silver energy — they blend together as the body becomes lighter; is associated with purity of purpose and love; helps to clarify purpose area through balancing and blending; emphasizes service to the plan, keeps lighting up the plan.

Indigo: identifies a deep Source-level connection and holds a focus on it; helps to clear issues of separation; has often been associated with the Christ consciousness energy; seeks to blend spiritual perspectives through a decrystallizing process: decrystallizes the surrender area, has seven levels that decrystallize as one "ascends" through them.

Violet: transformation; purification; transmutation; what has been called ceremonial "magic" or invoking through an integration of all of the other colors and what they represent; helps integrate all of what has been learned on Earth; helps heal polarity splits; helps heal the emotional body through its association with the spiritual body; helps cleanse and purify the physical structure; helps align the mental and spiritual perspectives; closely associated with St. Germain; closely associated with the New Age.

Pink: associated with the heart energy and its characteristics, particularly love, compassion, and gratitude; helpful in softening any crystallization in the will area; helps the surrender process and reaches into and supports what is new, what has begun; thus is helpful in realizing divine support; associated with the angelic kingdom.

Silver: a symbol for the electrical energy of the soul; symbolizes the use of the soul's energy; works with being in the flow; will seek to break up or decrystallize blocks in the use of electricity in all of its forms, including all electrical and electronic devices used on the Earth; many times is associated with the angelic kingdom; addresses the lightening perspective; helps deal with blocks in the electrical flow of the physical structure through a penetrative process; helps anchor more of the soul's energy on the cellular level.

Gold: the perfect integrator; the accepting of the soul level is emphasized; the accepting of wholeness on every level is emphasized; emphasizes linkage systems; deals with full abundance; helps to integrate the cocreator level; deals with putting together the pieces of any area that has seemed scattered; connects through Sanat Kumara or the planetary link directly to Helios or the Solar Logos consciousness level; helps to develop through decrystallization more heart radiance; seeks to help soften perspectives that need blending so they blend more easily; deals with "kingship/queenship"; deals with assuming one's full power through the true identity level; awakens within one the true reality level; broadens the creative base through allowing it to flow; accelerates blending of levels of creativity; often acts as a "launching" into an integrated level of creativity.

A Simplified Understanding of Colors

Violet. . . . . Spirituality
Indigo . . . . Intuition
Blue . . . . . Religious Inspiration
Green . . . . Harmony and Sympathy
Yellow . . . . Intellect
Orange . . Energy
Red . . . . . Life

Color	Music Note	Chakra (Energy Body); Location, Function, Behavior	Color's Effects	Problems Treated
Red	C	First – base of spine; creativity, sexuality, restorative process, transmutation	energizes, vitalizes, heats, and promotes circulation; stimulates adrenalin, red blood cell production, menstrual flow and sexual power; strengthens will power and courage	anemia infertility/impotence colds and chills weak menstruation (not in fevers or nervous problems)
Orange	D	Second – below navel; emotions, purification	warms and cheers, frees bodily and emotional tension; aids mental function	lung ailments epilepsy mental problems rheumatism kidney troubles
Yellow	E	Third – solar plexus; thinking, ambition	inspires and awakens the mind; strengthens the nerves; helps reasoning; aids self-control; aids elimination; improves skin; stimulates cerebrum and nerves	stomach troubles indigestion, gas constipation liver problems eczema nervous exhaustion
Green	F	Fourth – heart area; sensitivity, feelings, compassion, harmony	harmonizes and balances, soothes and restores; is a tonic; stimulates the heart; soothes the nerves, brain, heart, and eyes; helps elimination; refreshes	headaches heart ailments ulcers ulcers eye problems nervous conditions
Blue	G	Fifth – throat area; communiction, self-expression	cools, sedates, relaxes, and soothes; helps stop bleeding; helps with nutrition and building the skin and body; promotes truth, loyalty, and reliability; is an antiseptic	all inflammations throat problems fevers, infections burns spasms, pain headaches, diarrhea
Indigo	A	Sixth – pineal-pituitary area, third eye; perception, realization	is electric, cooling, astringent; has an anaesthetic effect; builds white blood cells; increases activity of the spleen; depresses heart and nervous system	pneumonia mental problems convulsions eye, ear, and nose problems
Violet	B	Seventh – crown (top of head); universal consciousness, oneness	stimulates spiritual nature and intuition; elevates inspiration; expands divine understanding	mental disorders neuroses neuralgia concussions cramps tumors scalp problems

Color Healing Using Candles

There are many ways color can be utilized. The first method I would like to suggest is lighting colored candles. Light a candle of the color that is appropriate for what you are attempting to manifest.

If you want truth and purity, light a white candle. If you want to gain knowledge, light a yellow candle. Light a pink candle to send love. Light a blue candle for the resolution of a spiritual problem. Green candles are good for all monetary and material concerns. Lavender candles are especially good for healing. Silver candles are good for protection.

As you light the candle, say a prayer and state what you need. It is important to be specific. Thank God for granting you what you need. The candle and the color it is radiating keep your prayer manifesting that specific energy as long as the candle is lit.

Color Healing Using Lamp Radiation

Colored lamplight is a wonderful method that I have often used. All you need is a small lamp and colored light bulbs. Sometimes light bulbs of certain colors are hard to find; at photography stores you can buy colored gels that can be taped over the lamp instead. Let yourself bask in the colored light as you read or sleep.

If you are reading and you want more energy, use an orange light bulb or gel. If you need physical healing, use a green light. If you want mental stimulation, use a yellow light. If you want a more spiritual feeling, use a blue or violet light. It is really fun to play with the colors and it is easy to switch them around.

Colored Water Healing

Using colored water is a wonderful healing modality. The idea is to place the colored gels I spoke of above around a clear glass bottle of water. Place the closed glass water bottle with the gel covering it outside in the sun. The sun will shine through the colored gel into the water and energize it both with the sun's energy and with the color frequency of that particular gel.

You can drink water permeated with the green healing vibration or with the qualities of whatever color you have chosen. The water will not change color but will most definitely contain the frequency of the chosen color.

Color Breathing

Another method of utilizing color is to breathe different colors into your body. Red, orange, and yellow are magnetic and should be visualized as flowing up from the Earth toward the solar plexus. Blue, indigo, and violet are electrical and are breathed in from the ethers downward. Green is the balancer of the spectrum and flows into the system horizontally. When breathing, breathe deeply, bringing air into the lower abdomen. The best time to practice this technique is before breakfast or dinner.

Color Visualization

Visualize yourself bathed in the color you choose to resonate with. It can be seen as a ball of light or a tube of light. You might just affirm to yourself, "I am now filled with emerald green." You are God, and anything you affirm or visualize takes place, for your word is law, and you create with your mind.

Radiant Color Magnetism

You can channel color through your hands for healing purposes. You can do it on yourself or on a friend, animal, or plant you want to heal. It is just a matter of affirming and visualizing that you are doing this and it will be done.

Color Healing and the Rays

One of the most powerful ways of doing color healing is by calling forth from God one of the twelve rays. This can be done by calling forth the actual color of the ray, the number of the ray, or the spiritual quality of the ray.

For details, I refer you again to *The Complete Ascension Manual*; for convenience I will list the twelve rays and their corresponding colors here.

First ray	Red
Second ray	Blue
Third ray	Yellow
Fourth ray	Emerald Green
Fifth ray	Orange
Sixth ray	Indigo
Seventh ray	Violet
Eighth ray	Seafoam Green / Violet luminosity
Ninth ray	Blue-Green
Tenth ray	Pearlescence
Eleventh ray	Orange / Pink luminosity
Twelfth ray	Gold

Just call these rays in from Source and see and feel yourself bathed inwardly and outwardly in their energy. They are always available; all you have to do is ask for them. Study the information in the other book if you need a refresher course on the soul qualities that each of these colors embodies. Calling forth the rays is a most powerful color-healing technique.

Color Healing and the Twenty-two Chakras

A color healing process that in actuality is just as powerful as calling in the twelve rays and their colors is to call down your twenty-two chakras from the higher dimensions into your physical and etheric bodies.

Each of your twenty-two chakras embodies a particular color. As you evolve spiritually, your chakras descend downward. Once you master your third-dimensional chakras, the fourth-dimensional chakras begin to descend into your body. Once you master your fourth-dimensional chakras, the fifth-dimensional chakras begin to descend. One of the fastest ways to accelerate your spiritual growth is to call these higher chakras down into your body to experience them and their corresponding vibrations. They are happy to come down; however, they must be asked.

They look like bodies of Light. Once anchored in your body, they will run their high-level color frequencies through your body to help you raise your vibration. They will not remain fully anchored until you are spiritually ready, for they don't want to burn out your body circuits. They will bring in only as much high-frequency color energy as you can handle.

Ask your monad and Mighty I Am Presence to guide the whole color chakra meditation process. In *Soul Psychology* I have gone into great detail in explaining all twenty-two chakras; for convenience, I will list them and their corresponding colors here.

The Chakras and Their Colors

Chakra	Color	Evolved Color
One	Red	Violet
Two	Orange	Indigo
Three	Yellow	
Four	Green or Pink	
Five	Blue (Djwhal Khul has recommended blue with an orange triangle in the center)	
Six	Indigo or Gold	
Seven	Violet or Rainbow White	
Eight	Emerald Green and Purple	
Nine	Blue-Green	
Ten	Pearlescence	
Eleven	Pink-Orange	
Twelve	Gold	
Thirteen	Pale Violet-Pink	
Fourteen	Deep Blue-Violet	
Fifteen	Light Golden-White	

Sixteen . . . . . . Light Violet-White
Seventeen. . . . . Multi-White
Eighteen. . . . . . Pink-Gold
Nineteen . . . . . Magenta
Twenty . . . . . . Violet-Gold
Twenty-one . . . Blue-Gold
Twenty-two . . . Platinum

Color Healing through Clothing

When you want to embody or cultivate a certain quality, consciously wear clothes of that color and wear jewelry or carry gemstones that hold the same vibration. I might also suggest that you have an analysis done to see if your physical body resonates best with Summer, Autumn, Winter, or Spring colors.

The Planets and Color Healing

Sun . . . . Gold, Bright Yellow
Moon . . . . Silver
Earth . . . . Lavender-blue
Mercury . . . . . Yellow, Orange
Venus . . . . Blue, Blue-Green
Mars. . . . . Red
Jupiter . . . . . . Purple, Violet
Saturn . . . . . . Olive Green
Uranus . . . . . . Electric Blue, Pale Green, Citrine
Neptune . . . . . Dark Blue, Indigo, Grays, Green
Pluto . . . . Yellow, Pale Green, Navy Blue

Astrology and Color Healing

Aries . . . . Red
Taurus . . . . . . Yellow
Gemini . . . . . . Violet
Cancer . . . . . . Green
Leo . . . . Gold
Virgo . . . . Purple
Libra . . . . Yellow
Scorpio . . . . . . Crimson Red
Sagittarius . . . Deep Clear Blue
Capricorn. . . . . Black and White
Aquarius. . . . . . Blue with Silver Lights
Pisces . . . . Soft Azure

Music Notes and Their Corresponding Colors

C . . . . Red
D . . . . Yellow
D# . . . Glint of Steel
E . . . . Pearly Blue
F . . . . Dark Red
F# . . . Bright Blue
G . . . . Rosy Orange
G# . . . Purple
A . . . . Green
A# . . . Glint of Steel
B . . . . Soft Blue
C . . . . Violet

Classical Music Compositions of Tremendous Healing Value

This music might be thought of as music of the spheres. You cannot help but be healed and uplifted by listening to this kind of music. In fact, music was used in healing temples of Atlantis for just such a purpose. In the future, doctors will heal using the science of sound and music.

Schuber . . . . . . "Ave Maria"
Mozart . . . . . . *The Magic Flute*
Verdi . . . . *Aïda*
Beethoven . . . . *The Nine Symphonies*
Tchaikovsky . . . *Swan Lake* and *Sleeping Beauty*
Wagner . . . . . . *Parsifal* and *Lohengrin*
Handel . . . . . . *Messiah*
Mendelssohn. . . *A Midsummer Night's Dream*
Bach. . . . . *The Passion of St. Matthew*
Wagner . . . . . . *Tannhauser*
Pachelbel . . . . . Canon in D Major

I would recommend that you get a set of tuning forks at your local music or metaphysical store. You can tune your chakras and clean out unwanted negative energies by using them.

Note	Color	Kundalini Chakra
C	Red	Muladhara
D	Orange . . .	Svadhisthana
E	Yellow	Manipura
F	Green	Anahata
G	Blue	Visuddha
A	Indigo	Ajna
B	Violet.	Sahasrara

There is now a form of healing in which practitioners, with the use of a specialized computer, can listen to your voice and tell you what notes you are missing or overusing. From this information they can do an entire personality workup that is accurate. They then teach you to reintegrate the missing tones and demphasize the overused tones, which changes the personality and results in healing.

Color Music

In a wonderful book called *Healing with Music and Color*, Mary Bassano has done some interesting research that correlates certain pieces of music with the basic color spectrum. This information will allow you to put on red music or green music — music of whatever color suits your mood. I would also like to acknowledge Heline Corinne for her book *Color and Music in the New Age*.

Red Music

Classical
> "March Militaire" by Schubert
> Sousa Marches
> "The Sailor's Dance" from *Red Poppy Ballet Suite* by Glière

New Age
> "Mars" from *The Planets* by Holst
> "On the Edge" by Mickey Hart
> "Diga Rhythm" by Mickey Hart

Orange Music

Classical
> Hungarian Dance No. 5 by Brahms
> "Habanera" from *Carmen* by Bizet
> "Capriccio Espagnole" by Rimski-Korsakov

New Age
> "Winterfall Music" by Paul Warner
> "Jupiter" from *The Planets* by Holst
> "Eagle's Call" by Bruce Hurnow

Yellow Music

Classical
> "Arabeske" by Schumann
> *Fountains of Rome* by Respighi
> Piano Concerto No. 26 by Mozart

New Age
> "Lemurian Sunrise" by Paul Warner
> "Dawn" by Steven Halpern
> "Kitaro Ki" by Kitaro

Green Music
Classical
> Melody in F by Rubenstein
> Violin Concerto in E Minor by Mendelssohn
> "Clair de Lune" by Debussy

New Age
> "Pan Flute" by Za Mir
> "Ocean" by Larkin
> "Fairy Ring" by Mike Rowland

Blue Music
Classical
> Air on a G String by Bach
> "Ave Maria" by Schubert
> "The Swan" by Saint-Saens

New Age
> "Divine Gypsy" (instrumental arrangement of Yogananda's cosmic chants)
> "A Crystal Cave (Back to Atlantis)" by Upper Astral
> Vocal Selection: "Be Still" by Rosemary Crow United Research, Black Mt., N.C.

Indigo Music
Classical
> "Traumerei" by Schumann
> Adagio from Symphony No. 1 in C Minor by Brahms
> Poème for Violin and Orchestra by Chausson

New Age
> "Angel Love" by Aeoliah
> "Inside" by Paul Horn
> "Venus" from *The Planets* by Gustav Holst

Violet Music
Classical
> Piano Concerto in B Minor by Tchaikovsky
> "Liebestraume" by Liszt
> Gregorian Chants

New Age
> "The Great Pyramid" by Paul Horn
> "Neptune" from *The Planets* by Holst
> "Eventide" by Steven Halpern

43

Brahma, Vishnu, and Shiva

*The mind may be said to be
of two kinds, pure and impure. Driven by the
senses it becomes impure, but with the senses
under control, the mind becomes pure.*

The Vedas

Hinduism is the world's third largest religion with over five hundred million followers. It began in India, and over two-thirds of its followers live in India. They believe that Hinduism goes back over four thousand years and is the oldest of all religions.

The objective of Hinduism is to achieve union with the one, all-pervading God, Brahman. Brahman is then divided into Brahma, the creator aspect, Vishnu, the preserver, and Shiva, the destroyer. The term "Atman" refers to the Eternal Self which is your true identity. The sacred Hindu writings called the Upanishads point out that Brahman and Atman are one.

According to Hindu doctrine, the ideal life consists of four stages:

1. The period of discipline and education;
2. The life of the householder and active worker;
3. The retreat for the loosening of the bonds;
4. The life of the hermit, preparing for death and union with God.

Hindu worship is individual as contrasted with the group and congregational worship of some of the other major religions. Most houses have a room or a corner of a room for worship called a puja where there are pictures or a statue of a particular image of God.

Hinduism recognizes tens of thousands of lesser gods that all come under the umbrella of the one God, Brahman. Hinduism also recognizes the divine descent of avatars, God-realized beings living on Earth. The two main avatars of Hinduism are Rama and Krishna.

Rama lived over twenty thousand years ago and Krishna lived around 5000 B.C. There have been other avatars, but these two are the most well known and most highly revered. Mahatma Gandhi said in his autobiography that one of the keys to his success was the continuous chanting of the name of God; the name he chanted was Ram or Rama. Gandhi was also greatly influenced by the sacred Hindu book, the *Bhagavad-Gita*, which is the part of the larger work, the *Mahabarata*, that tells the story of Krishna. The story of Rama is told in the *Ramayana*.

Sai Baba, who is now living in India, is the most popular avatar since Krishna. (Krishna, of course, was a past-life incarnation of the Lord Maitreya who is head of the Great White Brotherhood.) Sai Baba is actually much more popular than even Krishna or Rama because they lived at times when their lives had to be focused in small villages, so not very many people realized that they were divine incarnations. Sai Baba, because of modern media and travel, has been able to reach far more people than Krishna or Rama ever could have at the time they lived. Of course, after their deaths their legends spread widely through the *Ramayana* and the *Bhagavad-Gita*.

Hinduism recognized that many people need a personal God they can feel close to and visualize in their minds. This has often, unfortunately, been construed to be polytheism, which is not the case at all. The fact is that God's infinite universe does have infinite numbers of lesser gods that run the universe at stepped-down levels of frequency. Hindus recognize that the many lesser gods are all a part of Brahman.

Hindus recognize Brahman first and then the famous Hindu trinity of Brahma, Vishnu, and Shiva. There are three main sects of Hindus: those who worship Brahma, those who worship Vishnu, and those who worship Shiva. Brahma is the creator aspect of the trinity. Vishnu is the preserver and Shiva is the destroyer.

Brahma was once an important god but he has declined in popularity over the centuries. Vishnu is worshiped in the form of the avatars. He has supposedly had ten incarnations, the two most famous being Rama and Krishna. Sai Baba has said that he is an incarnation of Vishnu also, and he has also said that he is an incarnation of the Lord Dattetreya, who is the incarnation of Brahma, Vishnu, and Shiva. Sai Baba also embodies the Shakti energy. There has never been another like him in the Hindu tradition, as he is all four major deities in one body. Worshiping Shiva is also a very popular path.

Another smaller Hindu sect worships the Divine Mother aspect of God. She has been described as the embodiment of Shakti energy. Among the aspects of the Mother energy most widely worshiped is that of the wife of Shiva, Parvati. Vishnu's wife is Lakshmi, the goddess of good luck and good fortune. The great Hindu saint of the nineteenth century, Rama Krishna, was for a time a devotee of the Divine Mother aspect of God.

There are many minor gods that the Hindus worship, pay homage to, and call on as needed. One is Ganesh, the elephant-headed god. Hindus call on him when they have obstacles in their lives. Hanuman, the monkey god, is the embodiment of and perfect example of selfless service, for it was Hanuman who helped Rama rescue his wife, Sita, when she had been kidnapped by an evil demon. Some of the other minor gods are Durga, the warrior goddess; the goddess Kali, bringer of war and destruction; Indra, the war and water god; Surya, the Sun god; Chandra, the Moon god; Saraswati, the goddess of wisdom; and Agni, the god of fire. As you can clearly see, Hinduism is quite a colorful religion. There are pictures of the gods and goddesses in almost every home and shop, and the smell of sweet incense is everywhere.

Hindu wisdom is not collected into a single book like the Bible or the Koran or the Dhamapada of Buddhism. There are, rather, many different sets of books: the *Ramayana*, the *Mahabarata* which contains the *Bhagavad-Gita*, the Vedas, the Upanishads, the Puranas, and others.

The main message of the Upanishads, which elaborate on the Vedas, is that each soul, or Atman, is part of the world soul, or Brahman. Brahman is within all things. Through the cycle of reincarnation, man finally realizes Brahman through the understanding that he is the Eternal Self, or Atman.

The *Bhagavad-Gita*, which means "Song of God," was written by Vyassa, who was an incarnation of the Buddha. It is a conversation between Krishna and his disciple, Arjuna, who represents the spiritual warrior. Krishna is Arjuna's spiritual teacher and charioteer during the time before a great battle between two sects of Arjuna's family. Arjuna loses his faith and clarity and is consumed by negative ego just as the battle is about to begin. The *Bhagavad-Gita* tells how Krishna reawakens Arjuna to the divine realities of life.

There are many universal ideals in Hinduism such as truthfulness, kindness, unconditional love, the fulfilling of your dharma (mission), and selfless service. One of the keys to understanding Hinduism is to acknowledge the primary desire of all Hindus to achieve moksha (liberation) from the wheel of rebirth. The idea is to get rid of all desire except for that one, all-pervading desire which is fulfilled through the realization of the Atman, the Eternal Self, a state in which the seeker is at last free from the bondage of karma. It is achieved, in part, through the renunciation of identification with the material world.

Another set of teachings that is intimately involved with the path of

Hinduism is that of yoga. The Hindus recognize many paths back to the Creator and this is evidenced in the many forms of yoga, which is such a broad subject that I have dedicated an entire chapter to it.

During morning, afternoon, or evening worship, the devout Hindu sits in front of his altar and meditates, prays, and reads spiritual texts. Incense is often lit, and flowers and food are sometimes placed on the altar. Hindus believe that the sacred text of the Vedas was revealed by God to seers called rishis in ancient times. Sai Baba attests to the truth of this.

Five thousand years ago, it was predicted that an avatar called the Kalki Avatar would arrive at the end of the Iron Age. Sai Baba is that avatar the Hindu religion has been waiting for. The unique thing is that he transcends Hinduism, for he says that he is in all forms and will come to you no matter what form of God you worship, even if it isn't one of the Hindu gods.

Another key principle of the Hindu faith is the need to overcome maya, or illusion, the state of consciousness that is overidentified with the material universe, hence creating the illusion of separation and absence of unity with God. There are many paths to achieving this transcendence, including the many forms of yoga.

Hindus very much believe in the law of karma. The physical body that your soul will live in during the next life is determined by your actions in this life. If you do good deeds, you will be reborn at a higher level. This leads to an understanding of the Hindu caste system, for it is tied to the understanding of rebirth.

Hinduism divides society into four large classes. At the top are the Brahmins (as differentiated from Brahman and Brahma) who are considered the purest and who perform all religious ceremonies. Next are the Kshatriyas who are the rulers and warriors. The third group is the Vaishyas who are the traders and craft workers. Fourth are the Shudras, the ordinary workers. The fifth group is outside the caste system; called the untouchables, they do all the dirtiest jobs. This classification has been outlawed in modern India but attitudes are sometimes slow to change. Caste plays an important part in the life of a Hindu. It would probably determine your job, whom you married, your economic status, and whom you would share food with.

Respect for elders is also a very important part of the Hindu value system. It is the elders who actually choose marriage partners for their children or grandchildren. The bride then usually goes to live in the groom's home. American retirement homes are very shocking to the Hindus.

For every newly born child, an astrological horoscope is cast, a ritual I think is a fantastic service to the child. The name the child is given usually has a special religious meaning. The most important ceremony of child-hood is the initiation of the sacred thread which usually takes place between the ages of eight and eleven. It is a sacred ceremony in which the Brahmin priest hangs a long loop of thread made of several strands twisted together over the boy's left shoulder and under his right arm. This sacred thread is then worn from that day forward, for the rest of the boy's life. This ceremony is looked at as being a rebirth. Those who wear the thread are called "twice born." After this ceremony, the boy begins to study the sacred writings and religious rituals.

The schools in India do not have courses in Hinduism but teach the morals and ethics of all religions (an aspect that is sadly lacking in the American educational system). Displays and plays honor all the different religious leaders.

An astrology reading is also done before all weddings to determine the ideal time for the ceremony. The Hindu understanding of marriage is different from that in America. Love is expected to grow gradually after marriage, not before. It would have to be this way since marriages are so often arranged by elders.

Spiritual pilgrimages are a very important part of the Hindu religion. They are not required, but many devout Hindus strongly desire to make them. The Ganges River is by far the most holy place. The water of the Ganges is said to wash away a person's sins. Most Hindus try to bathe in it at least once in a lifetime.

Mount Kailas in the central Himalaya Mountains is also a sacred place for many Hindus, for it is sacred to Shiva. One of Hinduism's greatest temples is the spectacular Jagannatha Temple in the city of Puri. Hundreds of thousands of pilgrims gather there for a festival held in June or July. Jagannatha is a form of Vishnu. At this festival an image of Jagannatha is carried through the streets of the city in a procession.

Cremation after death is a standard practice for all Hindus. The body is placed on a raised platform and covered with sandalwood. Rituals are performed and hymns sung to remind the mourners that the body dies, but the soul is eternal. To Hindus death is a celebration, not a sad occasion as in Western culture. The Hindus recognize that the incarnated personality is now a free spirit and they are very joyous about this new life for their loved one. The actual lighting of the funeral pyre is done by the elder son or by another family member.

Hinduism teaches compassion for all living things. Gandhi exemplified this in his teachings of nonviolence, and it is also demonstrated by the sacred cows that wander the streets of India unharmed.

In Hindu cosmology, a universe projects from Brahman and endures only for a cycle of four billion three hundred twenty million human years.

Then it is breathed back into the heart of Brahman. This process is repeated over and over again. In Hindu cosmology, Brahman appears in the form of Brahma to create each universe, in the form of Vishnu to sustain it, and in the form of Shiva to eventually destroy it.

Integral to every Hindu's worldview is seeing God in everything; that includes trees, rivers, cows, and ants. This ideal of nonviolence applies to animals as well as to humans — most Hindus are vegetarians. It is also worthy of mention that nowhere else in the world is asceticism considered such a national ideal as in India.

Since liberation from the wheel of rebirth is the highest ideal for all Hindus, death is the biggest event in their lives. This is why many Hindus travel to the holy city of Benares when they are about to die.

44

The Bhagavad-Gita

Give up your unmanliness and get up and fight.
This self-pity and self-indulgence are unbecoming
of the great soul you are.

Krishna
to Arjuna

The *Bhagavad-Gita* is one of the holiest and most sublime books that exists on Planet Earth. If I were told that I had to get rid of all books but one, I would save the *Bhagavad-Gita*. It is really the book of books. Sai Baba has called it the cream of the Upanishads, the wisdom teachings of the Vedas. It is the sublime story of Sri Bhagavan Krishna and his disciple, Arjuna.

Krishna is the Christ of the Eastern world and, in reality, is the Christ of the Western world, too, because Krishna is none other than the Lord Maitreya, the Planetary Christ. He is the teacher of teachers, for he is the head of the Great White Brotherhood and the Spiritual Hierarchy.

This great teacher and leader is here again as he was seven thousand years ago as Krishna and two thousand years ago as the being who overshadowed Jesus; now he is physically incarnated in London, England. He is the World Teacher that all religions have been waiting for.

The *Bhagavad-Gita* is Krishna's sublime teachings to Arjuna as expressed by Vyassa. It is interesting to note that the soul that was Arjuna was later Vyassa and subsequently incarnated as Gautama Buddha. So the *Bhagavad-Gita* is the story of the relationship between the Lord Maitreya and Gautama Buddha. The Lord Maitreya, according to the channelings of The Tibetan Foundation, is the highest being ever to graduate from this planetary school. (He isn't the highest being ever to have come here but is the highest to graduate.) In his life as Krishna more than seven thousand years ago, he attained his fifth initiation. In his life overshadowing Jesus, he took his ascension, or sixth initiation. Who better to teach the wisdom of the ages than Lord Maitreya and Gautama Buddha?

Lord Maitreya was the teacher of Jesus, Kuthumi, El Morya, Saint Germain, Hilarion, Serapis Bey, and many other great masters. He is the teacher of both angels and men. In the *Bhagavad-Gita*, he is humanity's teacher.

The *Bhagavad-Gita* is part of a larger book called the *Mahabarata* which is the story of a great war. It is against the backdrop of this great battle between two armies that Krishna teaches the science of liberation and God-realization. The actual meaning of "Bhagavad-Gita" is "Song of God." The two opposing armies are the divine nature and the demonic nature with which all must come to terms and master. Arjuna, as the unfolding incarnated soul, is being pulled in opposite directions by his higher and lower natures which is crippling him both spiritually and psychologically.

The story begins with Arjuna, who is the leader of the divine army, falling into despondency and depression because he doesn't want to fight the demonic army since he knows many of them personally. Arjuna has been overcome by maya, illusion, glamour, and negative ego. The *Bhagavad-Gita* is Krishna's attempt to awaken Arjuna to the reality and perspective of his Eternal Self.

The Wisdom Teachings of Sri Bhagavan Krishna

The first lesson Krishna teaches is that the wise person does not grieve for the living or the dead because the indweller of the body is none other than the Eternal Self. The Eternal Self is never born and never dies. It is unborn and changeless. It cannot be killed, even if the body is slain. When the physical body is worn out it puts on a new one, like a new set of clothes. Weapons cannot hurt it nor fire burn it nor water drown it.

The Eternal Self is invulnerable, indestructible, and immortal. The true yogi lives in a state of transcendence of duality, or transcendence of the pairs of opposites. What this means is that the true yogi lives in even-mindedness and equanimity whether he or she is experiencing pleasure or pain, profit or loss, victory or defeat, criticism or praise, cold or heat. The yogi stands detached from all greed and attachment.

As Arjuna was to say later in his incarnation as the Buddha, "All suffering comes from attachment." The yogi remains in a state of unconditional love, joy, and inner peace at all times, regardless of what is going on outside of himself. This state of equilibrium is called yoga.

One of the key teachings of the *Bhagavad-Gita* that is repeated over and over again is that a person has a tremendous need to perform his duty and service in life without being attached to the fruits of his actions. In other words, taking action in life is essential, but it must not be taken to achieve some kind of material or spiritual reward. Action is taken out of duty, for a mission, and in worship of God who lives in all humans, plants, and animals as the Eternal Self. The true yogi sees the Eternal Self in all beings and all forms. Action without attachment to results is yoga.

A true knower of the Self casts away all material desire and is satisfied only by the Eternal Self. The yogi has no craving for pleasure and is free from passion, fear, and anger. He has total mastery of his physical body, emotions, mind, intellect, and five senses. Intuitional awareness cannot be obtained without self-control.

All desire for pleasure, power, and the acquiring and hoarding of material objects is removed. All selfish attachment is removed. The yogi is free from lust and has control over his sexuality. The yogi is neither elated by good fortune nor depressed by bad fortune. He is totally free from attachment and aversion to people and things.

The yogi has been released from the ego cage of "I," "me," and "mine." The path to Self-realization is one of renunciation — renunciation of the above-mentioned negative qualities, not renunciation of acting in life. The yogi lives in this world but is not of this world. The yogi fights the holy fight and lives as a spiritual warrior, thinking only of the Eternal Self and incurring no sin.

There are two paths to Self-realization: Jnana Yoga, the contemplative path of spiritual wisdom and Karma Yoga, the active path of selfless service. Both of these paths lead to Brahma (God). Every selfless act is born from Brahma, just as every selfish act leads away from Him. Through devotion to selfless work in service of humanity you attain the supreme goal of life. It is better for a person to perform his or her own dharma (path) imperfectly than to try to perform another person's perfectly. Each person must find his own dharma and not compare or compete with others.

Desire and anger are seen by Krishna as the all-consuming, all-polluting enemy of the world. Desire is the destroyer of wisdom and discrimination. Senses are superior to the body; the mind is superior to the senses; the intelligence is superior to the mind. Superior even to the intelligence is the Eternal Self. The ego has one belief: "I am the doer." The reality is that there is no separate I outside of the Eternal Self. The *Bhagavad-Gita* states, "Perform all actions for my sake [Krishna, the Eternal Self], completely absorbed in the Self and without expectations; fight, but stay free from the fever of the ego."

When a person lets himself be run by his senses, he is conditioned to be attracted to the pleasant and to have aversion to the unpleasant. The true yogi living in the consciousness of the Eternal Self does his duty and remains the same. The yogi lives in contentment regardless of what comes. The yogi lets the Atma (Eternal Self) rule the ego and slay selfish desire.

It is through humility, self-inquiry, and service that the yogi is led to those who will impart great knowledge. The true yogi is fearless, devoted, and free from envy and all self-doubts. He knows himself and others as the Divine Self and not just as separate physical bodies. The yogi is free from all sense of expectation and all sense of possession. The mind is fixed on knowledge and all work is performed in the spirit of service. Brahman is attained by those who see Brahma in every action.

The true sanyasin (renunciate) neither hates nor desires. He or she is free from the pairs of opposites. The self is seen as one with all other selves. All deeds are performed as an offering to God. A person of knowledge looks with equal eye on a Brahmin priest, a cow, an elephant, a dog, an outcast. The Eternal One is essentially the same in all.

The knower of the eternal doesn't rejoice on meeting pleasant experiences nor grieve on meeting unpleasant experiences. The person who withstands the impulses originating from lust and anger is a true yogi and a happy person. The yogi's only desire is for liberation and Self-realization. The true yogi is unaffected by likes and dislikes and the bondage of self-will. The goals of knowledge and service are unified. The yogi is free from delusion and not dependent on any external support.

The true yogi is filled with wisdom and knowledge and looks at a lump of earth, a stone, and a piece of gold as the same. All are just incarnations of God and the yogi sees beyond all appearances. The yogi has an equal regard for friends, companions, enemies, neutral people, hateful people, relatives, saints, and sinners. The yogi has an iron will that is used to abolish self-will. Will, or personal power, is used only in service of the Eternal Self.

Krishna very much preached the middle way. In one passage he says, "He who eats too much, he who fasts too much or sleeps too much or too little cannot perform yoga." Krishna taught the ideal of moderation in recreation, effort, actions, sleep, and wakefulness. The yogi's mind is calm, passions are stilled, and he has attained purity. He realizes that he is within all beings and all beings are within himself. The supreme yogi feels the pains and joys of all beings as if they were his own joys and pains. The yogi has trained his mind to rest only in the Eternal Self.

Krishna says that among thousands of men and women, hardly one strives for perfection, and of these successful strivers, only one really knows him. The Eternal Self is the Om. Krishna has delineated four types of virtuous people who seek God: the person in distress, the person seeking knowledge, the person seeking wealth, and the person aspiring to wisdom.

All four types are seen as virtuous, but the person seeking wisdom is the most virtuous. The person of wisdom has a steadfast mind and is focused on the Eternal Self as his supreme goal. The Eternal Self resides within all forms of God and religion.

At the time of leaving the body upon death (or sleep), a person will travel to the last thought in his mind. Therefore, the yogi keeps his mind on God at all times so that it is to God he will go when he dies. At the time of departure he says the word Om so he will enter the highest path.

Krishna says the Eternal Self is easily attainable by a steadfast yogi whose mind is fixed on the Eternal Self and who constantly remembers the Eternal Self. This is attained by complete devotion to God. The Eternal Self is easily attained by those who are attached to nothing but the Eternal Self. There are two paths in life: one leads to liberation and the other to rebirth. Choose whom ye shall serve.

The ignorant cannot see the Eternal Self when it inhabits a human form, but the yogi, seeing beyond form, has the eyes to see and the ears to hear. The Eternal Self is embodied in His Holiness, the Lord Sai Baba, but many are fooled by his seeming normal actions of walking around in an average-looking physical body. It is through constant striving, firmness, an undivided mind, and unbroken vows that the Self is attained.

The true yogi worships the Eternal Self in all beings. The Eternal Self does not find favor or disfavor in any being. Even the greatest sinner who begins to worship is counted as righteous. No devotee is ever rejected. Those who worship and meditate on the Eternal Self without any other thought will have their needs provided for. Those who fail to realize the true nature of the Eternal Self must be reborn. It is through single-minded devotion that one can see the Self and enter into the Self and become the Self.

Those who worship the Self with a fixed mind and with faith and courage and those who are steadfast are perfect yogis. They are totally devoted to the welfare of all beings. All actions are performed as if they were being performed for God. This is the path to perfection.

The true yogi never hurts any person or creature in the world and is never hurt by the world. The true yogi is modest, sincere, harmless, forgiving, straightforward, balanced in the mind in favorable and unfavorable conditions, free from pride and deceit, gentle, upright, pure, filled with inner strength, detached from sense objects. The true yogi does not get compulsively entangled, even in his home and family. He enjoys solitude, not following the crowd. Some realize the Self through the practice of meditation, some through the path of wisdom, some through the path of service, and some through all three paths practiced in integration and balance.

The Three Gunas

Krishna has put forth a fantastic model for understanding oneself and other people. He has divided the qualities that make up the phenomenal world into three categories, called gunas: the sattvic, the rajasic, and the tamasic. The sattvic quality has to do with law, harmony, purity, and goodness; the rajasic with energy and passion; the tamasic with inertia and ignorance. The ideal is to be sattvic – although, in truth, the Eternal Self is beyond all three qualities of energy. Even the sattvic nature can become negative if it becomes attached to happiness and wisdom. The rajasic nature binds through the passion arising from selfish desire and attachment. The tamasic nature binds through ignorance, indolence, and sleep. In essence, the sattvic person finds happiness, the rajasic person finds action, the tamasic person finds distorted understanding and delusion. When the sattvic quality predominates in a person's personality, the Light of wisdom shines. When the rajasic quality predominates, a person pursues selfishness and greedy purposes. When the tamasic quality predominates, a person lives in darkness, slothfulness, and confusion.

Dying with a sattvic nature, the yogi attains the pure worlds of the wise. Those dying in a rajasic state are reborn among people driven to work. Those dying in a tamasic state are conceived in the wombs of the ignorant. In my understanding, the sattvic nature is balanced, the rajasic nature is too yang, and the tamasic nature is too yin. The rajasic nature might be looked at as being the top dog, or superiority complex, while the tamasic nature might be considered the underdog, or inferiority complex. This is very simplified, but it might be helpful in putting Krishna's system into perspective.

The fruit of good deeds is sattvic: suffering is rajasic; ignorance and insensitivity are tamasic. The sattvic quality brings understanding, the rajasic brings greed, and the tamasic brings confusion, infatuation, and ignorance. The sattvic quality goes upward, the rajasic quality remains the same, and the tamasic quality sinks downward.

The true yogi ultimately goes beyond the three gunas, feeling no aversion when the forces are active nor any craving when the forces subside. The yogi remains impartial and undisturbed by the action of the gunas. The yogi does not vacillate but when dealing with form manifests the sattvic nature. Such a one is fit for union with Brahman. The yogi avoids malice, lack of morals, insatiable desires, scheming, anxiety, hoarding money, hypocrisy, arrogance, conceit, cruelty, harshness, self-glorification, a fragmented mind, obstinance, violence, demonic, evil thoughts, impure motives, stubbornness, and the intoxication of wealth. According to Krishna, the gate that leads to hell is built of lust, anger, and greed.

Sattvic people enjoy food that is mild, tasty, substantial, agreeable, and nourishing and that promotes health, strength, cheerfulness, and longevity. Rajasic people like food that is salty, bitter, hot, sour, and spicy and that promotes pain, discomfort, and disease. Tamasic people like overcooked food that has lost its taste and nutritional value.

Sattvic people perform sacrifices without thought of reward. Rajasic people perform sacrifices for the sake of show and for the goodwill it will bring to them. Tamasic people perform sacrifices but ignore both the letter and the spirit of the law.

Krishna states that the disciplines of the body are to offer service to the gods, to the good, to the wise, and to your spiritual teacher and to be pure, honest, continent, and nonviolent. The disciplines of speech are to offer soothing words, to speak truly, kindly, and helpfully, and to study the scriptures. The disciplines of the mind are calmness, gentleness, silence, self-restraint, and purity. When these three levels of discipline are practiced without attachment to results and in the spirit of great faith, the sages call the practice sattvic.

Giving simply because it is right to give, without thought of return, is sattvic. Giving with regrets or expectations of receiving something in return is rajasic. Giving at an inappropriate time, in inappropriate circumstances, or without affection or respect is tamasic.

Self-sacrifice, giving, self-discipline, and taking responsibility for one's life and world are sattvic. Avoiding action out of fear of difficulty or physical discomfort is rajasic. The sattvic person is not intimidated by unpleasant work, nor does he seek a job because it is pleasant. The true yogi does what God guides him or her to do and remains even-minded and not attached to the results. Those who renounce selfish desire and the desire for personal reward go beyond the reach of karma.

Sattvic knowledge sees the Eternal Self in all beings. Rajasic knowledge sees all people and animals as separate. Tamasic knowledge sees one small part and mistakes it for the whole.

A sattvic worker is free of egotism and selfish attachment, is full of enthusiasm, and has fortitude in success and failure alike. A rajasic worker has strong personal desires, wants rewards for his actions, and is easily swept away by good or bad fortune. The tamasic worker is undisciplined, vulgar, stubborn, deceitful, dishonest, lazy, depressed, and prone to procrastination.

The sattvic intellect knows when to act and when to refrain from action and knows what brings freedom and what brings bondage. The rajasic intellect confuses right and wrong actions and cannot distinguish what is to be done from what should not be done. The tamasic intellect is clouded in darkness and has utterly reversed right and wrong.

The true yogi is ever joyful and beyond the reach of desire and sorrow.

The yogi has become united with Brahman and has equal regard for every living creature. The yogi has abandoned all outer supports and looks totally to God for protection. The yogi shares his wisdom only with those with whom it is appropriate to do so. Those who teach the supreme mystery of the *Bhagavad-Gita* teach it to all who love God and perform the greatest act of love.

Krishna's Declaration to Arjuna and Arjuna's Response

As Arjuna began to become awakened from the delusion of his ego, Krishna said to him, "Get up. Give up your unmanliness and get up and fight. This self-pity and self-indulgence are unbecoming of the great soul that you are."

He is speaking to everyone. Arjuna did get up and he continued to listen to and absorb Krishna's teaching. Finally, at the end of Krishna's teaching Arjuna said, "My delusion is dissolved. I have become aware of my reality, which is God."

45

The Vedas: God's Revelation

*If one fails to realize Brahman (God)
in this life before the physical sheath is shed, he
must again put on a body in the world of
embodied creatures.*

The Vedas

The Hindus have received their religion as a direct revelation from God. No human author is credited with the work, as is the case in most other religions because no human wrote the Vedas. His Holiness, the Lord Sai Baba, has said that the Vedas came as a direct result of the hearing of the divine sounds of God by the rishis, the seers and prophets of ancient India. The Vedas are the scriptures in which this divine knowledge was written down.

The term "veda" comes from the root word that means "to know." When it is applied to scripture it means "book of knowledge." The Hindu religion based upon the Vedas is by far the oldest of all the major religions.

The Vedas are the earliest testaments to the victory of man over himself in discovering the underlying unity of all creation. Sai Baba has called the Vedas "the Breath of God." They have no describable origin for, in truth, they are timeless. They lead the seeker on the path to the realm of eternal bliss where no birth or death exists. The Vedas have also been referred to as "Sabda Brahma," the Sound of the Universal Absolute.

The Vedas are the philosopher's stone that turns all metals into gold, all students into aspirants, and all aspirants into sages. They are to be studied reverently and practiced in daily life, for they are the embodiment of truth. Recitation of the Vedas purifies the environment and strengthens the will to be true. Sai Baba says that every syllable of the Vedas is a name of God and that they are the source of all scripture.

The Vedas are not just for the people of India but are for all the people of the Earth. They enable the human to see a vision of the Lord. They are eternal messages from God caught by developed consciousness in the silence of meditation.

The Vedas are divided into four great books: the Rig-Veda, the Yajur-Veda, the Sama-Veda, and the Athaarva-Veda. Each Veda consists of four parts: the Mantra-Samhitas, or hymns; the Brahmanas, or explanations of mantras and rituals; the Aranyakas; and the Upanishads. The four subdivisions of the Vedas are symbolic of the four stages in a person's life.

The essence of the Vedas is that which is present everywhere and manifests itself under all circumstances as the Eternal Self. This Self lives in all people, animals, plants, minerals, and objects in the world. There is nothing but the Self. The purpose of being here is to realize your identity as the Self and to serve the Self in all beings and things.

You are here to learn discrimination so you can identify with that which is permanent rather than impermanent. You are here to recognize that God is one, not two. Immortality, or liberation, can be won only through renunciation of the material world. You must learn to live in the world but not be of the world. This can be achieved only through the development of nonattachment, self-control, and mastery over your thoughts, feelings, physical body, sexuality, and senses and over your identification with physical vision, or appearances. The essence of the Vedas is love and that all men are brothers.

The philosophy of the Vedas is known as Vedanta. Vedanta is merging with the Om, which leads to Veda (knowledge) - anta (end). Vedanta, hence, is the end of knowledge which is liberation, Self-realization, and immortality. Vedanta means the final product of the fund of knowledge that leads to liberation from the wheel of rebirth. Vedanta teaches that the mind can lead you either into the prison of petty desire or into the vastness of spiritual realization. Vedanta is wisdom that leads to release from the bondage of the material world. It is based on the knowledge of the Self. It is through right living, balanced living, and unconditional love that you achieve the bliss of God-realization. The wisdom of the Vedas is the supreme attainment that can be earned in life, for it leads to realizing the Self.

The Upanishads

The Upanishads are the most important sections of the Vedas. They contain the essence of the Vedas. Few books on Planet Earth are as soul-inspiring. The Upanishads are the products of the highest wisdom, the supreme divine knowledge. They provide a detailed description of the nature of the Eternal Self and Atman. They teach methods of attaining Brahman (God).

The Upanishads are eternal and come directly from Brahman. They serve as a means of freedom from Earthly bondage. Knowledge of the Upanishads allows you to attain Self-realization and merge with Brahman. It is this Self-realization alone that can eliminate ignorance and restore immortality, eternal peace, and bliss.

Only knowledge of Brahman can remove sorrow, illusion, and pain. It is only through discrimination, detachment, self-control, and a deep yearning for liberation that Brahman and Self-realization can be obtained. The term "upanishad" actually means secret teachings or secret doctrine.

Instead of trying to explain the Upanishads myself, I have looked through the Upanishads in the four sections of the Vedas and chosen some of my favorite stanzas for your enjoyment and spiritual edification. The translation of these quotations is from a book called *The Upanishads* by Eknath Easwaran, a book I would highly recommend if you are desirous of doing more spiritual study in this area.

Quotations from the Upanishads

Everything is loved not for its own sake, but because the Self lives in it.

This Self has to be realized. Hear about this Self and meditate upon Him. When you hear about the Self, meditate upon the Self, and finally realize the Self, you come to understand everything in life.

Separateness arises from identifying the Self with the body, which is made up of elements; when this physical identification dissolves, there can be no more separate Self.

As a great fish swims between the banks of a river as it likes, so does the sinning self move between the states of dreaming and waking.

The Self is free from desire, free from evil, and free from fear.

The Self is, indeed, Brahman, but through ignorance people identify it with intellect, mind, senses, passions, and the elements of Earth, air, fire, water, and space. This is why the Self is said to consist of this and that and appears to be everything.

As a person acts, so he becomes in life. Those who do good become good. Those who do harm become bad. Good deeds make one pure. Bad deeds make one impure. So we are said to be what our desire is, so is our will. As our will is, so are our acts. As we act, so do we become.

We live in accordance with our deep, driving desire. It is this desire at the time of death that determines what our next life is to be. We will come back to Earth to work out the satisfaction of that desire. But not those who are free from desire. They are free because all their desires have found fulfillment in the Self. They do not die like the others; but realizing

Brahman, they merge in Brahman.

Those who realize the Self enter into the peace that brings complete self-control and perfect patience. They see themselves in everyone and everyone in themselves.

The fourth is the superconscious state called Turiya, neither inward nor outward, beyond the senses and the intellect, in which there is none other than the Lord. He is the supreme goal of life. He is infinite peace and love, realize Him!

Turiya is represented by Aum.

Realize the Self, the shining goal of life! If you do not, there is only darkness. See the Self in all, and go beyond death.

Well, have you renounced these passing pleasures so dear to the senses and turned your back on the way of the world which makes mankind forget the goal of life? Far apart are wisdom and ignorance. The first leads one to Self-realization; the second makes one more and more estranged from his real Self.

It is but few who hear about the Self. Fewer still dedicate their lives to its realization. Wonderful is the one who speaks about the Self. Rare are they who make it the supreme goal of their lives.

Blessed are they who, through an illumined teacher, attain Self-realization. The truth of the Self cannot come through one who has not realized that he is the Self. The intellect cannot reveal the Self beyond its duality of subject and object. They who see themselves in all and all in them help others through spiritual osmosis to realize the Self, themselves.

The wise, realizing through meditation the timeless Self, beyond all perception, hidden in the cave of the heart, leave pain and pleasure far behind. Those who know they are neither body nor mind but the immortal Self, the Divine Principle of existence, find the source of all joy and live in joy abiding.

I will give you the word all the scriptures glorify, all spiritual disciplines express, to attain which aspirants lead a life of sense mastery. It is Om. This symbol of the Godhead is the highest. Realizing it, one finds complete fulfillment of all one's longings. It is of the greatest support to all seekers. Those in whose hearts Om reverberates unceasingly are indeed blessed and deeply loved as one who is the Self.

Hidden in the heart of every creature exists the Self, subtler than the subtlest, greater than the greatest. They go beyond sorrow who extinguish their self-will and behold the glory of the Self through the grace of the Lord of Love.

The Self cannot be known by anyone who desists not from unrighteous ways, controls not his senses, stills not his mind, and practices not meditation.

The senses derive from objects of sense perception, sense objects from mind, mind from intellect, intellect from ego, ego from undifferentiated consciousness, and consciousness from Brahman. Brahman is the first cause and last refuge. Brahman, the hidden Self in everyone, does not shine forth. He is revealed only to those who keep their mind one-pointed on the Lord of Love (Self) and thus develop a superconscious manner of knowing. Meditation enables them to go deeper and deeper into consciousness, from the world of words to the world of thoughts, then beyond thoughts to wisdom in the Self.

If one fails to realize Brahman in this life before the physical sheath is shed, he must again put on a body in the world of embodied creatures.

There are two selves, the separate ego and the indivisible Atman. When one rises above I and me and mine, the Atman is revealed as one's real Self. When all desires that surge in the heart are renounced, the mortal becomes immortal.

As long as we think we are the ego, we feel attached and fall into sorrow. But realize that you are the Self, the Lord of Life, and you will be freed from sorrow. When you realize that you are the Self, Supreme Source of Light, Supreme Source of Love, you transcend the duality of life and enter into the unitive state.

Those who dwell on and long for sense pleasure are born in a world of separateness. But let them realize they are the Self and all separateness will fall away. Not through discourse, not through the intellect, not even through study of the scriptures can the Self be realized. The Self reveals Himself to the one who longs for the Self. Those who long for the Self with all their heart are chosen by the Self as His own.

Not by the weak, not by the un-earnest, not by those who practice wrong disciplines can the Self be realized. The Self reveals Himself as the Lord of Love to the one who practices right disciplines.

Before the world was created, the Self alone existed. Nothing whatever stirred. Then the Self thought, Let me create the world. He brought forth all the worlds out of Himself.

Practice right conduct, learning and teaching. Be truthful always, learning and teaching. Master the passions, learning and teaching. Control the senses, learning and teaching. Strive for peace always, learning and teaching. Rouse the Kundalini, learning and teaching. Serve humanity, learning and teaching. Beget progeny, learning and teaching. Be truthful always, master the passions, learning and teaching. Learning and teaching are necessary for spiritual progress.

This is the essence of essences, the highest, the eighth rung, venerated above all that human beings hold holy. Om is the Self of all.

The universe comes forth from Brahman and will return to Brahman.

Verily, all is Brahman. A person is what his deep desire is. It is our deepest desire in this life that shapes the life to come. So let us direct our deepest desires to realize the Self.

The Self is sure, free from decay and death, free from hunger and thirst, and free from sorrow. The Self desires nothing that is not good, wills nothing that is not good. Seek and realize the Self! Those who seek and realize the Self fulfill all their desires and attain the goal supreme.

It is truth the body is perishable, but within it dwells the imperishable Self. This body is subject to pleasure and pain. No one who identifies with the body can escape from pleasure and pain, but those who know they are not the body pass beyond pleasure and pain to live in abiding joy.

The world is the wheel of God, turning round and round with all living creatures upon its rim. The world is the river of God, flowing from Him and flowing back to Him. On this ever-revolving wheel of being the individual Self goes round and round through life after life, believing itself to be a separate creature, until it sees its identity with the Lord of Love and attains immortality in the indivisible whole.

The Lord of Love holds in His hand the world, composed of the changing and the changeless. The manifest and the unmanifest. The separate self, not yet aware of the Lord, goes after pleasure, only to become bound more and more. When it sees the Lord, there comes an end to its bondage.

All is change in the world of the senses, but changeless is the Supreme Lord of Love. Meditate on Him, be absorbed in Him, wake up from the dream of separateness.

Dedicate yourself to the Lord of Life, who is the cause of the cosmos. He will remove the cause of all your suffering and free you from the bondage of karma.

Those who attain the supreme goal of life, realizing the Self and passing beyond all sorrow, shine bright as a mirror which has been cleansed of dust.

In the supreme climax of Samadhi they realize the presence of the Lord within their heart. Freed from impurities they pass forever beyond birth and death.

Not female, male, nor neuter is the Self. As is the body, so is the gender. The Self takes on a body, with desires, attachments, and delusions. The Self is born again and again in new bodies to work out the karma of former lives.

Hard to reach is the supreme goal of life, hard to describe and hard to abide in. They alone attain Samadhi who have mastered their senses and are free from anger, free from self-will and free from likes and dislikes, without selfish bonds to people and things.

Brahman cannot be realized by those who are subject to greed, fear, and anger. Brahman cannot be realized by those who are subject to the pride of name and fame or to the vanity of scholarship. Brahman cannot be realized by those who are enmeshed in life's duality.

The mind may be said to be of two kinds, pure and impure. Driven by the senses it becomes impure, but with the senses under control, the mind becomes pure.

It is the mind that frees us or enslaves. Driven by the senses we become bound. Masters of the senses become free. Those who seek freedom must master their senses.

When the mind is detached from the senses one reaches the summit of consciousness. Mastery of the mind leads to wisdom. Practice meditation. Stop all vain talk. The highest state is beyond reach of thought, for it lies beyond all duality.

Keep repeating the ancient mantra Om until it reverberates in your heart.

He faces heat and cold, pleasure and pain, honor and dishonor with equal calm. He is not affected by pride, jealousy, status, joy or sorrow, greed, anger or infatuation, excitement, egoism, or other gods, for he knows he is neither body nor mind.

The aspirant who is seeking the Lord must free himself from selfish attachments to people, money, and possessions. When his mind sheds every selfish desire, he becomes free from the duality of pleasure and pain and rules his senses. No more is he capable of ill will. No more is he subject to elation, for his senses come to rest in the Self. Entering into the intuitive state, he attains the goal of evolution. Truly, he attains the goal of evolution.

46

The Sacred Paths of Yoga

Care not for criticism when you are on the right path. Yield not to flattery.

Swami Sivananda

The purpose of this chapter is to provide a brief overview of the sacred paths of yoga. "Yoga" means "union with God." There are, however, many ways that can be achieved. I will attempt to describe them briefly:

Hatha Yoga	Sabda or Nada Yoga
Bhakti Yoga	Sankirtan Yoga
Raja Yoga	Ashtanga Yoga
Karma Yoga	Agni Yoga
Jnana Yoga	Eco Yoga
Mantra Yoga	Shiva Yoga
Kundalini, Laya, or Asparsha Yoga	Integral Yoga
Tantra Yoga	Yoga of Synthesis
Taraka Yoga	Mansa Yoga
Yantra Yoga	Siddha Yoga
Kriya Yoga	Lambika Yoga

There are seven root races that make up this current world cycle and there is a specific yoga connected with each time periods:

Polarian, Hyperborean, and Lemurian: Hatha Yoga
Atlantean: Bhakti Yoga
Aryan: Raja Yoga
Meruvian: Agni Yoga or Ashtanga Yoga
Paradisian: Unknown

Although there are many minor paths and off-shoots, these might be considered the major paths of yoga because Hatha Yoga correlates with the physical, Bhakti Yoga with the emotional, and Raja Yoga with the mental.

All the yogas might be considered spokes of a wheel with God in the center. They all lead to the same place. I practice what might be termed a yoga of synthesis which integrates all the yogas, extracting the best and finest teachings from each.

Hatha Yoga

Hatha Yoga was the form of yoga focused upon in the Lemurian epoch of Earth's history. It is a yoga concerned with physical purification and training. Its goal is to bring the physical body into a perfect state of health so the soul has a fitting vehicle of expression to work through.

Hatha Yoga embraces many practices, including physical postures and breathing exercises which also act upon the physical nervous system and the etheric body which is considered a corollary aspect of the physical body. Hatha Yoga also helps to bring the vital energies of the physical and etheric bodies under control.

This is an indispensable yoga for everyone to practice on some level and it is intimately tied to passing the first initiation which has to do with physical mastery.

The word "hatha" actually means the conjunction of the Sun and the Moon. It is these macrocosmic and microcosmic principles that must be balanced within the human body. There are eight main steps in the process of Hatha Yoga:

1. Abstinence,
2. Observance,
3. Sitting postures,
4. Breath control,
5. Nonattachment to possessions.

Hatha Yoga includes many muscular contractions which are called bandhas and physical gestures which are called mudras. It also includes the science of pratyahara which has to do with learning to withdraw your senses from external objects, truly the key to effective meditation.

If you would like to learn more about Hatha Yoga there are many wonderful books on the market. Two that I would particularly recommend are *The Practice of Yoga* by Swami Sivananda and *Yoga: Mastering the Secrets of Matter and the Universe* by Alain Danielou.

Bhakti Yoga

Bhakti Yoga was the yoga of the Atlantean period which dealt with emotional attunement. For this reason it is the yoga of love and devotion. It has also been, to a great extent, a major yoga of the Piscean Age. It is a good yoga for you if you are identified with your emotional body.

Its method of reintegration with Source is love. There are nine steps in Bhakti Yoga:

1. Listening,
2. Singing of praise,
3. Meditation,
4. Worship of the feet,
5. Ritual worship,
6. Prostration,
7. Being a slave to God,
8. Being a friend,
9. Self-surrender.

Two well-known spiritual masters who seem to embody this devotional aspect of yoga are Paramahansa Yogananda and Sathya Sai Baba.

Two forms of Bhakti Yoga are the Way of Passionate Attachment and the Way of Transcendent Love. The Angirasa Daiva Mimansa sutra says, "That form of devotion which makes use of emotions and brings joy and peace is called the Way of Passionate Attachment. The Way of Transcendent Love sees the whole universe, animate and inanimate, as being pervaded by divinity. It says, "Thou art that." This Way is summed up as follows: "He who, with his whole being, sees divinity in all existing things and all things in divinity, stands highest among the devotees of the Lord."

Followers of Bhakti Yoga often personalize God, as the followers of Krishna and Rama did. They often are very involved with rituals, flowers, incense, beautiful buildings, and other forms that aid in cultivating love for God, rather than being interested in intellectually understanding God.

As you can see, these yogas relate strongly to the four-body system and how you relate to and identify with your physical, emotional, mental, and spiritual bodies.

Bhakti Yoga is also very much involved with service. If you are on the spiritual path, it is essential for you to practice some form of Bhakti Yoga; otherwise you are disowning your emotional body in your pursuit of God-realization.

No form of yoga is better than another, although different yogas suit certain people better than do others at certain stages in their lives and spiritual evolution. Bhakti Yoga is the way of the heart, which is the most important spiritual practice of all.

Raja Yoga

It has been said that the purpose of Hatha Yoga is to make Raja Yoga possible. Raja Yoga cannot be achieved without the training of Hatha Yoga, and of Bhakti Yoga, too, for that matter. Raja Yoga is the yoga of the Aryan

Age. For this reason it is the yoga that deals with controlling the mind and concentrating, which is the main lesson of this current root race. It is through concentration that you gain knowledge and mastery of all things.

There are fifteen main steps in Raja Yoga:

1. Abstinence,
2. Observance ("I am the principle of all things, the Brahman"),
3. Renunciation,
4. Silence,
5. Solitude,
6. Proper use of time,
7. Postures,
8. Root contraction (mula-bandha),
9. Strengthening the body,
10. Straightening the body,
11. Spiritual sight,
12. Breath control,
13. Pratyahara ("Seeing divinity in all perceptible forms brings delight to the mind and its faculties. Know this as the withdrawal which should be practiced every moment"),
14. Contemplation ("The one changeless thought, 'I am the principle, the Brahman,' with no other notion, is known under the name of contemplation and is the giver of supreme bliss." – The Upanishads),
15. Identification ("When the very notion of contemplation is forgotten, this is known as identification." – The Upanishads).

Raja Yoga means Royal Yoga, and it refers specifically to the yoga system of Patanjali. (For an in-depth study of the teachings of Patanjali, see the chapter on his Yoga Sutras.) I have found Patanjali's teachings to be very profound. It is a system of study somewhat similar to *A Course in Miracles*, even though it was written over five thousand years ago. Raja Yoga is especially relevant now because of the current period of planetary history.

Karma Yoga

Karma Yoga achieves union with God through right action and through service. Sai Baba's famous quote applies here: "Hands that help are holier than lips that pray." Karma Yoga can also be summed up in a statement by Sri Bhagavan Krishna in the *Bhagavad-Gita*: "Worshiping Him with proper actions, a man attains realization."

One key to Karma Yoga is the performance of right action and service for its own sake, without consideration of the immediate or apparent results. Karma Yoga literally means "action yoga." It consists of the sacred work of performing your daily activities in harmony with the soul's wishes and desires.

All actions are to be done with an attitude of self-surrender and with no regard for the fruit of those actions – no egoistic attachments. You could say that Mahatma Gandhi perfectly embodied the ideals of Karma Yoga.

It is the gospel of Krishna in the *Bhagavad-Gita*. A Karma Yogi is an instrument of God in the affairs of the world. It is essential to integrate Karma Yoga along with the other yogas into your daily life.

Jnana Yoga

Jnana Yoga is the yoga of the philosopher and thinker who wants to go beyond the visible, material reality. The Jnana Yogi finds God through knowledge. Jnana Yoga is summed up in the Upanishads by the following statement: "In the method of reintegration through knowledge, the mind is ever bound to the ultimate end of existence which is liberation. This method leads to all attainments and is ever auspicious."

Jnana Yoga teaches seven stages of knowledge. Four states of mind and seven obstacles have to be faced.

The four states of mind are:

1. The dispersed state,
2. The past approach,
3. The grasped state,
4. The merging state.

The seven obstacles are:

1. Good will,
2. Reflection,
3. Subtlety of mind,
4. Perception of reality,
5. Freedom from leaning toward the world,
6. Disappearance of visible forms,
7. The unmanifest state.

Jnana Yoga is the path of insight or wisdom based on what Vedanta refers to as higher knowledge rather than lower knowledge. Djwhal Khul might refer to this as the difference between the knowledge of the higher mind and the knowledge of the concrete mind.

The Vedas support Jnana Yoga which is based on the spiritual concept of nondualism. Jnana Yoga is the path of Self-realization through gnostic understanding that teaches the ability to discern the real from the unreal. To the Jnana Yogi, will power and inspired reason are the two guiding principles by which he can attain enlightenment. Jnana Yoga has been described as a straight but steep course.

Vedanta lists six principles of Jnana Yoga that lead to liberation:

1. Discrimination,
2. Renunciation,
3. The three accomplishments (tranquillity, sense restraint, actions totally in harmony with God),
4. Endurance,
5. Mental collectedness,
6. Faith.

Other practices of Jnana Yoga include listening, redemption, the sacred teachings, and pondering on the importance of meditation. Jnana Yoga, in essence, is the cultivation of the eye of wisdom.

Mantra Yoga

Mantra Yoga finds union with God through the proper use of speech and sound. It is the power of the word to create or destroy that Mantra Yoga emphasizes. It utilizes the focused intent to make every word you speak be in harmony with God and with your own soul.

Mantra Yoga also uses mantras as an indispensable part of the practice. In the East, the Mantra Yogi usually uses Aum, So Ham, Om Namah Shivaya, or Hram, Hrim as his favorite mantra. The most important mantra is the syllable Aum. It is considered the greatest of all mantras. After that, there is the Gayatri Mantra, which is considered the mantra of eternal wisdom in the Vedas.

Rhythmic repetition of a mantra is called japa, which is why this type of yoga has also been called Japa Yoga. One of the greatest proponents of this practice is His Holiness, Lord Sai Baba. He considers the constant repetition of the name of God and the visualizing of your favorite form of God to be an indispensable spiritual practice. Most spiritual teachers in the East and West integrate some form of Mantra Yoga into their teachings.

The practice of Mantra Yoga requires constant vigilance over every thought you think and every word you speak, for every word you speak in your daily life, in truth, is a mantra and a word of power. There are different kinds of japa:

1. Daily japa, which is usually done in the morning and evening;
2. Circumstantial japa, which is usually done on festival days;
3. Japa that is done for some specific desired goal;
4. Forbidden japa, which is done without discipline and with wrong pronunciation;
5. Japa that is done for penance.
6. Moving japa, which is done through the day and which is

what Sai Baba has recommended;

7. Voice japa, which is done out loud for others to hear, if appropriate;

8. Whispered japa;

9. Bee japa, in which the mantra is murmured so it sounds like the hum of a bee – the lips and tongue do not move and the eyes are usually closed;

10. Mental japa, which is done solely in the mind and is an indispensable method to use in your daily life;

11. The uninterrupted japa, which is for those who have renounced the world. Japa is done continuously; when tired, the yogi meditates, and when tired of meditating, he goes back to japa. When tired of both, he thinks of the Supreme Self;

12. Japa that is done with beads or a rosary.

There are sixteen steps in Mantra Yoga:

1. Devotion;

2. Purity;

3. Posture;

4. Observance of the calendar which is based on an astrological understanding and which defines celebrations, fasts, and so on;

5. The ways of conduct;

6. Concentration;

7. The search for the inner divine countries. These inner countries are considered the abodes of deities, masters, and gurus on the inner plane;

8. Breath control;

9. Gesture;

10. Water offering;

11. Fire offering;

12. Ritual sacrifice (fruit);

13. Ritual worship, which usually utilizes scents, flowers, incense. a lamp, and food of some kind;

14. Repetition of mantras, words of power, and names of God;

15. Contemplation;

16. Identification (samadhi), which is achieved when the meaning of the mantra has been realized and the mind dissolves into the deity of the mantra. There becomes no separation between the seeker and that which is sought. With identification, the seeker has achieved his goal.

Kundalini, Laya, or Asparsha Yoga

Kundalini Yoga is the method by which certain spiritual practices are utilized to purposely and consciously raise the coiled energy at the base of the spine up through the chakras to the third eye and crown chakras in an attempt to achieve Self-realization. This type of yoga has also been called Asparsha Yoga. It utilizes eight basic steps:

1. Observances and abstinences,
2. Purification,
3. Courage,
4. Steadiness,
5. Endurance,
6. Subtlety,
7. Direct evidence,
8. Thoughtless identification.

It also utilizes certain specific breathing exercises, mudras, and bandhas in the process of awakening the kundalini.

I have written in great detail about the practice of Kundalini Yoga in *Soul Psychology*, so I will not repeat myself here. I do want to emphasize that the forced awakening of the kundalini is a very dangerous proposition unless it is done under the guidance of a qualified, Self-realized teacher, which, in truth, is hard to find.

The raising of the kundalini is important; however, it will activate quite naturally and at the proper time in the well-balanced, committed, integrated disciple on the path, no matter what path you are following. Trying to force the awakening of the kundalini is literally playing with fire. This is not a type of yoga to experiment with haphazardly on your own. Raised prematurely, this energy will activate and then shoot out of your lower chakras and create worlds of problems. Before practicing this form of yoga, you must have mastery over your energies. I would say it shouldn't be focused upon until after the third initiation at the earliest, and again, only with a qualified spiritual teacher.

Tantra Yoga

Tantra Yoga seeks to find union with the divine through the spiritual use of sexuality. It seeks to use sexual energy as a means of attaining self-mastery. Tantric philosophy states that you can achieve the same result through celibacy or through sexual union. It is the spiritual science of learning to raise sexual energy up the chakras while making love with your partner or spouse. Tantra Yoga embodies the concept that sexual energy must be controlled, mastered, and utilized, not run away from. Sexuality is seen as a sacred energy to be used, but only under the guidance of the soul, not the lower self.

In *Soul Psychology* I have dedicated a chapter to the spiritual aspects of sexuality, so I will not repeat myself here. It is my opinion, however, that this is a kind of yoga that almost all the people on this planet need to come to terms with.

Tantra Yoga provides a midpoint between the two extremes of celibacy and being run by the carnal lower self. Tantra Yoga is the spiritual science of how to properly utilize your sexual energy in the service of God. Many traditions and fundamentalist religions consider sexuality a bad thing, which just isn't true. When used properly it can accelerate your path to God-realization.

Taraka Yoga

Taraka Yoga is based on the nondualist philosophy of Advaita Vedanta. It is thought to have been started by Shankara.

The word "taraka" actually means "that which delivers." Taraka Yoga delivers the practitioner to the unconditioned reality of the absolute. This is achieved through the recognition of there being only one single being living in the infinite universe whose name is Brahman, or Atman.

The goal of Taraka Yoga is to convert your ordinary consciousness to a continuous awareness of this absolute reality. It is achieved, to a great extent, through a series of exercises in which Light phenomena play a decisive role.

The inner Light is produced by a technique known as Shambhavi-mudra. The yogi fixes his or her attention on the third eye and learns to see and experience the Light phenomena of the inner dimensions of reality. There are discernible stages of development in this yogic path which have been loosely designated as the inner sign, the external sign, and the intermediate sign.

There is a whole science of these Lights and sounds. If you are interested in this form of yoga, I recommend reading a book called *Sacred Paths* by George Feuerstein.

Yantra Yoga

Yantra Yoga is the path of union with God thorough geometric visualization. A yantra is a geometric design. They are highly efficient tools for contemplation, concentration, and meditation. This type of yoga might also be called Mandala Yoga.

The Buddhists are masters of this type of yoga as can be seen in their mandalas, icons, tankas, and sand paintings. The American Indians used this type of yoga, also. The Kabbalistic Tree of Life might be put in this category as well.

By tuning into the different aspects of a yantra you can tap into certain deities or creative force centers in the universe. The yantra is like a microcosmic picture of the macrocosm. It is a focusing point and an outer and inner doorway.

The yantras are often focused on a specific deity. They can be drawn on paper, wood, metal, or on the Earth itself or they can be three-dimensional.

The yantra provides a focal point that is a window into the absolute. The idea is to make the yantra so real, inwardly and outwardly, that it becomes alive. In that way it absorbs the practitioner's complete attention, and he can no longer tell if the yantra is within himself or if he is within the yantra.

The most celebrated yantra in India is the Sri Yantra, or Auspicious Wheel. It is a symbol of the entire cosmos that serves to remind the practitioner of the nondifference between subject and object.

Sri Yantra

Kriya Yoga

Kriya Yoga is the form taught by Babaji and Paramahansa Yogananda. I have written about it in *The Complete Ascension Manual* in the chapter called "Babaji, the Yogi Christ" so I am not going to repeat the same information here. I will say, however, that Paramahansa Yogananda has referred to it as "the airplane method to God." I have been initiated into this type of yoga and have found it to be extraordinarily valuable.

Sabda, or Nada, Yoga

Sabda, or Nada, Yoga is the method of achieving union with God through sound. One of its greatest proponents was Kabir, the poet-saint. Eckancar is a modern-day mystery school based upon Sabda Yoga. The practice of this kind of yoga has to do with learning to tune in and listen to the inner sounds that emanate from the different dimensions of reality. In the chapter on soul travel in this book I have listed these sounds.

Sabda Yoga also includes intoning certain mantras and sacred sounds that allow you to soul travel and attune to the dimensions from which the mantras come. This sublime form of yoga is the basis of the Sikh religion.

Sankirtan Yoga

Sankirtan Yoga seeks to find union with the Divine through the singing and chanting of bhajans, or devotional songs, which are also called sankirtan. Sai Baba is one of the strongest proponents of this kind of yoga. Not only are the songs filled with the sacred names of God, but they have very beautiful melodies which allow the emotional body of the practitioner to get involved.

Practitioners of Bhakti Yoga would especially love this type of yoga. The joy and bliss that come from singing devotional songs with a loving, supportive spiritual community are awe-inspiring. I have a whole set of devotional songs from the Sai Baba Foundation and I play them constantly.

Sai Baba has said that the singing of devotional songs is the best spiritual practice for getting rid of the blemish of ego. Devotional songs are a way of practicing Mantra Yoga and Japa Yoga, but doing it with a melody makes it more enjoyable. Temptation doesn't arise when your mind is constantly affirming, chanting, and singing your love, devotion, and praise of God!

Ashtanga Yoga and Agni Yoga

There is not a lot of information available on Ashtanga Yoga, but it is an important path of yoga because Djwhal Khul has said that Asntanga Yoga is the yoga for the coming Meruvian root race. Theosophical literature has designated Agni Yoga, or Fire Yoga, as the yoga of the next coming root race. It is for this reason that I have put the two together.

Ashtanga Yoga is a type of power yoga. The full name is Ashtanga

Vinyasa, and it is a very active, movement-oriented form of yoga.

Agni Yoga was made famous by Nicolas Roerich who in this century channeled a whole series of books on the subject from Ascended Master El Morya. I would guide anyone who is interested in this yoga to those books. The teachings were a dispensation much like those Madam Blavatsky and Alice Bailey channeled, except that they are probably more of the first ray than the second ray, since El Morya is the chohan of the first ray.

Eco Yoga

Eco Yoga is one of the newer yogas. It is the yoga of ecological and environmental sanctification and respect. It sees all life as being interconnected and interdependent. It is, hence, the study and practice of the interrelatedness among minerals, plants, animals, humans, and the environment.

This yoga might be one of the most important of all because if humans don't learn to respect and sanctify the Earth Mother and all the life that lives upon her, we will destroy the school that allows us to practice all the other yogas.

I have written about the need to take care of the environment and work cooperatively with the nature kingdoms. God lives as much in the earth, a river, a mountain, a city, a plant, a mineral, an insect, an animal, in the air, the forests, in the physical body as He does in higher dimensions of reality. Not to sanctify the environment is literally to deface and destroy God's physical body. You wouldn't do that to your own physical body; why would you show so little respect to His? The true spiritual path brings Heaven to Earth and recognizes the material universe as one of God's most beautiful and treasured heavens.

Shiva Yoga

Shiva Yoga is for those seekers who wish to merge with the Shiva aspect of the Hindu trinity of Brahma, Vishnu, and Shiva.

Shiva Yoga has five parts:

1. Knowledge of Shiva,
2. Devotion to Shiva,
3. Contemplation of Shiva,
4. Observances of the austerities connected with Shiva,
5. Ritual worship of Shiva.

Integral Yoga

Integral Yoga is the term given to the yoga created by Sri Aurobindo, the Self-realized master from India who lived earlier in this century. I am not well versed on his particular slant on the Vedic teachings, but I have always very much respected his contribution.

I am reminded of a story about him that occurred, I believe, on November 24, 1923. He was meditating when he received a vision that Krishna had incarnated into the physical world on the previous day; the previous day, Sathya Sai Baba had incarnated into a baby's body in southern India.

One of the integral teachings of Sri Aurobindo's yoga was his commitment to political action as well as to his inner spiritual work. In this regard he was more balanced than some of the Eastern spiritual traditions of noninvolvement with the material world.

He developed a lot of his teachings about Integral Yoga with his partner who was referred to as the Mother. If you are interested in studying his teachings in detail, I recommend reading his two-volume set of books called *Letters on Yoga*. He was a prolific writer and one of his teachers was Sri Sankara, the great Hindu master who lived in the eighth century.

Yoga of Synthesis

The Yoga of Synthesis is the form of yoga I recommend. It integrates all forms of yoga, all spiritual paths, all religions. It is an eclectic and universalistic path that gleans the best from each form of yoga and integrates it all into one cohesive, unified whole.

This is not to say that you might not emphasize a particular path during a certain phase of your life, or even during a certain incarnation. In the larger context, however, all paths are one; they are just different spokes on the same wheel, and one path of yoga is no better than any other. They are all important and all the knowledge they embody is essential for full and total realization of God.

I am grateful to the following authors for the information in their excellent books: Ronald Beesley, *Yoga of the Inward Path*; Alain Danielou, *Yoga*; George Feuerstein, *Sacred Paths*.

47

The Yoga Sutras of Patanjali

*By intense devotion to Ishvara [God],
knowledge of Ishvara is gained.*

Patanjali

The yoga sutras were given sometime between 820 B.C. and 200 B.C. The God-realized saint Patanjali was the first to write down the teachings; previously, they had been passed down orally. For this reason he is regarded as the founder of the science of Raja Yoga, "the kingly science of the soul."

His teachings are of particular importance because this is the Aryan Age, which holds the focus of mastery of the mind; Raja Yoga deals with the right use of the mind as an instrument for the soul and, hence, for Self-realization. It helps to bring about the mastery of the mental body and will lead humanity to the fifth initiation. In Alice Bailey's book *Light of the Soul: The Yoga Sutras of Patanjali*, she says that the three books every student should have on hand for study are the *Bhagavad-Gita*, the New Testament, and *The Yoga Sutras of Patanjali*.

The yoga sutras are a step-by-step system of gradually unfolded spiritual development. They remind me a little bit of *A Course in Miracles* by Master Jesus. Each sutra is a one-sentence aphorism, or teaching. There are one hundred ninety-five sutras in all, divided into four books. Book One deals with the problem of union. Book Two deals with the steps to union. Book Three deals with union achieved and its results. Book Four deals with illumination.

An interesting fact made known by Djwhal Khul in the Alice Bailey books is that these yoga sutras are the basic teachings of the trans-Himalayan school to which many of the masters of wisdom belong, certainly including Djwhal Khul, Kuthumi, and El Morya.

The yoga sutras form one of the six systems of Hindu philosophy. The Upanishads, the wisdom teachings of the Vedas, uphold the yoga sutras of Patanjali as being among the six systems containing the most efficacious methods for achieving direct perception of truth. The yoga system of Patanjali has been called the Eightfold Path that leads to the final goal of Kaivalya (absoluteness) in which the yogi realizes truth beyond all intellectual apprehension.

I would like to introduce you to these sutras. This graded series of lessons is one of the most valuable courses in spiritual development I have ever found. For the purposes of this chapter I have extracted what I consider to be the most valuable sutras and will share them with you in the order in which they are presented by Patanjali. After some I have provided a short commentary; otherwise, the meaning is straightforward and self-explanatory.

After reading this chapter you will have an excellent sense of the overall teachings. This translation of Patanjali's sutras is that of Djwhal Khul in the Alice Bailey book *The Light of the Soul*.

The Yoga Sutras of Patanjali

Book One

1.   Aum (Om). The following instruction concerns the science of union.

2.   This union (or yoga) is achieved through the subjugation of the psychic nature and the restraint of the chitta [mind].

> *The subjugation of the psychic nature which this lesson refers to is the control of the emotional body, desire nature, and subconscious mind.*

3.   When this has been accomplished, the yogi knows himself as he really is in reality.

> *Who the yogi really is, of course, is the soul and eternal spirit.*

4.   Up till now the inner man has identified himself with his forms and with their active modifications.

> *Man has seen himself as his physical, emotional, mental, and/or etheric bodies and/or all of the changes these bodies go through.*

7.   The basis of correct knowledge is correct perception, correct deduction and correct witness [accurate evidence].

> *This lesson deals with the correct use of the mind, the need for proper detachment, and the ability to see life from the soul's perspective, to perceive life from Christ consciousness, rather than from the negative ego's consciousness.*

8.   Incorrect knowledge is based upon perception of the form and not upon the state of being.

> *The choice for every person is to see himself and others as just a body (physical, emotional, or mental) or as the Eternal Self living within all bodies.*

12.   The control and modification of the internal organ, the mind, is to be brought about through tireless endeavor and through nonattachment.

> *Tireless endeavor is one quality that many aspirants on the path lose. It is tied up with the lesson of maintaining one's personal power and self-mastery at all times and it is all connected with what Patanjali calls "fiery aspiration toward God and Self-realization."*

13.   Tireless endeavor is the constant effort to restrain the modifications of the mind.

> *Sai Baba has referred to the "monkey mind." It is essential to maintain constant vigilance over it, since it is thoughts that create reality.*

14.   When the object to be gained is sufficiently valued, and the efforts toward its attainment are persistently followed without intermission, then the steadiness of the mind is secured.

> *The object the disciple is seeking is complete merger with the soul and spirit (the monad). This unceasing, persistent effort leads to learning to keep the mind "steady in the Light," as Djwhal Khul always likes to say.*

> *The disciple learns to remain in the Christ consciousness at all times as well as remaining attuned to the higher self and soul. This becomes an automatic process as the conscious and subconscious minds are reprogrammed to stay attuned to the superconscious always. It is a matter of where one keeps one's attention, or focus. Mastery is gained, and then the lower self, material desire, and negative ego literally die.*

15.   Nonattachment is freedom from longing for all objects or desires, either Earthly or traditional, either here or hereafter.

> *The idea is to die to material desire and make one's only desire that for ascension, or God-realization. All desires other than this are hindrances on the path.*

16.   The consummation of this nonattachment results in an exact knowledge of the spiritual man when liberated from the qualities, or gunas.

> *This nonattachment leads to the realization of the monad, or spiritual self. This is one step beyond soul-realization. Liberation from the gunas, or qualities, has to do with the three qualities of*

matter in Hindu thought: sattva (rhythm or harmony), rajas (activity), tamas (inertia). The disciple gains knowledge of the spiritual self because his detachment has led him to be the cause of his reality and the chooser of all form and qualities.

18. A further stage of samadhi [enlightenment] is achieved when, through one-pointed thought, the outer activity is quieted. In this stage the chitta [mind stuff] is responsive only to subjective impressions.

The disciple's total focus is only on the guidance from soul and spirit and not on the outer world and negative ego.

19. Other yogins [yogis] achieve samadhi and arrive at a discrimination of pure spirit through belief, followed by energy, memory, meditation, and right perception.

This lesson is pretty straightforward. The only thing I would add is that energy follows thought, and the memory function comes to be in service of the soul, which allows the disciple to maintain what the Buddhists call mindfulness of the things that God would have one be mindful of. Right perception comes from perceiving life with Christ consciousness, not ego consciousness. Meditation is essential for Self-realization.

21. The attainment of this stage [spiritual consciousness] is rapid for those whose will is intensely alive.

This lesson I believe to have two meanings, in terms of the word "will." First of all, the single most important quality for psychological and spiritual growth is the development of personal power which is will. The disciple who learns to own his power in all situations and at all times, in service to God, will make super-accelerated progress.

The second meaning of "will" is the monad, or Father in Heaven, who embodies the will aspect of the Creator. Spiritual consciousness as opposed to soul consciousness is an attunement to this energy. Soul consciousness carries the vibration of love/wisdom.

22. Those who employ the will likewise differ, for its use may be intense, moderate, or gentle. In respect to the attainment of true spiritual consciousness there is yet another way.

Every disciple must learn to own his power to achieve self-realization; however, how a disciple or master uses this personal power can vary. This reminds me of Paramahansa Yogananda and his guru, Sri Yukteswar. Sri Yukteswar was very severe and disciplined in the use of his will. Paramahansa Yogananda was much more loving and gentle. Each attained Self-realization, but their styles were different.

The path of yoga, as outlined by Patanjali, is to use the will and discrimination to determine the difference between the self and the not-self, or between the Christ consciousness and negative ego consciousness. This path is more of a mental path since, by definition, it is that of Raja Yoga and is appropriate for the Aryan root race. Some disciples might use another path such as the path of Bhakti (devotional) Yoga. Other disciples might use Ashtanga Yoga (Aquarian Age Yoga). (See the chapter on the paths of yoga.)

23. By intense devotion to Ishvara, knowledge of Ishvara is gained.

Ishvara is the son of God, the Cosmic Christ, or the realization of the soul. A disciple can realize the soul, or the Christ, through intense devotion, or bhakti.

24. This Ishvara is the soul and is untouched by limitation, free from karma and desire.

25. In Ishvara the germ of all knowledge expands into infinity.

26. Ishvara, being unlimited by time condition, is the teacher of the primeval lords.

The soul is beyond time and space. Time is a mental construct of the incarnated personality in the world of matter. The soul and spirit are the teachers of all disciples and all initiates.

27. The word of Ishvara is Aum (or Om). This is the pranava.

The word Aum is the sound of all forms existing in the physical plane. It is the word of glory. It is the pranava, the sound of conscious life itself. Aum is the arrow to Brahman. It is the sound that God hears as humans breathe. When rightly understood and spoken, it causes the Christ, or soul, aspect to shine forth. It is the sound that brings forth, in manifestation, the incarnated personality. It releases the soul from all limitations. It is the integrator and synthesizer of spirit, soul, and body. It is the word of the fifth root race (the Aryan race). The master, or God, within is the word Aum.

28. Through the sounding of the word and through reflection upon its meaning, the way is found.

29. From this comes the realization of the Self [the soul] and the removal of all obstacles.

30. The obstacles to soul cognition are bodily disability, mental inertia, wrong questioning, carelessness, laziness, lack of dispassion, erroneous perception, inability to achieve concentration, failure to hold the meditative attitude when achieved.

31. Pain, despair, misplaced bodily activity, and wrong direction [or control] of the life currents are the results of the obstacles in the lower psychic nature.

Pain occurs when the emotional body is not managed properly.

Despair is created by misuse of the mental body. Misplaced bodily activity occurs, obviously, on the physical plane. Life currents deal with the etheric body. When these four bodies are not managed properly by the conscious mind in service of the soul, these results take place.

32.   To overcome the obstacles and their accompaniments, the intense application of the will to some truth [or principle] is required.

In The Light of the Soul, *Alice Bailey and Djwhal Khul provide a small chart to help disciples to focus their energies on the one truth or principle that is needed.*

Obstacle	Remedy
1. Bodily disability	Wholesome, sane living
2. Mental inertia	Control of the life force
3. Wrong questioning	One-pointed thought
4. Carelessness	Meditation
5. Laziness	Self-discipline
6. Lack of dispassion	Correct analysis
7. Erroneous perception	Illumination

33.   The peace of chitta can be brought about through the practice of sympathy, tenderness, steadiness of purpose, and dispassion in regard to pleasure or pain, or toward all forms of good and evil.

Dispassion toward pleasure or pain and all forms of good and evil deals with the need for what Djwhal Khul has called "divine indifference." It comes from having detachment and what the Bhagavad-Gita *refers to as "transcendence of duality." Having God consciousness means having evenmindedness and equanimity in the face of pleasure or pain, profit or loss, sickness or health, criticism or praise.*

The disciple learns to stay in inner peace and joy at all times while maintaining compassion but not over-identified empathy. The disciple learns not to live on the emotional roller coaster of the subconscious mind, negative ego, mental, emotional, etheric, and physical bodies. The incarnated personality, now merged with the soul, is the divine observer and changeless, yet it deals with the form side of life appropriately.

34.   The peace of the chitta is also brought about by the regulation of the prana, or life breath.

This lesson deals with the importance of rhythmic and structured regulation of one's daily activities in life in terms of wise time and energy management. The second aspect of this lesson deals with the importance of breath itself. The breath is really the foundation of

> *all occult spiritual work. Not only do incarnated personalities
> breathe, but so do ascended masters and God Himself. God
> breathes in and breathes out the universe. In Hindu philosophy, the
> science of breath is called pranayama.*

36. By meditation upon Light and upon radiance, knowledge of the
spirit can be reached and thus peace can be achieved.

37. The chitta is stabilized and rendered free from illusion as the
lower nature is purified and no longer indulged.

> *Too many aspirants on the path indulge the lower self, emotional
> body, desire body, and five senses. As these are mastered, the four
> lower bodies (physical, emotional, mental, and etheric) become
> purified.*

38. Peace [steadiness of the chitta] can be reached through
meditation on the knowledge which dreams give.

> *This can refer to the dreams one has every night while sleeping and
> to the dreams, visions, and reveries that come in meditation. One is
> taught in this world to think of what is experienced during sleep as
> a dream. In truth, that may be more the reality and waking
> consciousness more the dream. The inner world is reality; the outer
> world we are just visiting and it is more the dream, in truth.*

39. Peace can also be reached through concentration upon that which
is dearest to the heart.

> *Concentrate on the soul and spirit at all times and peace will be
> attained, for you will merge with your consciousness if concentra-
> tion is unceasing.*

40. Thus his realization extends from the infinitely small to the
infinitely great. And from annu [the atom or speck] to the Atma [spirit] his
knowledge is perfected.

> *The microcosm is like the macrocosm. This lesson can be summed up
> by an ancient hidden scripture that states, "Within the speck God
> can be seen. Within the man God can reign. Within Brahma both
> are found; yet all is one. The atom is as God, God as the atom."*

41. To him whose vrittis [modifications of the substance of the mind]
are entirely controlled there eventuates a state of identity with and
similarity to that which is realized. The knower, knowledge, and the field
of knowledge, become one, just as the crystal takes to itself the colors of
that which is reflected into it.

45. The gross leads into the subtle and the subtle leads in progressive
stages to that state of pure spiritual being.

> *Matter is densified spirit, spirit is refined matter. The spiritual path
> leads one from the grossest matter through the seven levels of
> initiation to ascension where matter is transformed completely into*

Light, or pure spiritual being.

47.   When this super-contemplative state is reached, the yogi acquires pure spiritual realization through the balanced quiet of the chitta.

48.   His perception is now unfailingly exact.

When merger with the Self is reached, perception becomes perfect, and only truth exists.

49.   This particular perception is unique and reveals that which the rational mind (using testimony, inference, and education) cannot reveal.

Merger with the Eternal Self brings forth a means of processing information that utilizes the other 90% of the brain that the rational mind does not have access to.

50.   When this state of perception is itself also restrained [or superseded], then is pure samadhi achieved.

Samadhi is the state of consciousness in which one is not just thinking with the Christ mind but is actually completely merged with the Eternal Self. The omniscience, omnipresence, and omnipotence of Sathya Sai Baba or his past life as Shirdi Sai Baba are examples of what is possible when a being is merged in that state constantly. In Hindu thought there are levels of samadhi that relate to the dimensions of reality all the way up into the cosmic planes of consciousness.

Book Two
The Steps to Union

1.   The yoga of action leading to union with the soul is fiery aspiration, spiritual reading, and devotion to Ishvara.

One of the most important qualities a disciple needs to cultivate on the spiritual path is fiery aspiration and enthusiasm for God. They can be cultivated by spiritual reading and devotional love for God. Jesus said that the whole law could be summed up as follows: "Love the Lord thy God with all thy heart and soul and mind and might, and love thy neighbor as thou love thyself." This commandment contains the fiery aspiration and the devotion to God.

The yoga of action is Karma Yoga. The yoga of devotion is Bhakti Yoga. The yoga of the mind is Raja Yoga. The three of them combined include fiery aspiration, devotion, and spiritual reading. Patanjali was very exact in his science; hence the physical, emotional, and mental man.

2.   The aim of these three is to bring about soul vision and to eliminate obstructions.

Soul vision is another name for the Christ consciousness as opposed to negative ego consciousness.

3. These are the difficulties producing hindrances: Avidya [ignorance] and the sense of personality, desire, hate, and the sense of attachment.

> *Personality is the sense of negative ego, separateness, selfishness. The other qualities mentioned are self-explanatory.*

4. Avidya is the cause of all the other obstructions, whether they be latent, in process of elimination, overcome, or in full operation.

> *Ignorance stems from ego. As Sai Baba says, "God equals man minus ego." Ego manifests, as Djwhal Khul says, as glamour, maya, and illusion on the emotional, mental, and etheric planes and in those bodies.*

5. Avidya is the condition of confusing the permanent, pure, blissful, and the Self with that which is impermanent, impure, painful, and the not-self.

> *Is one a physical, emotional, and mental body or is one the Eternal Self living within these bodies?*

6. The sense of personality is due to the identification of the knower with the instruments of knowledge.

> *Again, is one the Eternal Self (the knower) utilizing the bodies, five senses, desires, emotions, thoughts, sensations, and feelings, or is one identified with and being victimized by these instruments of knowledge?*

7. Desire is attachment to objects of pleasure.

> *To pass the fourth initiation one must release all attachments and release all material desire. One's only desire should be to become desireless. Said in another way, one's only desire should be to achieve liberation so one may be of greater service.*

8. Hate is aversion for any object of the senses.

> *The true yogi feels neither aversion nor desire. They are two sides of the same coin. The true yogi remains in divine indifference.*

10. These five hindrances, when subtly known, can be overcome by an opposing mental attitude. The five hindrances are ignorance, sense of personality, desire, hate, and the sense of attachment.

> *This gets into the science of attitudinal healing. Patanjali's yoga sutras are really very similar to the lessons in A Course in Miracles which is about attitudinal healing. Emotions, be they positive or negative, come from the way one thinks. This is a fact; it is spiritual law. The easiest way to get rid of any negative quality is by using an "opposing mental attitude": Replace ignorance with knowledge. Replace grudges with forgiveness. Replace doubt with faith. Replace desire with desirelessness. Replace fear with love. Replace attachment with nonattachment or with preferences.*

11.   These activities are to be done away with through the meditation process.

The meditation process is a general term for doing the psychologi-cal and spiritual work of positive affirmations, visualizations, self-hypnosis, self-suggestion, mantras, words of power, repetition of the name of God, and meditation itself in the sense of attuning to the soul and spirit.

13.   So long as the roots [samskaras] exist, their fruitions will be birth, life, and experiences resulting in pleasure or pain.

The base of these negative or evil roots is ego. As long as ego, or separateness and fear, remain, future rebirth is insured, as are pleas-ure and pain. When negative ego, glamour, maya, and illusion are rooted out, liberation is achieved and duality is transcended. Duality and ego are one and the same also. When duality is transcended, evenmindedness, equanimity and unceasing joy are achieved.

14.   These seeds [samskaras] produce pleasure or pain according as their originating cause was good or evil.

All seeds, whether good or evil, are thoughts. Past-life karma or this-life karma are just thoughts that have been programmed into the subconscious mind. The most important concept is that all thoughts, be they from past lives or this one, can be reprogrammed. Wisdom, good thoughts, good feelings, and good deeds erase karma.

16.   Pain which is yet to come may be warded off.

This is achieved through a changed attitude of mind and the reprogramming of the conscious and subconscious minds in the pattern of the Christ consciousness. Did not the Bible say, "Let this mind be in you that was in Christ Jesus." The subconscious can be completely cleansed of all mental and emotional toxins, just as the physical body can be cleansed of physical toxins. If the four bodies are purified, pain and karma will be warded off.

21.   All that is exists for the sake of the soul.

The only purpose of Earth life is to realize the soul and then the spirit. Earth is a school for spiritual evolution. There is absolutely no other reason to be here but this. If for even a second, one considers any other reason, one is then moving into illusion. The ego will say that the world is for selfish, hedonistic, power-hungry, and pleasure-seeking purposes. One must choose whom to serve.

22.   In the case of the man who has achieved yoga [union] the objective universe has ceased to be. Yet it exists still for those who are not yet free.

One sees either with his spiritual eyes or with his material eyes (ego). One sees either the Eternal Self behind all appearances of form, or one sees and identifies with material form and hence does not see the soul behind all things. The spiritual master has achieved liberation from the three lower worlds. He can live in this world but be not of this world.

25. When ignorance is brought to an end through non-association with things perceived, this is the great liberation.

When self-mastery is attained through detachment, discrimination, renunciation, Christ (spiritual) vision, relinquishment of desire, transcendence of duality and ego, mastery of the five senses, and becoming a cause of one's reality in service of the soul and spirit, liberation is achieved.

26. The state of bondage is overcome through perfectly maintained discrimination.

One must discriminate between that which is of God and that which is not of God, that which is permanent and that which is impermanent, between the self and the not-self, between Christ consciousness and ego consciousness, between appearances and the reality that lies behind all appearances.

27. The knowledge [illumination] achieved is sevenfold and is attained progressively.

Hindu philosophy maintains that there are seven stages of illumination:

1. The stage of knowing all that is to be known. Nothing further remains to know. In other words, the basic lessons needed to be learned in this Earthly school have been learned.

2. The stage in which the disciple frees himself from every known limitation.

3. The stage in which the disciple's consciousness has shifted from the ego personality to that of the soul; hence, nothing remains to attract the disciple to the three lower worlds.

4. The stage in which the disciple fulfills his dharma (life path) and accomplishes his mission.

5. The stage in which complete control of the mind is achieved and the mind is at rest.

6. The stage in which the disciple realizes that matter, or form, has no power over him.

7. Full Self-realization which, in this case, would be the fifth initiation, or merger with the monad, or Eternal Self, in consciousness. The disciple now knows himself as the I Am that I Am, as the Eternal Self. The disciple has moved from soul-realization to Self-realization.

28. When the means to yoga have been steadily practiced and when impurity has been overcome, enlightenment takes place leading up to full illumination.

29. The eight means of yoga are the commandments, or yama; the rules, or niyama; posture, or asana; right control of life force, or pranayama; abstraction, or pratyahara; attention, or charana; meditation, or dhyana; and contemplation, or samadhi.

> *The yoga system of Patanjali is known as the eightfold path. It is differentiated from the eightfold noble path of Gautama Buddha:*
>
> > *1. The first step of Patanjali's path is yama, moral conduct: non-injury to others, truthfulness, non-stealing, sexual control, and non-covetousness.*
> >
> > *2. Niyama, religious observances, include purity of body and mind, contentment in all circumstances, self-discipline, self-study (contemplation), and devotion to God and guru.*
> >
> > *3. Asana, right postures, means the spinal column must be held straight and the body firm, in a comfortable position for meditation.*
> >
> > *4. Pranayama means control of prana, the breath and subtle life currents.*
> >
> > *5. Pratyahara means withdrawal of the senses from external objects.*
> >
> > *6. Charana is concentration, or holding the mind to one thought.*
> >
> > *7. Dhyana means meditation.*
> >
> > *8. Samadhi is superconscious direct experience.*
>
> *This eightfold path of yoga leads to the final goal of kaivalya (absoluteness) in which the yogi realizes the truth beyond all intellectual comprehension.*

30. Harmlessness, truth to all beings, abstention from theft, from incontinence (sexual control), and from avarice constitute yama, or the five commandments.

31. Yama constitutes the universal duty and is irrespective of race, place, time, or energy.

32. Internal and external purification, contentment, fiery aspiration, spiritual reading, and devotion to Ishvara constitute niyama, or the five commandments.

33. Thoughts contrary to yoga are: harmfulness, falsehood, theft, incontinence, and avarice, whether committed or approved of, whether arising from avarice, anger, or delusion, whether slight in doing, middling, or great. These result always in excessive pain and ignorance. For this reason the contrary thoughts must be cultivated.

35.   In the presence of Him who has perfected harmlessness, all enmity ceases. When the truth to all beings is perfected, the effectiveness of His words and acts is immediately to be seen.

37.   When the abstention from theft is perfected, the yogi can have whatever he desires.

Does not the Bible say, "Seek ye first the kingdom of Heaven and all things shall be added unto thee."

38.   By abstention from incontinence, energy is acquired.

Here the need is to raise the sexual energy and develop mastery over it.

39.   When abstention from avarice is perfect, there comes an understanding of the law of rebirth.

It is desire that causes a soul extension to have to incarnate into matter. When desirelessness is achieved, the need for rebirth ends.

40.   Internal and external purification produces aversion for form, both one's own and all forms.

Again, the shift to spiritual vision from material vision is the purification.

41.   Through purification comes also a quiet spirit, concentration, conquest of the organs, and ability to see the Self.

42.   As a result of contentment, bliss is achieved.

Bliss is the state of consciousness of union with the Eternal Self.

43.   Through fiery aspiration and through the removal of all impurity comes the perfecting of the bodily powers and of the senses.

44.   Spiritual reading results in a contact with the soul.

45.   Through devotion to Ishvara, the goal of meditation is reached.

Devotion is extremely important on the spiritual path because it brings forth one's emotions, most specifically, the emotion of love for God and all His kingdoms. God responds to a devoted heart.

46.   The posture assumed must be steady and easy.

47.   Steadiness and ease of posture are to be achieved through persistent light effort and through the concentration of the mind upon the infinite.

48.   When right posture [asana] has been attained there follows right control of prana and proper inspiration and expiration of the breath.

I highly recommend taking a Hatha Yoga class if you have never done so before.

54.   Abstraction [pratyahara] is the subjugation of the senses by the thinking principle and their withdrawal from that which has hitherto been their object.

55.   As a result of these means, there follows the complete subjugation of the sense organs.

Book Three
Union Achieved and Its Results

1.   Concentration is the fixing of the chitta [mind stuff] upon a particular object. This is dharana.

> *The object can be a mental ideal or idea, a quality, a visualization, an internal or external object, a spiritual master, a feeling, the third eye, or the consciousness behind the form.*

2.   Sustained concentration is meditation.

3.   When the chitta becomes absorbed in that which is the reality [the idea embodied in the form] and is unaware of separateness or of the personal self, this is contemplation, or samadhi.

4.   When concentration, meditation, and contemplation form one sequential act, then is sanyama achieved.

> *Sanyama means the synthesis or integration of the three stages of the meditation process.*

5.   As a result of sanyama comes the shining forth of the Light.

6.   This illumination is gradual; it is developed stage by stage.

18.   Knowledge of previous incarnations becomes available when the power to become thought images is acquired.

19.   Through concentrated meditation, the thought images in the minds of other people become apparent.

23.   Union with others is to be gained through one-pointed meditation upon the three states of feeling (compassion, tenderness, and dispassion).

25.   Perfectly concentrated meditation upon the awakened Light will produce the consciousness of that which is subtle, hidden, or remote.

32.   Those who have attained self-mastery can be seen and contacted through focusing the Light in the head. This power is developed in one-pointed meditation.

33.   All things can be known in the vivid Light of the intuition.

34.   Understanding of the mind consciousness comes from one-pointed meditation upon the heart center.

> *The spiritual understanding is always to think with one's heart not just with one's mind.*

35.   Experience of the pairs of opposites comes from the inability of the soul to distinguish between the personal self and the spirit. The objective forms exist for the use of the spiritual man. By meditation upon this arises the intuitive perception of the spiritual nature.

36.   As a result of this experience and meditation, the higher hearing, touch, sight, taste, and smell are developed, producing intuitional knowledge.

The following chart is also from Alice Bailey's book, The Light of the Soul. It depicts the psychic nature as it develops in the first five dimensions of reality.

Plane	Sense
Physical	1. Hearing
	2. Touch, feeling
	3. Sight
	4. Taste
	5. Smell
Astral	1. Clairaudience
	2. Psychometry
	3. Clairvoyance
	4. Imagination
	5. Emotional idealism
Mental	1. Higher clairaudience
	2. Planetary psychometry
	3. Higher clairvoyance
	4. Discrimination
	5. Spiritual discernment
	Response to group vibration
	Spiritual telepathy
Buddhic	1. Comprehension
	2. Healing
	3. Realization
	4. Perfection
	5. All knowledge

a. The First Sense: Hearing

1. Physical hearing
2. Clairaudience
3. Higher clairaudience
4. Comprehension (of four sounds)
5. Beatitude

b. The Second Sense: Touch or feeling

1. Physical touch
2. Psychometry
3. Planetary psychometry
4. Healing
5. Active service

c. *The Third Sense:* Sight
  1. *Physical sight*
  2. *Clairvoyance*
  3. *Higher clairvoyance*
  4. *Divine vision*
  5. *Realization*

d. *The Fourth Sense:* Taste
  1. *Physical taste*
  2. *Imagination*
  3. *Discrimination*
  4. *Intuition*
  5. *Perfection*

e. *The Fifth Sense:* Smell
  1. *Physical smell*
  2. *Emotional idealism*
  3. *Spiritual discernment*
  4. *Idealism*
  5. *All knowledge*

Many people don't realize that there are psychic senses on each plane of development.

37.   These powers are obstacles to the highest realization but serve as magical powers in the objective worlds.

Many disciples get caught in the glamour of the psychic world and, hence, fail to reach to the highest levels of the soul and the monad. It is not that these psychic senses are bad, it is just that they must be used only in service of the soul and monad and must not be used by the negative ego. There are many seekers on the path who are extremely developed psychically yet are totally run by their egos and lower selves. There are many people who are great channels, and the same phenomenon has taken place. There are many traps on the spiritual path. Djwhal Khul has called these the "glamours on the path." The psychic level is a level of development different from the spiritual level. I have known psychics who didn't even believe in God, if you can imagine that.

39.   By subjugation of the upward life there is liberation from water, the thorny path, and mire, and the power of ascension is gained.

Freedom from water is symbolic of being liberated from the emotional nature. Liberation from the thorny path symbolizes the path of physical life. Liberation from the mire symbolizes liberation from desire and the lower self. This is the first time Patanjali speaks of ascension, or the sixth initiation.

42. By one-pointed meditation upon the relationship existing between the body and the akasha, ascension out of matter [the three worlds] and power to travel in space are gained.

45. Through this mastery, minuteness and the other siddhis [powers] are attained; likewise, bodily perfection and freedom from all hindrances.

A yogi has the ability to make himself in consciousness as small as an atom or as large as the infinite universe. The siddhis, or powers, can also be a trap for initiates who have not yet achieved ascension. Sometimes the siddhis can become more important to an initiate than God. This will ultimately lead to the loss of these powers and to karmic repercussions.

49. The man who can discriminate between the soul and spirit achieves supremacy over all conditions and becomes omniscient.

This lesson deals with the understanding that at the third initiation, the disciple merges with the soul. However, at the fifth initiation and at the sixth initiation, the initiate merges with the spirit. Merging with the soul is just an intermediate step, albeit a supremely important one. The soul is the intermediary between the incarnated personality on Earth and the spirit, or monad, in Heaven. The soul is the higher self. The next step after merging with the spirit is to merge with God directly at the cocreator level in cosmic dimensions of reality.

55. When the objective forms and the soul have reached a condition of equal purity, then is at-one-ment achieved and liberation results.

When the four bodies are aligned with the soul and spirit and all are equally purified, liberation from the wheel of rebirth results. All lessons in this mystery school called Earth life have been learned.

Book Four
Illumination

1. The higher and lower siddhis [powers] are gained by incarnation, or by drugs, words of power, intense desire, or meditation.

These five methods for obtaining the siddhis relate to the five planes of consciousness. Incarnation is the physical-plane method. Drugs blast open the astral consciousness. (I am not recommending this method.) Words of power are the mental-plane method. Intense desire is the Buddhic-plane method. Meditation is the atmic-plane method.

2. The transfer of the consciousness from a lower vehicle into a higher is part of the great creative and evolutionary process.

The process of moving through the seven levels of initiation speaks to this process. At each state and initiation the disciple becomes polarized to or identified with the next higher dimension or vehicle (body).

The first initiation is focused on the physical vehicle. The second initiation focuses on mastery of the emotional vehicle. The third initiation deals with mastery of the mental vehicle. The fourth initiation becomes focused in the Buddhic vehicle and plane of consciousness. The fifth initiation is focused in the atmic vehicle and dimension of consciousness. The sixth initiation moves into the Lightbody, or ascension vehicle. At each initiation there is a transfer from a lower vehicle to the higher one just above it.

4.   The I Am consciousness is responsible for the creation of the organs through which the sense of individuality is enjoyed.

The I Am consciousness, of course, is the monad, or spirit.

5.   Consciousness is one, yet produces the varied forms of the many.

24.   The mind stuff also, reflecting as it does an infinity of mind impressions, becomes the instrument of the self and acts as a unifying agent.

The mind, when working properly, serves as a unifying agent. When the mind is serving the negative ego it serves as a separating agent. This is one of the keys to understanding Raja Yoga.

29.   The man who develops nonattachment, even in his aspiration after illumination and isolated unity, becomes aware, eventually, of the overshadowing cloud of spiritual knowledge.

It has also been referred to as "the raincloud of knowable things." This knowledge is held within the Lightbody. The idea is to call forth the Lightbody and merge with it so the knowledge becomes readily available in everyday existence. There are two levels of Lightbodies: there is the soul Lightbody and the monadic Lightbody.

30.   When this stage is reached then the hindrances and karma are overcome.

31.   When, through the removal of hindrances and the purification of the sheaths, the totality of knowledge becomes available, naught further remains for the man to do.

The purpose for incarnating has been fulfilled.

Summation

The profundity of these sutras is quite obvious. Meditating upon these lessons and the lessons in *A Course in Miracles* would give a person a supreme understanding of union with God through Raja Yoga. Those people who wish to study these lessons in a more in-depth fashion can purchase Alice Bailey's book *The Light of the Soul.*

Om Shanti, Shanti, Shanti, Om

48

The Church's Contamination by Ego

*He that is without sin among you,
let him cast a stone.*

Master Jesus

It must be understood that the most important relationship in your life is your relationship to yourself, not your relationship to God. This sounds blasphemous, but it is true. If you are not right with yourself, you will project your wrong relationship to self onto everything in your life, including your relationship to God. If you don't learn to control your lower self, or negative ego, it will interpret life for you.

This is true in all areas of life, including religion. The negative ego has been allowed to interpret the Bible and the teachings of Jesus. As Djwhal Khul has said in the Alice Bailey books, it isn't that Christ has failed; it is that the human element has prostituted the truth he presented.

Djwhal goes on to say, in the Alice Bailey book *Problems of Humanity*, that theology, dogma, doctrine, materialism, politics, and money have created a vast dark cloud between the churches and God. The two major factors responsible for the failure of the churches, according to Djwhal Khul, are:

1. the narrow theological interpretations of scripture and
2. the material and political ambitions of the clergy.

The teachings of traditional and fundamentalist Christianity are incredibly confused. They have been made by well-meaning, good people who have accepted a false doctrine made up by ignorant men. Some of the misconceptions are as follows.

The first great misconception is that Jesus is the *only* son of God and the rest of humanity are lowly, sinful worms. Every person on Earth or anywhere else is a child of God just as Jesus is. This is clearly what Jesus taught. There is no such thing as an original sin. Each person is the Eternal Self, the Christ. In truth, you are on the Earth to realize that.

Jesus, whom the Christian Church makes out to be more special than everybody else, in truth was only a third degree initiate when he incarnated onto Earth, and he died on the cross as a fourth degree initiate. He did not ascend, as the Christian tradition says he did.

The traditional Christian Church has completely missed the fact that the Lord Maitreya, the Planetary Christ and head of the Great White Brotherhood, was overshadowing Jesus during the last three years of his life. It was really Maitreya who performed all the miracles. It was Maitreya who ascended, not Jesus. Lord Maitreya was the realized Christ, not Jesus; Jesus was his instrument.

Traditional Christian belief holds that Jesus was crucified to redeem man from sin. Man has no sin, only mistakes and lessons and his own personal karma that must be balanced. This is another total misconception. *A Course in Miracles* teaches that Jesus was crucified to teach an extreme lesson of love and forgiveness.

Jesus' crucifixion could not take away your sins not only because you have no eternal stains on your character, but also because you are responsible for your own personal karma, and Jesus' crucifixion did not lift that responsibility.

Traditional Christianity believes that if you accept Jesus as your personal savior, you are saved and will go to Heaven and be with Jesus. Every one else will go to Hell, which is a place of eternal damnation, or will physically die and be obliterated. This is an incredibly confused doctrine.

First of all, there are many dimensions in God's creation and accepting Jesus is not necessarily going to get you anywhere. Where you go when you die is determined by the level of initiation you have obtained during your life on Earth.

Accepting Jesus or going to church on Sunday doesn't mean anything. It is what is in your heart and in your every thought, word, and deed throughout your life that will determine your spiritual progress. Your salvation is not up to God or Jesus; your salvation is up to you.

God has provided everything. He always has and always will. It is you who can choose to separate yourself from God through your own thinking. Each of you is the Christ, in truth, and you are here on Earth to demonstrate that truth.

You do not need a priest to serve as an intermediary and tell you how to interpret God's word or the Bible. The traditional Christian teaching says that the Bible is written by God. That is completely false. The Bible was written by men. The Bible is mostly man's interpretation of God, not God's direct revelation.

It must also be understood that the Bible was written two thousand years ago and is outdated to a certain extent. The Bible is a fantastic book; the problem lies in who is interpreting it. Traditional Christian interpretations of what the Bible says are confused and distorted. They will come to your door and tell you it is right there in the Bible. It is not right there in the Bible; it is in their interpretation of the Bible.

It is important to know that men in positions of power in the church actually extracted from the Bible statements they didn't like. An example of this is reincarnation. The Bible used to be filled with references to reincarnation. Then in 553 A.D. the Second Council of Constantinople issued a decree that all references to reincarnation be removed from the Bible. This is an indisputable fact, for it is in the minutes of the meeting, which can be looked up in the appropriate historical reference book.

Traditional Christians believe that anyone who disagrees with them is of the devil. First of all, there is no devil, there is only glamour, illusion, and maya. Secondly, this belief is just a product of incredible self-righteousness. They actually believe that the Bible and the teachings of Jesus are the only path to God and that all other religions and spiritual masters – including Buddha, Krishna, and Sai Baba, Hinduism, Judaism, and Islam – are of the devil.

They say they follow the teachings of Jesus who clearly preached unconditional love, yet these groups are among the most conditionally loving, judgmental, intolerant, attacking, self-righteous groups of people on Planet Earth. Their religion is based on fear and guilt. Anything that goes wrong, they believe, means God is punishing you. This, of course, is complete illusion, because God doesn't create your reality, you do. It is just a convenient weapon of the church higher-ups to control the people. They actually make God out to be judgmental, attacking, and angry, much like the Old Testament God of ancient Judaism: if you don't do what the Church says, you are destined for hellfire and eternal damnation.

They make the spiritual path out to be a path of suffering, and they teach people to be martyrs. The spiritual path, in truth, is a path of boundless joy and of balance. The Church teaches a type of conditional immortality that says you must do what the Church says or you will die. This is absurd because all people are immortal. Death is a complete impossibility, regardless of your level of evolution. Hell is not a place of eternal damnation; it is a state of consciousness that you can evolve out of.

Another abhorrent practice of the traditional Christian Church is teaching their followers to proselytize. They are taught to lay their trip on other people and not respect the beliefs or the personal space of others.

They believe in a last judgment in which Christ or God judges everyone and decides if you will be obliterated, go to Hell, or go to Heaven. This is totally absurd. God and Christ are incapable of judgment, by definition. The only judgment is done by yourself, and it would be more accurate to call it spiritual discernment. If you haven't learned your lessons then you will have to incarnate again and come back to school. The Church has no recognition of this fact or of the fact that Jesus has had many incarnations. These are listed in *The Complete Ascension Manual* in the chapter "The Untold Story of Jesus the Christ."

Another thing the Christian Church has conveniently failed to mention is the fact that Jesus studied Buddhism and was initiated in the Great Pyramid of Egypt. They also have purposely hidden the manuscripts telling of his life as an Essene. All these manuscripts are in the Vatican's secret libraries, but the general public will never see them because it would destroy the foundation of the entire Church if the information ever got out.

The fundamentalist Christian Church is incredibly judgmental and intolerant as is evidenced, for example, by their views on homosexuality and abortion. In considering abortion, they confuse the physical body with the incarnated personality who is only inhabiting the body. In respect to homosexuality, Jesus taught unconditional love and nonjudgmentalness; the fundamentalist Christians practice neither. Traditional Christianity has formulated a doctrine with which Jesus and the Lord Maitreya are not connected. It has created an actual tomb for true Christian teachings.

During its two-thousand-year life, the Christian Church has been militant, fanatical, and grossly materialistic. Look at the Crusades as one striking example. Look at the fanaticism of the pro-life groups. The churches have been more interested in building beautiful, ornate, glamorous churches than in helping the poor. The money they gather supports a powerful ecclesiastical hierarchy.

In the Catholic Church, the views of the Pope are seen as infallible, which is absurd when you look at some of the teachings such as the prohibition of condoms and all other forms of birth control.

The policy is to keep the masses of people ignorant and to turn totally against any new or evolutionary presentation of truth. The fundamentalist Christian churches are completely stuck in the past. There is no continuing revelation of God.

The Christian Church is doing the *exact* same thing the Jewish leaders did upon the appearance of Christ two thousand years ago: they remained stuck in the law and didn't allow themselves to evolve to the next dispensation of truth. Lord Maitreya, the Planetary Christ, is on the planet now, and when he declares himself, people will reject him. They believe Jesus is coming, and that is not true. They are waiting, in truth, for the Christ. He is here, but they will look at him as the devil because he doesn't correspond with their ignorant doctrine.

Then you have to look at the television ministers, who, for the most part (with a few exceptions) are interested in collecting money more than anything else. It is no accident that half of the famous ones have been caught having affairs.

The Church has no relationship to the ascended masters or to the true Spiritual Hierarchy that governs this planet. It is filled with bigotry, selfishness, greed, and narrow-mindedness. Something you might ask yourself is whether Jesus and the Lord Maitreya would feel comfortable in their own Church.

One of the worst teachings is that of prophecy. They are holding on to prophecies that were given in the Bible anywhere from two to four thousand years ago and are totally outdated. They are projecting an Armageddon to end the world. That is not going to happen. I am not saying that it was not a possibility when the prophecies were given in ancient times. However, humankind has evolved to the point where it has over-come the need for Armageddon. That is the whole purpose of prophecy: to warn humanity to change, using the free will God has bestowed. The ignorance of the Christian Church proclaims that if it is in the Bible it has to happen. What such believers are doing is projecting their mind power to create Armageddon and the end of the world. They will actually be disappointed if it doesn't happen.

In ending this chapter, I want to say that most of the people in the Church are good, well-meaning people who are being poisoned by a false doctrine and false teachings. The coming declaration of the Christ and the externalization of the Hierarchy will bring about the new world religion which will give the traditional people of the world a new alternative.

It will be a universalistic spirituality that accepts all religions as equally valid. It will cleanse all religions of the cancer of glamour, illusion, maya, and ego. The New Age movement has been the initial thrust that is leading the world in this loving and nonjudgmental direction.

49

An Esoteric Understanding of Judaism

Be still, and know that I am God.

Psalms

The religion of Judaism cannot be separated from the history of its people. The founder was the first great Jewish prophet, Abraham (Ascended Master El Morya). Abraham's teacher was the great spiritual master, Melchizedek (Master Jesus in a previous incarnation). Thus it is clear that Judaism, Christianity, and the Order of Melchizedek are inseparable.

In addition to this, Edgar Cayce, in channeling the Universal Mind, said that the Essenes, a Jewish sect, had true inception in the time of Melchizedek.

The Virgin Mary, her husband, Joseph, and John the Baptist (Elijah in a past life) were all Essenes. The same souls who started Judaism started Christianity. It was through Abraham, in his training from Melchizedek, that the first true understanding of monotheism began. Previous to that time, except perhaps for Hinduism, all other forms of religion had been polytheistic so it was a major breakthrough in the transformation of this planet.

Jesus' connection to Judaism continued after his incarnation as Melchizedek, when he came back as Joseph who had the coat of many colors and was dream interpreter for the Pharaoh. He later incarnated as Joshua, who led the Jewish people to the promised land after Moses died.

Any competition between the two religions is ludicrous since the same souls are involved with both religions. The two greatest prophets of the Jewish religion, in all its history, were Abraham and Moses.

What stands out as a key principle in understanding Judaism is the issue of the Jewish people's covenant with God. This covenant was first established by Abraham and later reestablished with Moses. At the time of Abraham, the name of God was El Shaddai. Later in Jewish history, God spoke to Moses on Mount Sinai and told him His name was I Am That I Am or just I Am. In Hebrew this is Ehyeh Asher Ehyeh or YHWH. Translators of the Bible later changed this to Jehovah, which is not really an accurate translation. In Hebrew it would be Yod Hay Wah Hay or Yod Hay Vav Hay.

The other name for God that was used over two thousand five hundred times in the Old Testament was Elohim. This is very interesting, given the fact that the elohim are the creator gods who helped God create the infinite universe. God was seen as having such a sacred name that Jewish teachings held that it could not be spoken. Given this fact, they often used the word "Adonai" to refer to God.

The Kabbalah, which is the mystic aspect of Judaism, and *The Keys of Enoch* both refer to God with all these names, but YHWH is the most commonly used.

Abraham's covenant with God can be found in the book of Genesis when God said, "And I will make of thee a great nation, and I will bless thee, and make thy name great; and thou shalt be a blessing." He was not afraid, for he had the promise of his God: "And I will bless them that bless thee, and curse him that curseth thee: and in thee shall all families of the Earth be blessed." (Genesis 12:2-3)

When Abraham was "ninety years old and nine," this covenant was reaffirmed when God said,

> "I am the Almighty God; walk before me, and be thou perfect. . . . And I will make my covenant between me and thee, and will multiply thee exceedingly. . . . As for me, behold, my covenant is with thee, and thou shalt be a father of many nations . . . and I will make nations of thee, and kings shall come out of thee. And I will establish my covenant between me and thee and thy seed after thee in their generations for an everlasting covenant, to be a god unto thee, and to thy seed after thee. And I will give unto thee, and to thy seed after thee, the land wherein thou art a stranger, all the land of Canaan, for an everlasting possession; and I will be their God. . . . thou shalt keep my covenant, therefore, thou, and thy seed after thee in their generations. (Genesis 17:1-9)

This is quite a powerful passage in the Old Testament and God has kept His word to this day. It is from this covenant that Judaism, Christianity, the Order of Melchizedek, the Essenes, and the Islamic religion were all born.

The Islamic religion is part of this story too, according to Mohammed, their prophet. He believed that Islam had its antecedents in the succession of the prophets Abraham, Moses, and Jesus. These prophets are all believed in by Moslems; however, they also believe that Mohammed was the greatest, or revealed the greatest revelation of God. Another connection is that Islam has its roots in Abraham's son, Ishmael, according to Islamic teaching.

Judaism has its roots in Abraham's sons, Isaac and Jacob. This covenant with Abraham, Isaac, and Jacob was reinforced five hundred years later with the coming of Moses, who is considered the greatest of the Jewish prophets.

Everyone knows the story of Moses so there is no need to go into it, except for one part. The most significant moment in Moses' life was his climbing of Mount Sinai when he spoke to God as symbolized by the burning bush. This story was always of great interest to me, and I had always been curious about who Moses had actually been speaking with. Was he speaking to his higher self, his monad, an angel, an ascended master? I asked Djwhal Khul about this, and he told me that Moses actually spoke to God.

This powerful revelation and reaffirmation of the covenant with the Jewish people is found in the Old Testament, in the book of Exodus:

And the angel of the Lord appeared unto [Moses] in a flame of fire out of the midst of a bush: and he looked, and, behold, the bush burned with fire, and the bush was not consumed. . . . God called unto him out of the midst of the bush, and said, "Moses, Moses." And he said, "Here am I." And he said, "Draw not nigh hither: put off thy shoes from off thy feet, for the place whereon thou standest is holy ground. . . . I am the God of thy father, the God of Abraham, the God of Isaac, and the God of Jacob." (Exodus 3:2-6)

Later, Moses asked what was God's name. The answer came: "I AM THAT I AM. . . . Thus shalt thou say unto the children of Israel, I AM hath sent me unto you." (Exodus 3:14) (See also the chapter on the Mighty I Am Presence.)

The highlight of this revelation came later when YHWH gave Moses the Ten Commandments:

I Am the Lord thy God, which have brought thee out of the land of Egypt, out of the house of bondage. Thou shalt have no other gods before me. Thou shalt not make unto thee any graven image, or any likeness of any thing that is in heaven above, or that is in the earth beneath, or that is in the water under the earth: Thou shalt not bow down thyself to them, nor serve them: for I the Lord thy God am a jealous God, visiting the iniquity of the fathers upon the children unto the third and fourth generation of them that hate me; and shewing mercy unto thousands of them that love me, and keep my commandments. Thou shalt not take the name of the Lord thy God in vain; for the Lord will not hold him guiltless that taketh his name in vain. Remember the Sabbath day, to keep it holy. Six days shalt thou labor, and do all thy work: but the seventh day is the Sabbath of the Lord thy God: in it thou shalt not do any work, thou, nor thy son, nor thy daughter, thy manservant, nor thy maidservant, nor thy cattle, nor thy stranger that is within thy gates: For in six days the Lord made heaven and earth, the sea, and all that in them is, and rested the seventh day: wherefore the Lord blessed the Sabbath day, and hallowed it.

Honor thy father and thy mother: that thy days may be long upon the land which the Lord thy God giveth thee.

Thou shalt not kill.

Thou shalt not commit adultery.

Thou shalt not steal.

Thou shalt not bear false witness against thy neighbor.

Thou shalt not covet thy neighbor's house, thou shalt not covet thy neighbor's wife, nor his manservant, nor his maidservant, nor his ox, nor his ass, nor any thing that is thy neighbor's. (Exodus 20:1-17)

It must be understood that at the time I am writing about, civilization and consciousness were not very advanced. It was the purpose of Melchizedek, Abraham, and Moses to establish this covenant between the Jewish people and God and to lay down the laws by which they would live.

Part of the Jewish teaching was the looking forward to the coming of the Messiah. Melchizedek, Abraham, and Moses were the great spiritual teachers and masters of the astrological age of Aries, in planetary astrology. Melchizedek and Abraham began this dispensation in approximately 2000 B.C. Planetary astrology dictates the coming of an avatar or great spiritual teacher every two thousand years.

Jesus was born into a Jewish family who were members of the Jewish community known as the Essenes. (See the chapter on the Essenes.) Many people forget that Jesus was a Jewish rabbi. Jesus was the Messiah that the Jewish people were looking for; the problem was that the Sanhedrin and other Jewish authorities were holding too tightly to the law. as set down by Moses and the Jewish prophets, to see that Jesus was bringing the next dispensation of the Jewish religion.

Jesus taught the understanding that love was even greater than the law. Some Jewish people recognized him as the Messiah, but most of those in control did not. This is no judgment, just a simple statement of fact. That created the schism between Judaism and Christianity which, in truth, are the same religion at core.

The Jews, for the most part, did not recognize Jesus as the son of God, the Christ. The problem occurred later when Christians distorted Jesus Christ's teachings, saying he was "the only son of God." The truth is, of course, that we are all the Christ.

The Jewish people didn't allow their religion to continue to evolve. In truth, this can be said about almost all the major religions. They arose two to three thousand years ago, and many of the understandings are outdated, as they were brought forth specifically for that time period.

It is important to understand that religion and consciousness evolve. Djwhal Khul said of the Alice Bailey books that some of the material would be outdated in twenty or thirty years. At each initiation you go through, you have to die to a certain level of understanding and be reborn to a new one. This is true of races of people as a whole, too. Each root race bring through a new level of understanding and attunement. Too many religions are trying to hold on tightly to the past instead of building upon it. Jesus was not trying to create a new religion; he was trying to build upon the wonderful foundation Abraham, Moses, and other prophets had laid down.

People's low level of consciousness during the past two thousand years has caused the Jewish people and the Christians to misinterpret what the great prophets were really saying. Because of wrong relationship to self and lack of control of their own negative egos, they projected onto God human qualities. This has occurred in Judaism, Christianity, Islam, Buddhism — really, in all religions.

In Judaism this projection is seen in the angry and jealous Old Testament God; in Christianity, in the fundamentalist Christian understanding of God. Buddhism went so far as to not even believe in God. In Islamic teachings, the vengeful God was portrayed. This is not to judge these religions but, rather, to indicate the natural process of man's wrong relationship to himself and the corresponding projection that, hence, has to take place.

The issue of the Messiah has again come to the forefront today. Two thousand years have gone by and humanity is at the end of another age, the Piscean Age, and at the beginning of the Aquarian Age. Again, it is time for the spiritual avatar to return. The Jews are again prophesying the coming of the Messiah. The Christians are prophesying the coming of Jesus. The Moslems are prophesying the coming of the Imanmadhi. The Buddhists are prophesying the coming of Buddha Maitreya. Humanity is in exactly the same position it was in two thousand years ago.

The Messiah is here. He is Lord Maitreya, head of the Great White Brotherhood. Will the Jews recognize him? With no judgment intended, I doubt it. Will the fundamentalist Christians recognize him? He is not Jesus, so I doubt it. Will the Buddhists and Moslems recognize him? It is unlikely that the Moslems will; the Buddhists' choice remains to be seen.

That is part of the reason Lord Maitreya has not declared himself. Those people who are involved with traditional religion are still too stuck in their separative traditions to see that the Spiritual Avatar and World Teacher they seek is right before them, but they don't have the eyes to see or the ears to hear. This is part of the reason why the New Age movement is so important.

A very important subject I want to tackle here is the issue of "the chosen people" and why Jews have suffered and been persecuted so greatly throughout history. These points are two different subjects in reality, but there is some correlation.

First it must be understood that the Jewish people are *not* chosen people. As *A Course in Miracles* says, "All are chosen, but few choose to listen." The Jewish people chose God and chose to follow His commandments. This statement has been misinterpreted at times by both Jews and Christians to be some kind of egotistical statement of superiority. If the Jewish people used it in that way, then, as the Bible says, "After pride cometh the fall." Some Jewish people have used the statement in this way but it can cause nothing but a karmic backlash. Non-Jews might have interpreted the statement to indicate pride, which caused them to fight back out of their own false pride.

Another reason for the Jewish people's suffering and persecution was the strict set of laws they were required to live by which made them different from other people. It is the nature of the negative ego to dislike people who are different.

Suffering could also be caused by the issue I spoke of earlier of holding on to the law and tradition so tightly and being unwilling to let their religion and understanding evolve. This too creates a kind of separateness.

In addition, there is a clannishness that gets reinforced one thousand times over each time Jews are persecuted. I was raised in the Jewish tradition and I sense a certain need in Jewish people to keep themselves separate on some level. This can only create a backlash. However, it might be changing somewhat in modern times among most of the Jewish population living in America.

By no means do I mean to be critical of Jewish people or of the religion by making these points. The same can easily be said about certain aspects of Christianity such as the fundamentalist movement. I could make these points about Hinduism with its caste system; I could make the same points about the Islamic fundamentalist teachings. There is no judgment or blame in any of this. I am attempting to use the sword of spiritual discernment and discrimination to separate out the glamour, illusion, maya, and negative ego that have infiltrated the true teachings of all religions and led to misinterpretation.

In the future it will be essential for all the world religions to move into a more universal understanding of religion and let go of the ego that says theirs is the only true way. The ego has infiltrated all the world's religions; that is a fact. It is why so many people have left religion and have instead sought what I would call spirituality.

I am attempting to bridge the gap by understanding the antecedent causes of the schism so religion can take its true and proper place in the world. Religion is a wonderful thing as long as the negative ego isn't its guide and organizer.

The Great White Brotherhood and the Spiritual Hierarchy, in their infinite compassion, understand these problems clearly, and that is why, within the next ten years, it is sending the Jewish people their own personal Messiah as well as the Lord Maitreya.

This will basically be true of all the world's religions. Specific masters working under the Lord Maitreya will be sent to reform religions in the directions I mentioned above. Jesus will be reforming Christianity from the inner plane. Two Buddhist masters will be reforming Buddhism. A new world religion is coming that will incorporate all religions as valid paths back to the Creator.

The Old Testament and Noah's Ark

The story of Noah's ark in the Old Testament is making reference to the destruction of Atlantis. The prophets of Atlantis knew Earth changes and destruction were coming, so they guided those who served the Law of One to leave.

Noah's ark is a literal and symbolic depiction of this story. A friend recently told me about an hour-long documentary on PBS that actually told the story and showed the discovery of the ark. If I am not mistaken, they found it on top of Mount Ararat in Turkey. It is frozen in the snow on the top of the mountain and can clearly be seen in the summer when the snow melts. The ark has split in half, but the compartments inside and the overall shape of it are apparent.

Moses and the Parting of the Red Sea

I have always been curious as to the truth of the story about Moses parting the Red Sea to escape the pharaoh's army. I asked Djwhal Khul about this and he told me that it is a true story. It didn't happen exactly as the movie portrayed it, but the Red Sea did part for Moses to allow the Jewish people to escape. I asked Djwhal how Moses did it and he said that it was "an act of God." Moses prayed for help and God responded with what we would call a miracle.

While I was on the subject, I also asked Djwhal Khul about the ten plagues Moses called forth to convince the pharaoh to let the Jewish people go. He told me they did happen and that it was the power of God Moses had called forth that caused them. These are not just stories.

Adam and Eve

According to the Universal Mind as channeled through Edgar Cayce, Adam and Eve were physical beings. Adam was an incarnation of Jesus. His fall was the story of an actual personal as well as a symbolic story for all humankind.

The Teachings of Judaism

Judaism is a strongly Earth-focused religion. It is more concerned with this life than with an afterlife. Much like Confucianism, its main focus is that of ethics and doing God's will. The heart of the Jewish religion is set down in the Torah which is the five books of Moses. However, Judaism also relies on the Talmud which sets down teachings, legends, and laws by which the Jewish people are to live. Some of them are quite practical and deal with all areas of life, including spiritual, mental, emotional, and practical, Earthly levels.

A central concept of Judaism is the ideal of mitsvah, doing good deeds. Ancient rabbis listed six hundred thirteen mitzvahs ranging from visiting the sick to studying the Torah. Judaism sees man as having free will and being constantly faced with the choice between good and evil.

The Jewish path is one of loving God and trying to be like Him, which means loving your fellow man. Traditional Judaism does not accept reincarnation, but there is some vague belief in an afterlife. It is interesting, however, that in the Kabbalistic aspect of Judaism, which is Jewish mysticism, reincarnation is embraced. The problem is that the Kabbalistic teachings are not presented to the general public as they are considered secret; they are similar to the beliefs of the Essenes.

Kabbalistic teachings are so exciting and so filled with the true spirit of God that I was very happy to find that the Jewish religion is tremendously rich if you delve a little deeper into the teachings. Even though I was raised Jewish, I see myself as a universalist who believes in all religions and all spiritual paths. How can you choose among Abraham, Melchizedek, Moses, Jesus, Krishna, Buddha, Rama, Sai Baba, Lord Maitreya, Mohammed, Confucius, Lao-tzu, Zoroaster? They are all so incredibly beautiful it is impossible to choose just one! I have reconciled this by choosing them all.

I like what Sai Baba says in this regard: "Whatever religion you are involved in, keep it, for I am in all of them." Whatever form you call on, he will respond. I enjoy shifting from one to another at different phases of my life, for each brings forth a different flavor, a feeling that is unique. According to Jewish law, a person does not cease to be a Jew simply because he or she lapses from observance. Raising a family is a sacred duty for most Jewish people. It is through this family loyalty that they express loyalty to Judaism. Jewish families are very enthusiastic about celebrating the rich Jewish heritage and tradition that are embodied in the celebration of the various Jewish holidays.

There are three branches of Judaism: orthodox, conservative, and reform. The three branches agree on most matters of theology but not on how Judaism should be practiced. Also, there are many Jewish people who look at Judaism as more of a cultural heritage than a religion. This is not discussed a lot, but in my observation it is quite widespread.

The acknowledged foundations of Judaism are the Principles of Faith, the Ten Commandments, the Golden Rule, and the Laws of Holiness. Few religions can boast of having such closely knit families as are found in the tradition of Judaism. In Judaism, the physical world is seen as good and it is meant to be enjoyed.

Sabbath services are held in a synagogue on Friday evenings and Saturday mornings. There are no pictures or images of God in the temples because of the commandment against graven images. The chief officer in the synagogue is the rabbi, or teacher. The Jewish state is called Israel which means Jacob, son of Abraham. The children of Israel were, first of all, his twelve sons which made up the twelve tribes.

The prophets are the exponents of the highest elements in the Hebrew religion. Some of the major prophets were Isaiah, Jeremiah, Ezekiel, Samuel (Saint Germain), Joshua (Jesus), Elijah (John the Baptist), Amos, Hosea, and Micah. The Talmud is the later Jewish interpretation of the Bible; in it was developed a belief in life after death, as ancient Judaism was very weak on this point. The Biblical command to "love thy neighbor as thyself" also runs through the Talmud.

Moses Maimonides, a Jewish philosopher in the twelfth century A.D., set out thirteen principles that have been accepted as a summary of the Jewish creed and that are incorporated in the authorized daily prayer book. These thirteen articles of faith are the following:

> Faith in God, the Creator,
> His Unity,
> His Incorporeality,
> His Eternity;
> To Him alone worship is due;
> Belief in the words of the prophets;
> Moses as the greatest Jewish prophet;
> The revelation of the laws of Moses;
> The law as unchanging;
> Belief in God's all-knowledge,
> His rewards and punishments;
> The coming of the Messiah;
> The resurrection of the dead.

The most famous book of the Kabbalah is the *Zohar, the Book of Splendor,* attributed to Moses of Granada, who died in 1305. It is from the Kabbalistic teachings that the understanding of the Tree of Life has come.

There are approximately twelve million Jews in the world today, over half of them living in the United States. This is true despite over six million Jews' having been massacred by the Nazis during World War II. Out of that carnage, one creative event did occur: the establishment of the Jewish State of Israel in 1948. It was the fulfillment of God's covenant with Abraham over four thousand years ago.

Judaism

Judaism is a wonderful religion with a very rich tradition. I have much appreciation for all I have gained from the experience of being incarnated into a Jewish family. The glamours and illusions of Judaism are quite interesting, too.

Djwhal Khul has said that the Jewish race actually came from the previous solar system (there are apparently seven progressive solar systems perceived by those who have studied occult knowledge in depth), having been the most advanced beings of that solar system. The major glamour has been their not allowing themselves to assimilate, hence creating separation.

The Jewish people performed a great service from the time of Abraham and the greatest Jewish prophet, Moses: they carried forth God's law. The only problem was that when the new dispensation of the Piscean Age arrived, they stayed stuck in that law and didn't allow the next revelation to be acknowledged.

50

The Essene Brotherhood

*Do not try to take the speck
out of the eye of your brother when you have a
log in your own eye.*

Jesus Christ

The Essene brotherhood had its inception at the time of Melchizedek, the great spiritual master who lived on this planet around 1973 B.C. and was an incarnation of Jesus Christ. Thus, Jesus actually began the Essene movement, as well as facilitating the start of the Jewish religion through Abraham and beginning the Christian religion himself with the help of the Lord Maitreya.

The development of the Essene brotherhood over the next two thousand years is embodied in the development of the Jewish religion. The Essenes were a Jewish sect representing an esoteric aspect of Judaism, or Jewish mysticism. The Jewish mystics studied the Kabbalah, which taught belief in reincarnation, astrology, channeling, prophecy, soul travel, psychic development, and angels and which organized itself around the Tree of Life.

The Historical Background of the Essenes

Since the Essene Brotherhood evolved within Judaism, its history can be traced by looking at the development of the Jewish religion. It begins at the time of Melchizedek and the establishment of the Order of Melchizedek; it continues with Abraham (El Morya); it continues onward through Jacob (the story of Jacob's ladder and of his wrestling with the angel); it continues through Joseph, an incarnation of Jesus, and his coat of many colors, his jealous brothers, and his eventually becoming the dream interpreter of the Pharaoh; it continues through the great spiritual master Moses, who led the Jewish people out of bondage in Egypt and spoke to God in the burning bush on Mount Sinai, which was a direct revelation of the Godhead, according to Djwhal Khul. Moses was told that God's name was "I Am That I Am," and was given the Ten Commandments — which are very similar to the original teachings that Melchizedek (Jesus) gave to Abraham. Upon Moses' death, when he ascended, Joshua, an incarnation of Jesus, took over and led the Jewish people into the Promised Land.

The development of Judaism then arrives at the incarnation of Jesus, when the great Jewish prophets lived and carried forth this mystical lineage — prophets such as Samuel, Isaiah, Jeremiah, Ezekiel, Hosea, Joel, Amos, Obadiah, Jonah, Micah, Nahum, Habakkuk, Zephaniah, Haggai, Zechariah, and Malachi. Carrying forth this lineage were the writings of Elisha, Daniel, Ezra, and Nehemiah. Then there were the great Jewish kings, King David and King Solomon; there was Enoch, another incarnation of Jesus, who wrote "The Book of Enoch" as well as the recent publication, *The Book of Knowledge: The Keys of Enoch;* there was Elijah (John the Baptist) who began the school of the prophets on Mount Carmel.

The Essene, Jewish, Melchizedek, and Christian lineages are, in truth, one lineage which sets the stage for next dispensation of spiritual teachings for humankind.

Moses brought forth the law. Buddha, five hundred years earlier, had brought forth the wisdom of God. Jesus and the Lord Maitreya carried forth the law of Moses and the wisdom of the Buddha and added the love principle.

Jesus was a Jewish rabbi who had purposely incarnated into a Jewish family that was involved with the Essenes. Jesus was the Messiah the Jewish people were waiting for, but it was only the Essenes who recognized that.

The Recorded History of the Essenes

Recorded history of the Essenes begins around 200 B.C. and ends around 100 A.D. The Edgar Cayce information from the Universal Mind tells us that Mary, Joseph, John the Baptist, the innkeeper at Bethlehem, and Jesus himself were all Essenes. He also suggests that Zebedee, John, James, and Andrew all had close ties with the Essenes. The discovery of the Dead Sea Scrolls in 1947 provided tangible proof of the Essenes' existence, although Cayce had been correct about the location of the Essene community eleven years before the scrolls were discovered.

The Dead Sea Scrolls were found in Qumran, on the northwest coast of the Dead Sea. Excavations began in the Qumran ruins in 1949 and continued for five years. What was uncovered was an Essene establishment that included a monastery, a house of studies, and a school. According to Edgar Cayce, only a fraction of the Essenes lived in the monastery; thousands of them lived normal lives throughout the Middle East. They were bound together by the conviction that the Messiah would be born within their ranks.

The Words of Philo

In 20 A.D., Philo, the Jewish philosopher, wrote of a Jewish sect numbering about four thousand whom he called Essaie because of their saintliness. He said they were worshipers of God who did not practice animal sacrifice. They regarded a reverent mind as the only true sacrifice. No slaves were found among them because they saw all men as brothers. Moral philosophy and ethics were their chief preoccupations. The seventh day was their Sabbath. They taught piety, holiness, justice, and the art of regulating home and city, but the essence of their teaching was love of God, virtue, and love of humankind. They were indifferent to money, worldly possessions, and pleasure. Their love of humanity, kindliness, equality, and fellowship passed beyond description. All money was placed within a common fund out of which the sick were supported when they could not work.

The Words of Josephus

Josephus, writing around 80 A.D., said that the Essenes were Jews by birth but seemed to have a greater affection for one another than did the Pharisees and Sadducees. They rejected pleasure as evil and greatly valued self-control and discipline over the passions. They clothed themselves in white garments. Their piety toward God was quit extraordinary. Before the sun rose they would not speak of profane matters but began their days with prayer, ritual bathing, and baptism. The priest would always say grace before meals and praise God after meals. They were ministers of peace. They spent a great deal of time studying the writings of the ancients.

Each candidate to become an Essene passed through a period of preparation and purification that extended over three years. First, he or she was required to turn over all property to the common treasury. The candidate was then given the ordinances and rules, a spade, an apron, and a white robe. After a year of probation the candidate was allowed to enter the second stage during which he enjoyed closer fellowship with the other candidates and was involved in more of the ceremonies and closed rites. At this second stage he could not hold office or sit at the common table. The candidate entering the third stage was required to take a solemn oath never to reveal the secrets of the Essene order and to practice piety toward God and charity toward his fellow humans. Also required was a vow that he would do no harm to his fellow man, either of his own accord or at the command of others. He would at no time abuse his authority or put himself above others. Any Essene caught committing a crime would be cast out of the society. It was only after the third year that a candidate was allowed to be present at the hadoth, the secret meetings.

Josephus went on to describe the Essenes as being accurate and just. They did not pass sentence in their communal court of law with fewer than one hundred members present. What they most honored, after God, was the law of Moses. They were stricter than any other Jewish sect about resting from their labors on the seventh day.

They lived long lives, often beyond one hundred years. When captured and tortured by the Romans, they could not be made to shed a tear or flatter their tormentors. Their doctrine was that their physical bodies were corruptible, but their souls were immortal and continued forever. Many of the Essenes were great prophets of the future and were seldom wrong in their predictions.

Pliny, a Roman who wrote about the Essenes, said, "Toward the west of the Dead Sea, the Essenes establish their communities. They are a Hermetical society, marvelous beyond all others throughout the whole Earth."

The Essenes at Qumran conducted a religious service every morning during the rising of the Sun. They were aware of their role in the preparation, birth, and training of Jesus. They were well versed in the concepts of reincarnation. The Essenes considered women to be equals with men. Membership in the Essenes was based on free choice.

Elijah's school of the prophets on Mount Carmel in past times had been a part of the Melchizedek training, as had the work of the prophet Elisha who was a disciple of Elijah (an incarnation of John the Baptist). This work was also carried on by the prophet Samuel (an incarnation of Saint Germain).

The life of the Essenes was given to good deeds and missionary activities, according to Edgar Cayce. The daily life in the monastery of the Essenes was austere and strict, but both Josephus and Philo attest to the fact that the Essenes were a happy, industrious, and optimistic people. They were also very clean; they wore special clothes for their two daily meals, one at eleven in the morning and the other after sunset. Their members were not to argue, bear grudges, or be critical of anyone. If a disagreement developed they were to discuss it in a loving way between themselves. If no compromise could be reached, a third person was to listen and try to settle the matter. If this failed, they were to go before a council of twelve elders and three priests whose decision was law. Punishments for infractions were very severe: speaking brusquely was punishable by rationed food for a year; for falling asleep or spitting in a public session it was rationed for a month.

The head of the Essenes, called Judy by Edgar Cayce, was incarnated in this century and went to Cayce for a reading. Among her many functions had been that of recordkeeper of the Essene material. In some of Edgar Cayce's readings, the Universal Mind said that he was actually reading from the Akashic Records some of the records that Judy herself had written at that time.

Cayce also said that there were sects within the Essene movement itself. The philosophical dividing point seemed to be whether man could make things happen or whether only God could make things happen. (The truth, of course, is that both are true, although you do cause your own reality.)

The Essenes were opposed to taking oaths; they were taught that a simple yes or no, given in common conversation, was the only oath they needed to make, for their word was as good as law. The Essenes had the highest level of integrity. The Dead Sea Scrolls established the fact that they revered "The Book of Enoch" (as differentiated from *The Book of Knowledge: The Keys of Enoch*).

The Dead Sea Scrolls provide absolute confirmation that the Essenes had a great understanding of astrology. One of the scrolls describes the influence of the heavenly bodies on the physical and spiritual characteristics of those born in certain sections of the zodiac.

Some people of the time referred to the Essenes as "the silent ones" because of the silence they kept during their morning rituals and prayers. The Essenes also believed in the spiritual importance of baptism. They had an initiatory form of baptism and a daily, more personal form of it. In the excavations at Qumran were found meeting rooms, classrooms, a kitchen, a room for copying scrolls, and, around the buildings, a series of pools connected by canals.

The Essenes were also known as people of "hidden strength." Josephus stated that through superior mental will, they seemed to be above pain. The treasures in which the Essenes were interested were those that were stored in Heaven (in the causal body, or soul body). The Essenes were expert Kabbalists. They believed in tithing. Some of them were celibate, and some were householders. No Earthly subjects were discussed until the morning prayer and baptism service had been completed. They were quite adept at dream interpretation as well as receptive to divine revelation.

The principal teacher for the Essenes was the rabban, or rabboni, which means master. The rabban's assistant was known as the rabbi, or teacher. The rabbi was assisted in his duties by one known as the rab, or assistant teacher. The rabban, rabbi, and rab are symbolically associated with the monad, soul, and personality.

In order to preserve their sacred records from the Romans and other profane groups, the Essenes hid such records in caves and crypts inside pottery jars especially made for the purpose. It is scrolls such as these that were found in 1947 near the Dead Sea. Two of these scrolls were called "The Manual of Discipline" and "The War of the Sons of Light with the Sons of Darkness." A third, called "The Copper Scroll," listed the material possessions of the Essenes.

The Dead Sea Scrolls also refer to a "teacher of righteousness" who lived approximately one hundred years before the time of Jesus. He was a priest and a recipient of divine revelation. I have not yet been able to figure out who he was.

The Practici and the Therapeutici

The Essenes were loosely divided in two groups — the practici and the therapeutici. The practici, or practitioners, were focused on physical survival jobs such as making pottery and clothing, farming, and carpentry. The therapeutici were the healers.

The Essenes taught that the physical body was the temple of the soul. Their healing methods were divided into three categories. They were master herbalists, understanding the healing properties of herbs, roots, leaves, and barks. The second method of healing was the use of healing stones and hardened earth. Jesus prescribed that clay be placed on the blind man's eyes, something he probably learned in his training with the Essenes. The third healing method involved the use of the spiritual energy of the soul, the monad, and God.

The Gospel of Peace

The Gospel of Peace is an extraordinary source of information about the Essenes that is not well known. It is the original manuscript of St. Jerome's translation for the Pope in the middle of the fourth century. Although it had been thought lost, it had survived in the Benedictine Monastery of Monte Cassino and was discovered in this century in the "secret archives of the Vatican" by Edmond Bordeaux Szekeley.

There are further documents in these archives that refer to the Essenes, but I don't think the Catholic Church is too enthusiastic about releasing them; an understanding of the Essenes does change the Church's interpretation of what happened.

St. Jerome was one of the most brilliant scholars and translators of his time and was apparently quite gifted at soul travel. He had become the personal secretary for the Pope, which is how he had access to such extraordinary documents. Edmond Bordeaux Szekeley has eloquently presented his lifelong research into the Essenes and has brought to light profound teachings and understandings of Essene philosophy.

Angelology

The Essenes were particularly attuned to angels, and they developed the field of angelology. These invisible forces of the universe were considered sources of tremendous power and energy.

The Essenes developed a sort of tree of life that represented fourteen positive angelic forces. Seven of them were of a Heavenly nature and seven of a more Earthly nature. The tree of life had seven branches reaching toward Heaven and seven roots reaching into the Earth. Man was seen sitting in a sort of yoga posture half way between Heaven and Earth.

The esoteric significance of the number seven was acknowledged clearly. The seven Earthly powers and roots were the Earthly Mother, the Angel of Earth, the Angel of Life, the Angel of Joy, the Angel of the Sun, the Angel of Life, and the Angel of Air. The seven powers and branches in the Heavenly region of the tree were the Heavenly Father, the Angel of Eternal Life, the Angel of Peace, the Angel of Love, the Angel of Wisdom, the Angel of Power, and the Angel of Creative Work.

Contacting these fourteen angelic forces in their daily routine was fundamental to the overall lifestyle and spiritual development of the Essenes. Within this tree of life there is also a specific vertical correspondence between certain roots and certain branches of the tree:

The Heavenly Father . . . . The Earth Mother
The Angel of Eternal Life . . . . . The Angel of Earth
The Angel of Creative Work . . The Angel of Life
The Angel of Peace . . . . The Angel of Joy
The Angel of Power. . . . . The Angel of the Sun
The Angel of Love . . . . The Angel of Water
The Angel of Wisdom . . . . The Angel of the Air

This tree of life allowed the Essenes to understand that they were surrounded by invisible spiritual forces both in the heavens and in nature and the Earth. Every day the Essenes practiced certain prayer and meditative rituals, said to have originated with Enoch, wherein they would commune with these forces.

The morning communions were as follows:

The Earth Mother. . . . . Saturday morning
The Angel of the Earth. . . . . . . Sunday morning
The Angel of Life . . . . Monday morning
The Angel of Joy . . . . Tuesday morning

The Angel of the Sun . . . . Wednesday morning
The Angel of Water   . . . . Thursday morning
The Angel of the Air . . . . Friday morning

The evening communions were as follows:

The Heavenly Father . . . . Friday evening
The Angel of Eternal Life . . . . Saturday evening
The Angel of Creative Work . . Sunday evening
The Angel of Peace . . . . Monday evening
The Angel of Power. . . . . Tuesday evening
The Angel of Love . . . . Wednesday evening
The Angel of Wisdom . . . . Thursday evening

A third form of practice, the noon contemplations, took place each day
of the week, too:

Peace with the Body . . . . Friday noon
Peace with the Heavenly Father . Saturday noon
Peace with the Earthly Mother . Sunday noon
Peace with Culture . . . . Monday noon
Peace with Humanity . . . . Tuesday noon
Peace with the Family . . . . Wednesday noon
Peace with the Mind . . . . Thursday noon

In these noon contemplations the Essenes would call upon the Heavenly Father to send His angels of peace to balance and harmonize the various areas of their lives.

The Great Sabbath and Essene Vows

Every seventh Sabbath was called a Great Sabbath. It was a transcendental day that acknowledged all aspects of peace.

According to the research Edmond Bordeaux Szekeley describes in *From Enoch to the Dead Sea Scrolls*, candidates to become members of the Essenes entered a seven-year, not a three-year probationary period. Having finished this seven-year period, they then had to take the Great Sevenfold Vow — never to reveal the communions to anyone without permission and never to use the power and knowledge they had obtained for material or selfish purposes.

Prologue to the Communions

Before actually speaking the words of the communion to a particular angel on the tree of life, the Essene would say the following prayer/affirmation:

"I enter the eternal and infinite garden with reverence to the Heavenly

Father, the Earthly Mother, and great masters, reverence to the holy, pure, and saving teaching, reverence to the brotherhood elect."

Then they would actually perform a communion with an angel. For example, to commune with the Earth Mother on Saturday mornings they would say:

"The Earthly Mother and I are one. She gives the food of life to my whole body."

The Essene member would then meditate on the Earth Mother, the Earth energy, and the food and sustenance she supplies.

You can read *From Enoch to the Dead Sea Scrolls* in an hour and find in it the rituals the Essenes practiced. I have attempted to give you a skeletal outline and a feeling for the teachings and the lifestyle. My thanks to Edmond Bordeaux Szekeley for his wonderful research and the Light he has brought to humanity's understanding of the Essene brotherhood.

The Sevenfold Vow

The sevenfold vow, which the candidate for the Essene Brotherhood was required to take before being given the actual understanding of the tree of life and daily communions with the angels, is quoted in Szekeley's book:

1. I want to and will do my best to live like the tree of life planted by the great masters of our brotherhood, with my Heavenly Father who planted the eternal garden of the universe and gave me my spirit; with my Earthly Mother who planted the great garden of the Earth and gave me my body; with my brothers who are working in the garden of our brotherhood.

2. I want to and will do my best to hold every morning my communions with the angels of the Earthly Mother and every evening with the angels of the Heavenly Father, as established by the great masters of our brotherhood.

3. I want to and will do my best to follow the path of the sevenfold peace.

4. I want to and will do my best to perfect my acting body, my feeling body, my thinking body, according to the teachings of the great masters of our brotherhood.

5. I will always and everywhere obey with reverence my master, who gives me the Light of the great masters of all times.

6. I will submit to my master and accept his decision on whatever differences or complaints I may have against any of my brothers working in the garden of our brotherhood; and I shall never take any complaint against a brother to the outside world.

7. I will always and everywhere keep secret all the traditions of our brotherhood which my master will tell me; and I will never reveal to anyone these secrets without the permission of my master. I will never

claim as my own the knowledge received from my master and I will always give credit to him for all this knowledge. I will never use the knowledge and power I have gained through initiation from my master for material or selfish purposes.

Summation

I imagine that it would be difficult to avoid being deeply moved by the purity and devotion to God of the Essenes. What stands out most for me, however, is the tree of life and the incredible balance they achieved in integrating the Heavenly and Earthly aspects of life.

So many of the spiritual teachings of today are so top-heavy, strongly emphasizing the spiritual side but ignoring all understanding of Pan, the devas, the nature spirits, the elemental kingdom, the physical body, and the Earth Mother. This tree of life is a beautiful metaphor for a balanced process.

I would like to acknowledge with gratitude Edmond B. Szekely's books, *The Essene Gospel of Peace* and *From Enoch to the Dead Sea Scrolls*, and Glenn D. Kittler's book, *Edgar Cayce on the Dead Sea Scrolls*.

51

The Kabbalistic Tree of Life

Ehyeh Asher Ehyeh
I Am That I Am.

God, revealing His name to Moses

The Kabbalah is the secret doctrine, the esoteric, mystical aspect of the Jewish religion. I was raised in the Jewish religion in this particular lifetime but had no exposure to the Kabbalah until the past three or four years. The Jewish religion is very beautiful; however, it didn't really satisfy me spiritually until I uncovered this sublime metaphysical system. It has been through the Kabbalah, the Tree of Life, and the Keys of Enoch that I have discovered the spiritual goldmine of Judaism. It is one of the most profound systems of spiritual growth I have ever studied, and I consider myself just a beginner. In it is total understanding.

My purpose here is to give you a basic framework that will encourage you to explore its hidden mysteries more deeply. I will use the Kabbalistic Tree of Life as the foundation for the discussion. A series of diagrams of the Tree of Life will serve as a map for your inward journey.

Tree of Life Number One

The Tree of Life embodies the most sacred teachings of the Jewish religion. It had its antecedents in the time of the Order of Melchizedek and of Abraham, the Father of the Jewish people. Only a very small number of Jewish rabbis were Kabbalists.

The Tree of Life provides a visual understanding of the story of creation. The ten circles on the tree are called Sephiroth, or Lights. They are a tenfold division of creation. They are individualistic, but they make up a whole. In a sense they provide ten windows for looking upon God's creation. Djwhal Khul has said that you could study the Tree of Life for centuries and not uncover its vastness. It embodies the journey of existence through creation. If you start at the top of the tree and move down, you see spirit descending into matter; if you start at the bottom of the tree and move up, you see matter returning to spirit.

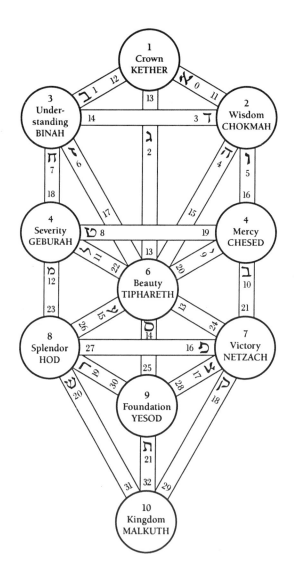

Diagram 51-1.
The Tree of Life

In this second diagram, you will note three terms have been added at the very top of the tree: Ain, Ain Soph, and Ain Soph Aur, meaning negative existence, undifferentiated illimitable one, and boundless universal Light. These three terms in Kabbalistic teachings refer to stages of the unmanifest spirit before the actual descending of spirit, or what you might call manifestation.

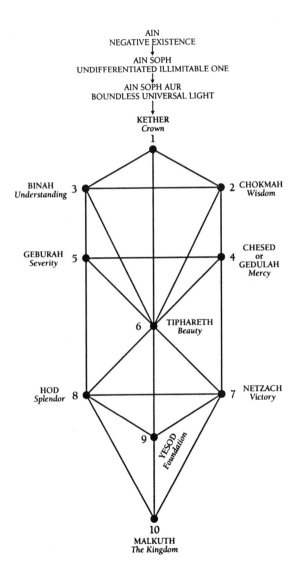

Diagram 51-2.
The Sephirothal Tree according to the Kabbalah

The actual point of manifestation on the Tree of Life is the very top Sephiroth, or Light, which the diagram depicts as Kether. Djwhal Khul has said its color is white. Kether can be equated with the point at which you emerged as a monad, or spiritual spark, from the Source, or from the nonmanifested state. As the monad emerges, it comes forth through the energies of the Kether, the crown of the tree. The power name of God for the Kether is Ehyeh (or Eheih) Asher Ehyeh which means I Am That I Am.

The next Sephiroth, on the upper righthand side of the tree, is known as Chokmah. Chokmah, according to Djwahl Khul, is the Light, or Sephiroth, that contains all of the potentialities of creation. Chokmah is considered the male, or father, aspect of the tree. The term that is associated with it is wisdom. The Hebrew power name of God that is associated with it is Yod Hay Wah Hay or Yod Hay Vav Hay which means Jehovah.

This leads the monad, on its continuing journey, across the tree to the upper lefthand side. This is the Sephiroth called Binah. It is associated with the term understanding. It is the mother, or female, aspect of the tree. The Hebrew power name of God that is associated with it is the word Elohim, the Divine Mother aspect of creation, which means, literally, All That God Is. Binah functions to receive what has been given. Whereas in Chokmah, the monad received the outline of creation, in Binah, the monad receives the purposes and the manifested ways in which it may serve on the spiritual plane.

These three Sephiroth — Kether, Chokmah, and Binah — form a triad that the Kabbalah calls the Supernal Triad. In the Alice Baily teachings, it is the upper spiritual triad the monad uses as it serves the Creator on the spiritual plane. Djwhal has referred to them as Atma, Buddhi, and Manas, or spiritual will, intuition, and higher mind.

As you begin to move down the tree, you move into the soul level of existence, wherein lies another triad. (Moving down the tree even farther, you come to the lower spiritual triad, the personality level, which I will speak of in a little while. Do you see how exciting this is starting to become? This tree of life is literally a map of creation.)

The Soul Level of Existence

The next three Sephiroth deal with the soul level of existence. The first one, on the middle righthand side of the tree, is known as Chesed, the next Geburah, and the next Tiphareth. These three have been termed mercy, severity, and beauty. This triad is related to the fifth and sixth initiations which deal with monadic merger and, of course, ascension. Studying this middle triad helps the incarnated personality to merge in consciousness with the higher self, or soul, and to understand which aspects within self must be developed in order to function here on Earth.

The Sephiroth of Chesed contains unconditional universal love. The Sephiroth of Geburah serves as the perfect balance for Chesed — divine will. The tree is balanced from top to bottom within the understanding of yin and yang. Unconditional love and divine will must be perfectly balanced if you are to realize the soul and monadic levels of consciousness.

The Sephiroth of Tiphareth is the center of the Kabbalistic Tree of Life. According to Djwhal Khul's interpretation of the Kabbalah (which is the system I am focusing on here), Tiphareth is the soul and the Christ consciousness. All the lines, or energy pathways, of the tree flow through it. Your true identity lies here.

If you are identified with the triad that lies below this one, you are identifying yourself as a personality or physical body rather than as a soul. As you evolve through the middle of the tree to the upper spiritual triad, you will eventually see yourself as soul and then as monad. You are steeped in glamour, illusion, and maya until you realize Tiphareth.

The Lower Spiritual Triad

The three Sephiroth that make up the lower spiritual triad are Netzach, Hod, and Yesod. In English they have been referred to as victory, splendor, and foundation, the three aspects of the personality. They are only a reflection of the soul level of existence, just as the soul level is a reflection of the monadic level of existence.

The Sephiroth of Netzach feels life and is associated with the doingness of the personality. The opportunity in Netzach is to transcend the less desirable feelings of the lower self and begin to manifest the feelings of the higher self and soul which, in essence, are unconditional love, compassion, and joy, thus enabling the incarnated personality to enjoy the more harmonious aspect of this Sephiroth.

Straight across the tree is Hod, the logical, rational, analytical mind, which is the perfect balance for Netzach, the feeling aspect. On the monadic level, the Divine Father and Divine Mother are balanced. On the soul level, divine will and divine love are balanced. On the personality level, feeling and thinking are balanced.

The next Sephiroth is Yesod. Yesod is the center of the personality level so, of course, it refers to the subconscious mind, the focus and controlling factor of the personality. The ideal is to raise the personality level and the subconscious patterns to the level of Christ consciousness.

The final Sephiroth is known as Malkuth. This Light deals with physical existence. Earth life can, hence, be considered to be one-tenth of total existence. If you are materialistic in your focus, you are missing literally nine-tenths of God's creation. Malkuth gives the incarnated personality the opportunity to launch itself upward on the Tree of Life.

Expanded Understanding

The chart below is from Ann Williams-Heller's book, *Kabbalah: Your Path to Inner Freedom*. In it she lists the ten Sephiroth along with the power name of God associated with each Sephiroth, the English interpretation of this name, and the astrological sphere associated with each Sephiroth.

The Ten Branches of the Tree of Life					
Number	English	Hebrew	God-Name	Meaning	Sphere
One	The Crown	Kether	Ehyeh	I Am That I Am I Shall Be There	The Prime Mover
Two	Wisdom	Chokmah	Jehovah	The Lord	The Zodiac (Uranus?)
Three	Under-standing	Binah	Jehovah Elohim	God of Gods	Saturn (Neptune)
Four	Mercy, Abundance	Chesed, Geburah	El	God, the Mighty One	Jupiter
Five	Justice, Severity	Geburah, Din, Pachad	Elohim Gabor	God of Battles God Almighty God the Potent	Mars (Pluto, Neptune?)
Six	Beauty, the King	Tiphareth	YHVH, Aloah wa Daath	God the Strong	Sun
Seven	Victory, Firmness	Netzach	Jehovah Tsabaoth	The Lord of Hosts	Venus
Eight	Glory in Splendor	Hod	Elohim Tsabaoth	The God of Hosts	Mercury
Nine	The Foundation	Yesod	Shaddel El Chai	The Almighty Living One God	Levanah, the Moon
Ten	The Kingdom	Malkuth	Adonai Malekh	The Lord and King, the Lord Made Manifest in Nature	The Four Elements, the Seven Planetary Powers

The Three Pillars

The Tree of Life can also be divided into three pillars or columns. The Sephiroth on the right side of the tree have been referred to as the Pillar of Mercy. The left column has been called the Pillar of Severity. The middle column has been called the pillar of Mildness or Equilibrium.

This reminds me of Buddha's Middle Path and also of the Hindu teachings dealing with the spinal column and the raising of the kundalini. The sushumna, the ida, and the pingla make up the etheric nervous system of the human being. The kundalini, when awakened, rises up the sushumna to the crown; the ida and pingala are the female and male aspects of the sushumna. There is obviously a macrocosmic/microcosmic correlation between the etheric nervous system and the Tree of Life.

Djwhal Khul teaches that there are two paths up the tree: the zigzag path and the path straight up the middle of the tree. The path up the middle relates to what I referred to in *The Complete Ascension Manual* as the short path of ascension. The zigzag path is the more complete path of ascension. Many incarnate personalities have taken the short path of ascension and are now returning to take the complete path of ascension which includes balancing all the opposites and ascending for your entire soul group and not just for yourself.

The Seven Dimensions of Reality

There are seven dimensions of reality, according to Djwhal Khul. These seven planes can be correlated with the ten Sephiroth:

Logoic Plane. . . . . . Kether
Monadic Plane . . . . Binah; Chokmah
Atmic Plane . . . . . . Geburah; Chesed
Buddhic Plane . . . . Tiphareth
Mental Plane . . . . . Hod; Netzach
Emotional Plane . . Yesod
Physical Plane . . . . Malkuth

These, of course, are the seven subplanes of the cosmic physical plane through which humanity is now evolving. This Tree of Life is a mirror, on this level of evolution, for the cosmic Tree of Life through which humanity will have to evolve later in its evolutionary progression.

The Archangels

Each of the ten Sephiroth is associated with a specific archangel:

Kether . . . . Metatron
Chokmah . . . . Ratziel
Binah. . . . . Tzaphkiel
Chesed . . . . Tzadkiel
Geburah. . . . . Khamael
Tiphareth . . . . Michael
Netzach . . . . Auriel

Hod . . . . Raphael
Yesod . . . . Gabriel
Malkuth . . . . Sandalphon

The Elements

There is an element associated with each Sephiroth:

Kether . . . . Hydrogen
Chokmah . . . . Uranium
Binah . . . . Oxygen
Chesed . . . . Carbon
Geburah . . . . Nitrogen, Steel, Iron
Tiphareth . . . . Gold
Netzach . . . . Copper
Hod . . . . Mercury
Yesod . . . . Quartz
Malkuth . . . . Earth, Air, Fire, Water

The Colors

A specific color is associated with each Sephiroth:

Kether . . . . White
Chokmah . . . . Gray
Binah . . . . Black
Chesed . . . . Blue
Geburah . . . . Red
Tiphareth . . . . Yellow
Netzach . . . . Green
Hod . . . . Orange
Yesod . . . . Purple
Malkuth . . . . Mixed Colors

The Angelic Hosts

Each Sephiroth has a connection with a particular group of angels:

Kether . . . . Hyos Ha Kodoish
Chokmah . . . . Auphanim
Binah . . . . Aralim (Thrones)
Chesed . . . . Chasmalim (Brilliant Ones)
Geburah . . . . Seraphim
Tiphareth . . . . Malachim
Netzach . . . . Elohim
Hod . . . . Beni Elohim

```
Yesod . . . . . . . . . . Kerubim
Malkuth . . . . . . . . Ahim (Soul of Fire)
```

The Lord's Prayer

Every phrase of the Lord's Prayer is associated with a Sephiroth:

```
Kether    . . . . . . . . Our Father
Chokmah . . . . . . . Which art in Heaven
Binah. . . . . . . . . . Hallowed be Thy name
Chesed    . . . . . . . . Thy kingdom come
Geburah. . . . . . . . Thy will be done
Tiphareth . . . . . . . On Earth as it is in Heaven.
Netzach . . . . . . . . Give us this day our daily bread
Hod . . . . . . . . . . . And forgive us our trespasses as we forgive
                        those who trespass against us.
Yesod . . . . . . . . . . Lead us not into temptation
Malkuth . . . . . . . . For Thine is the kingdom
Tiphareth . . . . . . . And the glory
Kether    . . . . . . . . Forever and ever. Amen
```

The Major Arcana of the Tarot

Between each of the ten Sephiroth are twenty-two pathways, lines of energy that connect the Sephiroth. These twenty-two pathways themselves have exact meanings. They have been related to the twenty-two cards of the Tarot's major arcana, as indicated in Diagram 51-3.

The Complete Tree of Life

In the Tree of Life in Diagram 51-4, I have attempted to include all of the most pertinent information in one diagram for your meditative pleasure. The little pattern at the bottom right corner, which I have called the lightning flash, refers to the zigzag path up the Tree of Life.

On the far left I have divided the Tree of Life into what Kabbalists call the four worlds — physical, emotional, mental, and spiritual. The only explanation that is missing here is the hidden Sephiroth in the upper middle portion of the diagram which has been referred to as "Daath." That I will explain in detail later on in the chapter.

The Tree of Life can also be seen as the human body, with the middle Sephiroth representing the chakras, Kether being the crown, Tiphareth the heart chakra, Malkuth the physical body, and Yesod, the second chakra. Daath, the hidden Sephiroth, might be the third eye.

You can be creative and come up with your own interpretations and insights. The Tree of Life provides literally infinite potentialities.

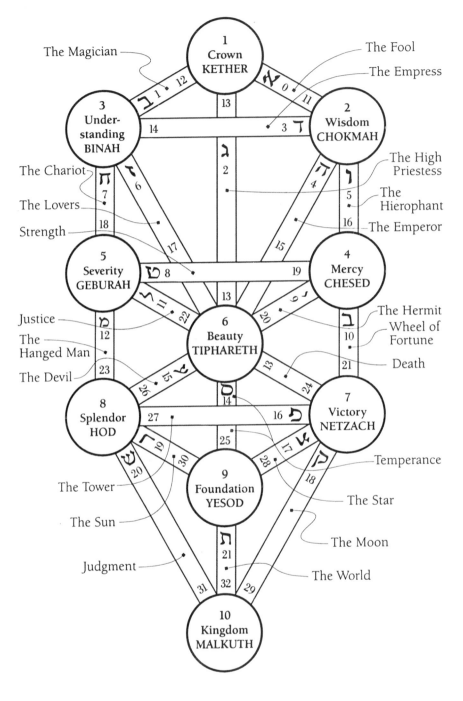

Diagram 51-3.
The Major Arcana of the Tarot Deck
and the Twenty-two Paths to God

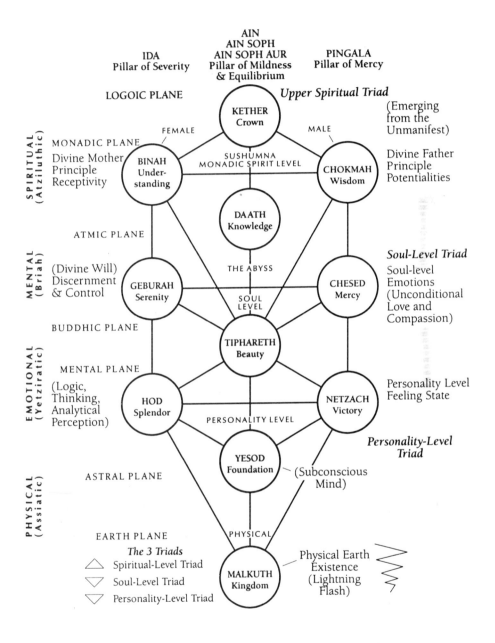

Diagram 51-4.
The Complete Tree of Life

Correlations of the Sephiroth

1. Kether	Experience:	Union with God
	Virtue:	Attainment
	Tarot cards:	The four aces
	Color:	Brilliance
	Magical Image:	Bearded king in profile

2. Chokmah	Experience:	The vision of God face to face
	Virtue:	Devotion
	Tarot cards:	The four twos
	Color:	Pure soft blue
	Magical Image:	A bearded male figure

3. Binah	Experience:	The vision of sorrow
	Virtue:	Silence
	Tarot cards:	The four threes
	Color:	Crimson
	Magical Image:	A mature woman

4. Chesed	Experience:	The vision of love
	Virtue:	Obedience
	Tarot cards:	The four fours
	Color:	Deep violet
	Magical Image:	A mighty crowned and throned king

5. Geburah	Experience:	The vision of power
	Virtue:	Courage
	Tarot cards:	The four fives
	Color:	Orange
	Magical Image:	Almighty warrior in his chariot

6. Tiphareth	Experience:	The vision of harmony
	Virtue:	Devotion to great work
	Tarot cards:	The four sixes
	Color:	Clear rose-pink
	Magical Image:	A majestic king, a child, a sacrificed god

7. Netzach	Experience:	The vision of beauty triumphant
	Virtue:	Unselfishness
	Tarot cards:	The four sevens
	Color:	Amber
	Magical Image:	A beautiful naked woman

8. Hod	Experience:	The vision of surrender
	Virtue:	Truthfulness
	Tarot cards:	The four eights
	Color:	Violet/purple
	Magical Image:	A hermaphrodite

9. Yesod	Experience:	The vision of the machinery of the universe
	Virtue:	Independence
	Tarot cards:	The four nines
	Color:	Indigo
	Magical Image:	A beautiful, naked, strong man

10. Malkuth	Experience:	The vision of holy guardian angel
	Virtue:	Discrimination
	Tarot cards:	The four tens
	Color:	Yellow
	Magical Image:	A young woman, crowned and throned

The Three-Dimensional Tree of Life

The diagram labeled 51-5 is from an old Theosophical book. I include it here not for intellectual purposes but rather for right-brained, aesthetic purposes. I cannot even begin to conceptualize what the meaning of a three-dimensional Tree of Life would be. Here is a meditation for the advanced students of Kabbalah, for sure.

Jacob's Ladder and the Hidden Sephiroth

Djwhal Khul has added to the Tree of Life an understanding that has to do with adding rungs, or overlaying a second Tree of Life on the already existing one, as in Diagram 51-6. This has been esoterically termed "climbing Jacob's ladder." It is done by moving the second tree one step upward from the previous one in terms of the ten Sephiroth. This diagram, from a book put out by The Tibetan Foundation and channeled by Janet McClure, called *Cabala*, clearly illustrates the process.

As you see, Malkuth, at the bottom of the first tree, has now moved up and overlies the Sephiroth of Yesod, with all the other Sephiroth on the new tree being raised up in a corresponding fashion.

The diagram shows the twelve rays and their corresponding Sephiroth. It is only when the new Tree of Life is added that rays eleven and twelve find a home, since there are only ten Sephiroth on the first Tree of Life. This causes a very interesting thing to happen. Yesod, in the first tree, is now raised to the level of Tiphareth. This is the personality merging with

the soul consciousness, or Christ consciousness. Tiphareth, in the first
Tree of Life, is now raised to the hidden Sephiroth of Daath. Daath has
been associated with hidden knowledge; in other words, the soul is raised
into the hidden knowledge. Daath, according to Djwhal Khul, is activated
only in the enlarged, evolutionary Tree of Life. To work with Daath, a
person must be approaching the third, or soul merge, initiation.

Geburah, in the first Tree of Life, is now raised to Binah. Logical
thinking is hence raised to divine will. Netzach is raised to Chesed;
personality-level feelings are raised to the unconditional love and compassion of Chesed. Geburah and Chesed move to Binah and Chokmah, the
soul level of experience now being raised to the monadic, or spiritual, level
of consciousness at the fifth and sixth levels of initiation.

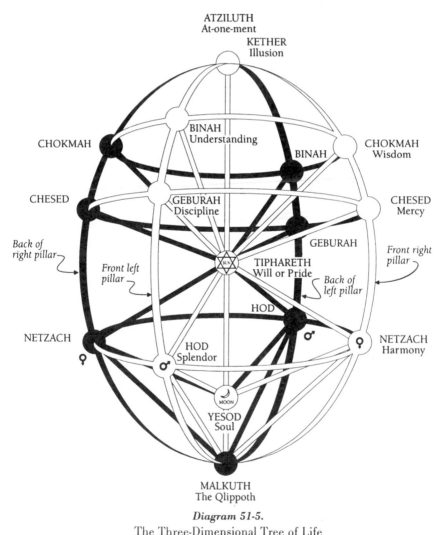

Diagram 51-5.
The Three-Dimensional Tree of Life

As you can see, there is endless material here for your contemplation. I am just providing skeletal basics for your continued study. The four books I recommend studying if you would like to learn more are *Cabala* by Janet McClure; *The Mystical Quabalah*, an incredible book by Dion Fortune, which might be the best book ever written on the subject; *Kabbalah, Your Path to Inner Freedom* by Ann Williams-Heller; and *The Book of Knowledge: The Keys of Enoch* by J.J. Hurtak. I am indebted to these authors for much of the material in this chapter.

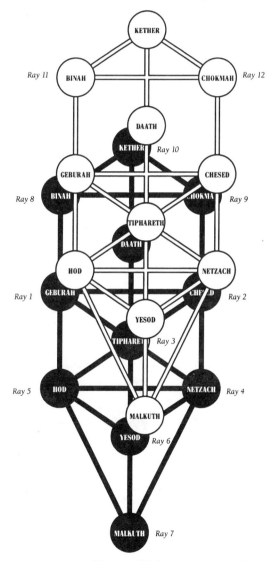

Diagram 51-6.
Climbing Jacob's Ladder: the Ray Correspondences

Summation

The Kabbalah embodies the true wisdom teachings of Israel; it might be considered "the Yoga of the West." It provides the foundation for modern Western occultism. The Tree of Life is an excellent meditation symbol for understanding the spiritual path. It reduces to a diagrammatic form every force and factor in the manifested universe that the monad, soul, and personality must deal with and balance. It is a spiritual map. It might be looked at as a dream symbol of the universal mind, a picture arising from the subconscious mind of God.

The tree applies not only to the macrocosm but also to the microcosm. Each individual symbol of the tree represents a cosmic force you can get in touch with through meditation. The Tree of Life as a whole is a composite symbol that represents the cosmos in its entirety and the soul of man as he relates to it. May it bring you many hours of beautiful meditation on the divine during your journey home.

52

The Keys of Enoch

*Kodoish, Kodoish, Kodoish Adonai Tsabayoth
Holy, Holy, Holy is the Lord God of Hosts.*

The *Book of Knowledge: The Keys of Enoch* is not a channeling of God, it is a revelation of God. It is truly one of the most profound books I have ever studied. It is not my purpose here to explain *The Keys of Enoch*, for that is beyond what can be taught. My purpose here is, rather, to give you a brief introduction to this profound teaching brought forth by J.J. Hurtak.

On the title page of *The Keys of Enoch*, the following inscription is found: "A teaching given on seven levels to be read and visualized in preparation for the Brotherhood of Light, to be delivered for the quickening of the people of Light."

The Keys of Enoch is not a spiritual self-help book but more like a science book of the metaphysical universe. It is a book that is best read as much with your right brain as with your left brain in order to facilitate an intuitive grasp of the material. I recommend reading the introduction and the glossary before attempting to read the actual text. I also recommend putting it under your pillow or mattress as you sleep at night so you can soak in the profound teachings on a subconscious level. I do not claim to be an expert on the keys, but I have read the book, which is no easy task, and I am constantly drawn back to it, feeling the desire to refer to it often.

The Keys of Enoch also serves as a wonderful reference book. It is especially good for those people who are drawn to the teachings of the Kabbalah and Jewish mysticism, for it is written from that cosmic vantage point. It is, however, universal in nature.

The sixty-four keys of Enoch were revealed to J.J. Hurtak in a profound out-of-body, soul travel experience. Hurtak was sitting in his room in a state of prayer when his room became filled with Light and the Ascended Master Ophanim Enoch appeared. Enoch asked Hurtak whether he was ready to go into the Father's midst, and he said he was. A great field of Light was placed around his body, and they immediately left in their soul bodies.

He was first taken through a region of stars known as Merak and Muscida and then up through the midway station of Arcturus. It was after this that Hurtak had to exchange his current body for a garment of Light, the vibration was so high. He was then guided up into what was referred to as the seventh heaven. It was here that he saw the elohim masters. He was then taken through the star field of Oronis and up through a field of Light called Mintaka, where he met the Archangel Metatron, the creator of the electronic outer Light in this physical universe. The Light was of such a high frequency that Hurtak would have been overwhelmed without Meta-tron's help.

Metatron then took Hurtak into the presence of the Divine Father. This was done by traveling through the spiritual door of Omega Orion, which served as a grand entrance to regions of pure energy. It was here that Hurtak said he saw the face of the Ancient of Days, the Divine Father, face to face. He described His throne as a pyramid of living Light. The Divine Father had flowing white hair, and His face was filled with overwhelming joy and love. He referred to the Divine Father as YHWH, and around Him Hurtak saw the twenty-four Elders of Light who were singing "Kodoish, Kodoish, Kodoish, Adonai Tsabayoth" (Holy, Holy, Holy is the Lord God of Hosts).

On the right hand of the Father, he saw Jesus Christ. Hurtak was told that his own work was part of the work of Enoch. He was also told that the time was at hand for the externalization of the Father's Hierarchy so that His kingdom will come to be on Earth as it is in Heaven.

Hurtak was then taken to many other regions of God's universe for instruction. While still at the throne, however, he saw a burning scroll that was rolled up into a cylinder. Out of this scroll a Light was projected into Hurtak's third eye; it embodied the sixty-four keys of Enoch, the basis for this sublime book.

The purpose of the keys, in part, is to make the Earth ready for the descent of the Melchizedek Brotherhood and for the descent of the one hundred forty-four thousand ascended masters who will help to redeem the meek and righteous of the Earth. Hurtak was shown how the seventy Brotherhoods of Light on the inner plane serve as a field of intelligence for the repairing of the universes so that they can evolve into the infinite wisdom and glory of the Eternal Mind of YHWH (God). Each key is encoded in fire letters so that a new spectrum of Light can biochemically respatialize humanity by activating the chemistry in the mind so that it can participate in the many dimensions of the reality of God.

Having received this vision, Hurtak returned to the Earth plane to write the words and information he had received into *The Book of Knowledge.*

The purpose of the sixty-four keys given by Enoch and Metatron is to help coordinate the sixty-four unique areas of scientific knowledge that are now being simultaneously advanced. Hurtak says that the keys have been given to assist all of the basic scientific disciplines in making a quantum leap forward into the new consciousness of Light. The keys are to focus scientific research on the planet with respect to the larger blueprint of life.

Hurtak was also told that to be able to work the keys, you must be able to go into the fourth dimension. Here the intellect must bow to the spiritual mind. Enoch also said that the keys are not only for this planet but have been given in preparation for work with other planets as well.

The actual keys were given on January 23, 1973, to prepare human-kind for the activation of events taking place in the thirty years leading up to the year 2003. They were given to Hurtak in an out-of-body experience on the higher spiritual planes so that they would not be contaminated by the fallen thought forms of collective humanity. The keys were given in a special sequence that allows them to connect mathematically with one another so as to explain the interpretation of universes and how spiritual intelligence works through the keys.

Enoch said the first fifty-four keys are the foundation for the ten commandments. The final ten keys contain the grid system of life and provide for the resurrection and respatialization of the collective humanity that will proceed into the universal I Am That I Am.

Summation

The purpose of this chapter is to give you a little taste of this revelation of God so as to inspire you to buy or borrow the book and work with it yourself in whatever way you are guided to. It is very difficult to read; however, don't let that stop you.

As I have already said, just reading the introduction, the glossary, and the sixty-four keys makes buying the book worthwhile, in my opinion. If you go on to read the book, approach it in advance with your right-brained, intuitive self, and you won't be overwhelmed.

I did a very interesting meditation with the keys of Enoch which I recommend that you try. After going into a deep meditation, call forth Helios, the Solar Logos, to anchor the sixty-four keys of Enoch into your consciousness in all five sacred languages. All you have to do is ask for this and it will be done on the subtle, inner-plane level. Then when you read the keys, the information in your subconscious mind will be triggered.

53

The Mighty I Am Presence

I am the resurrection and the life.

Jesus Christ's favorite affirmation,
according to Saint Germain

Of the many teachings and systems of spiritual study I have been involved with, one of the most interesting and useful is the "I Am" teachings of Saint Germain. *The I AM Discourses* are books that were channeled by Godfre Ray King in the 1930s and 1940s.

Godfre Ray King was trained as a channel and he brought forth from Saint Germain, and later from other ascended masters, beautiful teachings. My personal orientation is more closely in alignment with Djwhal Khul's teachings through the Theosophical Society, the Alice Bailey books, and The Tibetan Foundation. However, I find that the Saint Germain teachings dovetail perfectly with that material.

The teachings are simple and nondenominational. I believe that Saint Germain purposely wrote these books in a simple manner so the average person could read and understand them without being overwhelmed by massive amounts of occult information such as was presented in the Theosophical literature. I do not say this to criticize the Theosophical material, for I have benefitted greatly from it, but it is an obvious fact that many of the books are extremely difficult to read. The I Am teachings are just the opposite; they don't overwhelm the reader with a lot of Eastern or religious terminology.

The basic concept of the I Am teachings of Saint Germain is that the most powerful name of God in this world is the name I Am. When Moses climbed Mount Sinai to speak with God and saw the burning bush, God told him that his name was I Am That I Am.

Any time you use the words "I Am," you are affirming God's name and your own. When you say, "I am going to the store," you are really saying, "God is going to the store," without even realizing it.

Saint Germain and the other ascended masters suggest that whenever you make affirmations you use the words "I Am" to begin them. For example, I could say, "I Am the ascended master I wish to be now." The affirmation becomes much more powerful when you use the words "I Am." Saint Germain said that Jesus Christ's favorite affirmation was, "I Am the resurrection and the life!" He apparently used this affirmation often during his life in Palestine.

The following affirmations are from *The I AM Discourses* by Godfre Ray King, exactly as Saint Germain and the ascended masters channeled them. I highly recommend that you choose your favorite ones from the list and use them every day. I also recommend that you read the books by Godfre Ray King. Other teachings have followed in more recent times, but these were the first and in my opinion they are the purest. There are also I AM foundations and organizations in many locations such as Mount Shasta and Los Angeles.

I AM Affirmations of Saint Germain through Godfre Ray King

Be still and know I Am God!

I Am God living in this body as (your name).

I Am a fully liberated God living in this body as (your name).

I Am the Mighty I Am Presence!

I Am the Ascended Master (your name)!

In the name of the Beloved Presence of God, who I Am.

By the power of God, who I Am.

The Mighty I Am Presence is my real self!

I Am the resurrection and the life.

I Am the truth, the way and the life.

I Am the embodiment of divine love.

I Am the open door which no man can shut.

I Am God in action!

I Am the Scepter of Dominion, the Quenchless Flame, the Dazzling Light and Divine Perfection made manifest!

I Am the revelation of God.

I Am the baptism of the Holy Spirit.

I Am the ascended being I wish to be now.

I Am the realization of God.

I Am an open door to all revelation.

I Am the Light that lights up every room I enter.

I Am the Presence of God in action this day.

I Am That I Am!

I Am the eternal liberation from all human imperfection.

I Am a perfect channel and instrument of God.

I Am the presence filling my world with perfection this day.

I Am an invincible body of Light.

I Am the Light that lights every man that comes into the world.

I Am the victory in the Light!

Forgive them, Father, they know not what they do.

I Am the cosmic flame of cosmic victory!

The second basic concept of the I Am teachings is that of the Mighty I Am Presence. The Mighty I Am Presence is the first individualized spiritual spark that God created. In the Alice Bailey books and Djwhal Khul's Tibetan Foundation material, this was referred to as the monad.

Moses called this spark the I Am That I Am. In the beginning, God created trillions of monads, individual sparks of God, I Am Presences. When you pray to God, Saint Germain suggests in these books that you pray to the Mighty I Am Presence. I like the sound of it. In some ways I feel more comfortable praying to my Mighty I Am Presence than to my monad, although I use both terms, as they are interchangeable. When I say the words "my Mighty I Am Presence," I get a surge of power and energy that I really like.

Saint Germain and the ascended masters, as channeled through Godfre Ray King, strongly recommend that throughout your day, you pray and call to your Mighty I Am Presence for help.

The basic spiritual law of the universe is that God, spirit, and the ascended masters are not allowed to help you unless you ask for help. They are not allowed to impinge upon your free will or free choice. They desperately want to help and are just waiting for your request.

Spiritual Prayers

The following are some examples of Mighty I Am Presence prayers, as channeled by Godfre Ray King. I think you will find them very powerful.

Mighty I Am Presence! Charge my entire mind, emotions, and body with thy ascended master consciousness and keep it eternally sustained and all-powerfully active.

Mighty I Am Presence! I call you into action to charge your cosmic flame of cosmic victory into my thoughts, emotions, body, and world and wipe out all else!

Mighty I Am Presence! Take out of my feeling-world every single thing that seems to obstruct the way and release of your mighty, intelligent energy to go forth and produce the perfect results I desire!

Mighty I Am Presence! I call you into action to take dominion over my thoughts, feelings, emotions, body, home, world, and daily activities. Produce your perfection and hold your dominion!

Mighty I Am Presence! Take my love and let it flow in fullness and devotion to thee. Take my hands and let them work incessantly for thee. Take my soul and let it be merged in oneness with thee. Take my mind and thoughts and let them be in tune with thee. Take my everything and let me be an instrument of thy work.

Mighty I Am Presence! Take complete control of my being, world, and activity. See that I make my ascension in this embodiment, for I Am the resurrection, the truth, and the life! I Am the ascension in the Light!

Mighty I Am Presence! Charge, intensify, and expand your cosmic flame of cosmic victory around me. See that I feel naught but your ascended master victory.

Mighty I Am Presence! I call you forth to place around me the cosmic armor of the cosmic flame of cosmic victory!

Mighty I Am Presence! I face thy eternal sunrise and receive thy mighty radiance and activity visibly manifest in my experience now.

Mighty I Am Presence! Consume and dissolve in me all negative, egotistical qualities, their cause, effect, record, and memory, and replace them with the fullness of thy perfected spiritual qualities.

Mighty I Am Presence! Come forth and charge my being and world every second of this day and forevermore with ascended master perfection.

Mighty I Am Presence! Charge me so full of divine love that every person, place, condition, and thing I contact becomes instantly harmonious and obedient to the I Am Presence.

Mighty I Am Presence! See that this home and environment and all connected with them are governed harmoniously and that all who enter manifest only ascended master consciousness and activity.

Mighty I Am Presence! Fill me with your divine love, power, and perfect intelligent direction.

Mighty I Am Presence! Charge me and my world with the violet consuming flame of divine love which consumes all that is undesirable, and keep me clothed forever with thy almighty perfection.

Mighty I Am Presence! Consume in me and my world all doubt, fear, jealousy, pride, resentment, irritation, criticism, condemnation, and judgment and their cause, effect, record, and memory, replacing them with the fullness of the perfection which thou art, keeping it self-sustained in the ever-expanding Light of thy glorious presence.

Mighty I Am Presence! Descend into this, thy mind and body. Take full conscious control this instant of all its activities and hold thy dominion and victory here forever.

Mighty I Am Presence, come forth! Charge my being and world with that Light and love as of a thousand suns, and crowd my path with showers and showers of Mighty I Am Presence! Take complete possession of my attention and fill it entire with thyself!

Mighty I Am Presence! Protect me from the human suggestions of the outer world that I may go forth accepting only thy mighty self and thy perfection forever.

Mighty I Am Presence! Move everywhere before me today and do all for me and through me perfectly!

I feel deep gratitude to Godfre Ray King for his work in channeling these prayers and affirmations; I strongly recommend reading *The I AM Discourses*.

54

Sufism

*Prayer carries us halfway to Allah;
fasting takes us to the door of His palace; charity
gains us admission.*

Sufi scripture

Sufism began a century later than Islam as a struggle against the increasing distortions of the teachings of Islam. Sufism is very much a
part of Islam, but it represents the mystical aspects of the faith. Sufism
appeals to those who are interested in inner knowledge, inner awakening,
and enlightenment. It is a path of self-purification and purification of the
heart.

You might have heard of or participated in Sufi dancing, a group dance
that creates harmony and oneness through its designed movements.
Sufism has also been called a means of adopting every higher quality and
leaving lower qualities behind. It is a method of learning to behave in order
to be always in tune with and in harmony with Allah. It is concerned with
personal and universal courtesy. Sufi teaching emphasizes right relationship between man and Allah. It accepts the teachings of Mohammed and
begins with the following of Islamic law. However, Sufism goes beyond the
Islamic practices of following the outer law and attempts to go much
deeper. It aims to bring about the development of the whole person.

Since its inception, Sufism has often been denounced by the scholars
and leaders of traditional Islam, which has led to a great deal of persecution. Many different orders of Sufism have evolved, all of them more
oriented toward inner development and the unseen world than is traditional Islam.

Muslims take the outer laws very seriously and don't think the outer world should be renounced; Sufis attempt to achieve inner contentment in all situations and circumstances, teaching need for detachment and the surrendering of all material desire. Their focus is on that which is permanent — spiritual reality — rather than on the impermanence of the material world. Difficulties are seen as blessings, for they facilitate awakening. They see self-knowledge as the most difficult and most essential of all subjects for any human being to study.

Sufism could also be described as liberal Islam with a coloring of Vedanta. The Sufi mystic sees God in all people and in all objects. The Sufi mystic is free of all egoism, lust, greed, anger, and pride. The Sufi mystic consecrates all his acts to the unity of God, the brotherhood of man, and surrender to the Lord. The Sufi wants to stay very much in the world but to be above worldliness. The Sufi strives for absolute beauty, absolute love, and absolute bliss at all times.

The Sufi path is one of annihilation of the lower self and negative ego. The spiritual practices consist of concentration, meditation, obedience to a guru, poverty, discipline, fasting, doing penance, reciting the name of the Lord, using a rosary, rhythmic and controlled breathing, prayer, universal love, nonviolence, detachment, introspection, dispassion, purity of heart, and self-control with the goal of attaining union with God.

Quotations from Sufi Scripture

Prayer carries us halfway to Allah; fasting takes us to the door of His palace; charity gains us admission.

He needs no other rosary whose thread of life is strung with beads of love, service, charity, and renunciation.

Happy are the believers who humble themselves in prayer and who keep aloof from vain words, who do charitable acts, and who restrain their appetites.

Do good, because God loveth those who do good.

I recommend Shaykh F. Haeri's book, *Sufism*, if you are interested in additional details.

55

Shinto: the Way of the Gods

Even the wishes of an ant reach Heaven.

Shinto saying

Shinto means "the Way of the Gods" or "the God-like Way." It has been a path of worship in Japan since time immemorial. It is an all-pervading, indefinable way.

Shintoism is a religion of the heart. It permeates Japanese culture, family ethics, and national structure. It is the chief source of regeneration and revitalization for the social and religious life of Japan. It has a quality of being polytheistic because of the multitude of gods that are worshiped, but the Sun God, Amaterasu-omi Kami, is the Supreme Highest.

According to Shinto theology, Ame-no-mi-naka-nushi is the absolute Universal Self. The visible universe is Ken Kai. The invisible world is Yu Kai. Both of these have come into being from Ame-no-mi-naka-nushi and three subdieties.

Fundamental to this structure of the universe is absolute loyalty to the sovereign emperor who is regarded as a direct descendant and representative of the highest God. Also fundamental is respect for ancestors and love and respect for parents and children.

Purity is one of the most important ethics of Shintoism. It is broken down into outer purity, or purity of the body, and inner purity, or purity of the heart. A person with inner purity is seen as being able to attain God-realization. Another strong guiding principle is that of sincerity. There are ten main precepts, or ideals, in Shintoism:

1. Do not transgress the will of the gods.
2. Do not forget your obligation to ancestors.
3. Do not offend by violating the decrees of the state.

4.   Do not forget the profound goodness of the gods, through which calamity and misfortunes are averted and sickness is healed.

5.   Do not forget that the world is one great family.

6.   Do not forget the limitation of your own person.

7.   Do not become angry even though others become angry.

8.   Do not be sluggish in your work.

9.   Do not bring blame to the teachings.

10. Do not be carried away by foreign teachings.

One of the common Shinto prayers reads as follows: "Our eyes may see some uncleanliness, but let not our minds see things that are not clean. Our ears may hear some uncleanliness, but let not our minds hear things that are not clean."

Shinto Quotations

The heart of the person before you is a mirror. See there your own form.

Even the wishes of an ant reach to Heaven.

Leave the things of this world and come to me daily with your bodies and pure hearts.

A single sincere prayer moves Heaven. You will surely realize the Divine Presence through sincere prayer.

Where you have sincerity, there also is virtue. Sincerity is a witness to truth. Sincerity is the mother of knowledge. Sincerity is a single virtue that binds divinity and man in one.

Retribution for good or ill is as sure as the shadow after substance.

To do good is to be pure. To commit evil is to be impure.

To admit a fault is the beginning of righteousness.

The first and surest means to enter into communion with the Divine is sincerity. If you pray to a deity with sincerity, you will surely feel the Divine Presence.

56

Baha'i: The World's Newest Religion

All races and religions are one.

Bahaullah

One of the world's most recently established religions is called Baha'i. It is a worldwide religion of Iranian origin which holds to the belief that its teacher, Bahaullah, is the prophet of God for this age. The religion was founded by Bahaullah's teacher, Mirza Ali Mohammed, who lived from 1819 to 1850. Mirza had been involved with Sufism, the mystical aspect of Islam. He became a messiah, or what is called a mahdi, for the Sufis. His title was Bab; the religion he founded was known as Babism. The teachings spread rapidly, but the Persian government heavily persecuted the people involved and Mirza Ali Mohammed died a martyr.

Bahaullah had been his disciple. He declared to his followers that he was the next prophet of god whom Mirza Ali Mohammed had prophesied. The two men are considered cofounders, but Bahaullah represents the full culmination of the revelation.

The Baha'i faith emphasizes the spiritual unity of all humankind — all races and religions are one, and all the founders of all the religions (Jesus, Buddha, Krishna, Zoroaster, Moses, Confucius, Lao-tzu, and so forth) are manifestations and messengers of God. Each prophet is acknowledged as having brought forth from God the message that was needed at that particular time in history. Progressive revelation occurs throughout the centuries. Bahaullah is considered to have brought forth the next dispensation of teachings in a long line of great prophets and world teachers.

The key ideal of the Baha'i faith is to love and serve humanity and to work for universal peace and brotherhood. Any person who lives the teachings is considered to be a Baha'i; that means you could keep your

Christian faith, for example, and still be a Baha'i.

Although Baha'i accepts the existence of an afterworld, the main work is to focus on bringing the kingdom of God to Earth now. The teachings are very Christlike, even though they are not identified with the Christian religion. Baha'i loves and respects all religions, all nations, and all people, who are considered to be of one race, regardless of skin color, creed, or religious affiliation.

Baha'i teaches its followers to be truthful, hospitable, unconditionally loving, prayerful, clean-minded, modest, humble, self-effacing, selfless, patient, self-supporting, and joyous under all conditions. Baha'i also teaches the work ethic, sacrifice, service, enjoyment of Earthly life, acquisition of knowledge, the following of dietary laws, cooperation, equal rights for men and women, and the helping of the poor, sick, and disabled. Adherents are never to hurt others, are always to see the good in others, never the bad, are never to indulge in gambling, narcotics, alcohol, or carnal sexuality but are to be a good example to the community, leading a holy life through obedience to God and God's laws, nonattachment, acceptance, humility, the study of Baha'i writings, being nonjudgmental, turning the other cheek, loving their enemies, and spreading the teachings.

Marriage is encouraged in the Baha'i faith; however, chastity before marriage and absolute faithfulness to your partner are seen as essential.

An interesting concept in the Baha'i faith is the belief in the need for a universal language. The idea is that each country throughout the world would keep its main language but would also learn a second language agreed upon by the world community. This would allow all peoples of all countries to have a common language with which to communicate with the rest of the human race.

Baha'i teaching says true religion and science are always in agreement. In truth, they are two sides of the same coin. The faith concerns itself with social, economic, and political issues, which are not considered separate from religion. It states that society must not permit extremes of wealth or poverty. Bahaullah believed in an economic system based on graduated taxation. When a person was earning just enough to live a comfortable life he or she would not be taxed. The more a person made above his needs, the more he would be taxed. People who were ill or had bad harvests from their farms, for example, were to be helped out, so no human being would be permitted to live below a certain standard.

The Baha'i faith teaches religion without the need for clergy. There is a spiritual assembly that helps to run the community's affairs, but clergy aren't used as mediators between the individual and God.

Divorce is deplored but is permissible. No guilt is attached to it. After separating, Baha'i followers are not supposed to see other members of the opposite sex with a view to remarrying for a period of twelve months. The teachings suggest a need to strive toward reconciliation with one's legal partner during that time. After the waiting period, the spiritual assembly helps to facilitate divorce proceedings if that is what the couple still wants.

Members are encouraged not to become identified with political figures, political parties, or political discussions. The danger is that of creating separation or lack of unity and love among all people. It is considered important to support one's government and not join underground movements that might seek to overthrow those in power. Baha'i youth automatically ask for noncombat status when registering for military service.

All members are required to write a will and testament so as to avoid any possibility of legal problems or family friction. They are expected to educate their children in the Baha'i teachings and also to celebrate the nine Baha'i holy days.

The Baha'i faith is very community-oriented and it is very clear in the teachings that no man is an island unto himself. In terms of an afterlife, death is seen as the release from an outer shell into a new and even more wonderful world of experience. Heaven and hell are seen as states of consciousness, rather than as merely places. The soul, at birth, is seen as the bud of a flower that is waiting to grow. Its own good and bad deeds and thinking will determine whether it blooms or becomes retarded in its growth.

Summation

The three things about the Baha'i faith that stand out for me are the honoring and recognizing of all prophets of God and all religions; the tremendous focus on universal brotherhood among nations, religions, and people of all races, creeds, and colors; and the willingness to deal with the social, political, economic, scientific, and educational issues of the community.

In Western culture, there is a dichotomy of church and state, but religion and all ramifications of Earthly life cannot be separated, in truth. The key is for their integration to take place in a nonbiased, nonegotistical manner. Religion and politics have not been able to achieve this state of consciousness.

The Baha'i faith seems to have taken a giant step in transcending religious bias and in seeking to blend spirituality with some of today's pressing social, political, economic, and scientific problems.

I would like to acknowledge *The Baha'i Faith* by Jessyca R. Gaver as a source of information for this chapter.

For further information,
Dr. Joshua David Stone
can be contacted
through the publisher
or at
5252 Coldwater Canyon, #112
Van Nuys, CA 91410
(818) 769-1181

Bibliography

Anka, Darryl. *Bashar: Blueprint for Change.* Seattle, WA: New Solutions Publishing, 1990.

Bahree, Patricia. *The Hindu World.* Morristown, NH: Silver Burdett Co., 1982.

Bailey, Alice A. *Problems of Humanity.* New York: Lucis Publishing Co., 1993.

——. *The Light of the Soul.* New York: Lucis Publishing Co., 1988.

Bassano, Mary. *Healing with Music and Color.* York Beach, ME: Samuel Weiser, 1992.

Beaulieu, John. *Music and Sound in the Healing Arts.* Barrytown, NY: Station Hill Press, 1987.

Beesley, Ronald P. *Yoga of the Inward Path.* Marina del Rey, CA: DeVorss, 1978.

Bernard, Dr. Raymond. *The Hollow Earth.* New York: Citadel Press, 1969.

Bittleson, Adam. *Our Spiritual Companions.* Edinburgh: Floris Books, 1980.

Blavatsky, Helena P. *The Secret Doctrine.* Wheaton, IL: Theosophical Publishing House, 1993.

Cayce, Edgar. *Edgar Cayce on Atlantis.* New York: Warner Books, 1988.

Chaney, Earlyne. *Beyond Tomorrow.* Upland, CA: Astara, 1985.

——. *Initiation in the Great Pyramid.* Upland, CA: Astara, 1987.

——. *Revelations of Things to Come.* Upland, CA: Astara, 1982.

Cheney, Margaret. *Tesla: Man Out of Time.* New York: Bantam Doubleday, 1981.

Cooper, William Milton. *Behold a Pale Horse.* Sedona, AZ: Light Technology Publishing, 1991.

Daniel, Alma, et al. *Ask Your Angels!* New York: Ballantine Books, 1994.

Danielou, Alain. *Yoga.* Rochester, VT: Inner Traditions International, 1990.

Denaerde, Stefan, and Stevens, Wendelle C. *UFO: Contact from Planet Iarga.* Tucson, AZ: Wendelle C. Stevens, 1982.

Easwaran, Eknath. *The Bhagavad-Gita.* Petaluma, CA: Nilgiri Press, 1987.

——. *The Upanishads.* Petaluma, CA: Nilgiri Press, 1985

Elkins, Don; Rueckert, Carla; and McCarty, James A. *The Ra Material: An Ancient Astronaut Speaks.* West Chester, PA: Whitford Press, 1984.

Emerson, Willis George. *The Smoky God: A Voyage to the Inner World.* Mokelumne, CA: Mokelumne Hill Press, 1965.

Feuerstein, George. *Sacred Paths.* Burdett, NY: Larson Publications, 1991.

Findhorn Community. *The Findhorn Garden.* New York: HarperCollins, 1976.

Fortune, Dion. *The Mystical Qabalah.* York Beach, ME: Samuel Weiser, 1984.

Fry, Daniel, and Telano, Rolf. *The White Sands Incident.* Boscobel, WI: Horus House Press, 1992.

Gardner, Edward L. *Fairies.* Wheaton, IL: Theosophical Publishing House, 1983.

Gaver, Jessyca R. *The Baha'i Faith.* New York: Award Books, 1967.

Goelitz, Jeffrey. *Secrets from the Lives of Trees.* Boulder Creek, CA: Planetary Publications, 1991.

Goldman, Karen. *The Angel Book.* New York: Simon & Schuster, 1988.

Grant, Joan. *The Winged Pharaoh.* Alpharetta, GA: Ariel Press, 1985.

Haeri, Shaykh F. *Sufism.* Dorset, England: Element Books, 1990.

Haich, Elisabeth. *Initiation.* Palo Alto, CA: Seed Center, 1974.

Hall, Manley P. *The Secret Teachings of All Ages.* Los Angeles: Philosophical Research Society, 1978.

Harary, Keith. *Have an Out-of-Body Experience in 30 Days.* New York: St. Martin's Press, 1989.

Hawken, Paul. *The Magic of Findhorn.* New York: Harper & Row, 1975.

Heline, Corinne. *Color and Music in the New Age.* Marina del Rey, CA: DeVorss & Co., 1981.

Hodson, Geoffrey. *The Brotherhood of Angels and of Men.* Wheaton, IL: Theosophical Publishing House, 1982.

Katz, Ginny. *Gifts of the Gemstone Guardians.* Portland, OR: Golden Age Publishing, 1989.

Khul, Djwhal. *The Cabala.* Out of print.

King, Godfre R. *Unveiled Mysteries.* Schaumburg, IL: St. Germain Press, 1982.

———. *Ascended Master Light.* Out of print.

———. *The I AM Discourses.* Out of print.

Kirkwood, Annie. *Mary's Message to the World.* Nevada City, CA: Blue Dolphin Publishing, 1991.

Kittler, Glenn D.. *Edgar Cayce on the Dead Sea Scrolls.* New York: Warner Books, 1970.

Laberge, Stephen. *Lucid Dreaming.* New York: Ballantine, 1986.

Lawrence, Brother. *The Practice of the Presence of God.* Springfield, IL: Templegate, 1974.

Levi. *The Aquarian Gospel of Jesus Christ.* Marina del Rey, CA: DeVorss & Co., 1972.

Long, Max Freedom. *The Secret Science at Work.* Marina del Rey, CA: DeVorss & Co., 1953.

———. *The Secret Science Behind Miracles.* Marina del Rey, CA: DeVorss & Co., 1948.

———. *Growing into Light.* Marina del Rey, CA: DeVorss & Co., 1955.

———. *Huna Code in Religions.* Marina del Rey, CA: DeVorss & Co., 1965.

———. *Self-Suggestion.* Marina del Rey, CA: DeVorss & Co., 1958.

———. *Psychometric Analysis.* Marina del Rey, CA: DeVorss & Co., 1959.

Milanovich, Dr. Norma J. *We, the Arcturians.* Albuquerque, NM: Athena Publishing, 1990.

Montgomery, Ruth. *Alienss Among Us.* New York: Fawcett Crest, 1979.

Newhouse, Flower A. *Rediscovering the Angels and Natives of Eternity.* Escondido, CA: Christward Ministry, 1966.

Ossendowski, Ferdinand. *Beasts, Men and Gods.* New York: Gordon Press Publications, 1991.

Printz, Thomas. *The Seven Mighty Elohim Speak.* Mt. Shasta, CA: Ascended Master Teaching Foundation, 1986.

Purchit, Swami. *The Geeta.* London: Faber & Faber, 1935.

Ribera, Antonio. *UFO: Contact from Planet Ummo.* Tucson, AZ: Wendelle C. Stevens, 1985.

Robbins, John. *Diet for a New America.* Walpole, NH: Stillpoint Publishing, 1987.

Robinson, Lytle. *Edgar Cayce's Story of the Origin and Destiny of Man.* New York: Berkley Publishing Group, 1983.

Rodriguez-Montiel, Zithe, and Hernandez, R.N. *UFO: Contact from Andromeda.* Tucson, AZ: Wendelle C. Stevens, 1988.

Roeder, Dorothy. *The Next Dimension Is Love.* Sedona, AZ: Light Technology Publishing, 1993.

Royal, Lyssa, and Priest, Keith. *The Prism of Lyra.* Scottsdale, AZ: Royal Priest Research, 1992.

——. *Visitors From Within.* Scottsdale, AZ: Royal Priest Research, 1992.

Sedona Journal of Emergence. Sedona, AZ: Love Light Communications, Inc.

Sen, K.M. *Hinduism.* London: Penguin Books, 1961.

Singh, Isbar. *The Philosophy of Guru Nanak.* New Delhi, India: Atlantic Publishers, 1987.

Sivananda, Swami. *The Practice of Yoga.* India: Divine Life Society, 1984.

Stearn, Jess. *Edgar Cayce: The Sleeping Prophet.* New York: Bantam Books, 1967.

Steckling, Fred. *We Discovered Alien Bases on the Moon.* Vista, CA: GAF International, 1981.

Steiger, Brad, and Hansen, Sherry. *Starborn.* New York: Berkeley Books, 1992.

Stevens, Wendelle C. *UFO: Contact from the Pleiades.* Tucson, AZ: Wendelle C. Stevens, 1978.

——. *UFO: Contact from Andromeda.* Tucson, AZ: Wendelle C. Stevens, 1978.

Stranges, Dr. Frank E. *The UFO Conspiracy.* Van Nuys, CA: I.E.C. Publishing, 1985.

——. *Stranger at the Pentagon.* Van Nuys, CA: I.E.C. Publishing, 1991.

Szekely, Edmond B. *The Essene Gospel of Peace.* London: Int. Biogenic Soc., 1978.

——. *From Enoch to the Dead Sea Scrolls.* London: Int. Biogenic Soc., 1981.

Temple, Robert K.G. *The Sirius Mystery.* Rochester, VT: Inner Traditions, 1987.

Twitchell, Paul. *Eckankar: The Key to Secret Worlds.* Minneapolis, MN: Eckankar, 1969.

Tuella. *Ashtar: A Tribute.* Salt Lake City, UT: Guardian Action Int., 1980.

The Urantia Book. Chicago: Urantia Foundation, 1955.

Valerian, Valdimar. *Matrix I; Matrix II; Matrix III.* Yelm, WA: Leading Edge Research.

Williams-Heller, Ann. *Kabbalah: Your Path to Inner Freedom.* Wheaton, IL: Quest Books, 1990.

Wingo, E. Otha. *Huna: Twelve-Lesson Correspondence Course.* Marina del Ray, CA: DeVorss & Co., 1955

Wright, Machaelle Small. *MAP: The Co-Creative White Brotherhood Assistance Program.* Jeffersonton, VA: Perelandra, Ltd., 1994.

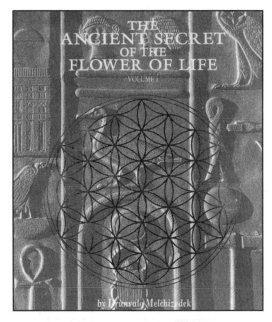

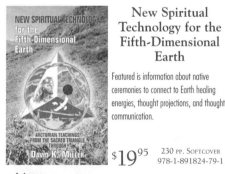

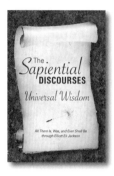

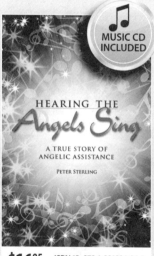

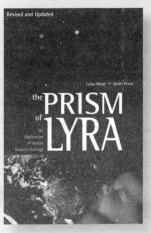

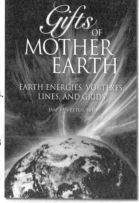

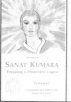

The Books of Jasmuheen

Ambassadors of Light

In this book, Jasmuheen offers practical solutions to world health and world hunger challenges through her Luscious Lifestyles Program and also effective ways to redirect global resources. This entails an in-depth look at global disarmament, the dissolution of prohibition, the forgiveness of Third World debt, holistic education programs, and the elimination of the need for personal pharmaceutical use through the elimination of all disease.

$16.95 | ISBN 13: 978-3-929512-70-0 | Softcover: 253 PP

Harmonious Healing and the Immortal's Way

This book details Jasmuheen's personal healing journey and includes information on the magic of meditation, plus pragmatic tools to reenergize and find the perfect program for healing. Today one in four adults dies unnecessarily from one of the seven deadly diseases. Perhaps this is due to a lack of holistic education, or perhaps it is just that person's time to die. But how do we know if what we are facing is our checkout time or just a life challenge?

$16.95 | ISBN 13: 978-1-891824-59-3 | Softcover: 194 PP

In Resonance

This book is a manual for personal self-empowerment and self-mastery. It is filled with inspirational information of experiential research and channeled guidance from Jasmuheen and the Ascended Ones. *In Resonance* offers practical tools utilizing specific programming techniques and tuning, and mind mastery for reality creation and creating a purposeful and passionate existence. It addresses issues from meditation to telepathy and the universal laws.

$24.95 | ISBN 13: 978-3-929512-36-6 | Hardcover: 312 PP

JUDITH K. MOORE

Crop Circles Revealed

Language of the Light Symbols

By Barbara Lamb and Judith K. Moore

Welcome to the world of crop circles, one of the most TANTALIZING phenomena in the world today. It is difficult not to be captivated by their beauty and complexity and by the questions and issues they provoke, including one that becomes more pressing everyday—what other INTELLIGENT life forms are out there trying to communicate with us.

$25⁰⁰

308 PP. SOFTCOVER
978-1-891824-32-6

A New Formula for Creation

Enak-Kee-Na and Laiolin through Judith K. Moore

What do I think? Wow! It's definitely a mind-expanding experience. I can only imagine how it must have stretched Judith during the 'birthing' process. Perhaps the holographic message within this book will finally generate the 'critical mass' necessary to elevate human thinking above the egocentric mind control still so prevalent today. One way or another, a new age is dawning! This book admirably reminds us that that drawing extends far beyond just the refreshment of our patient little Mother Earth. —Dr. Edwin M. Young

$16⁹⁵

214 PP. SOFTCOVER
978-1-891824-57-9

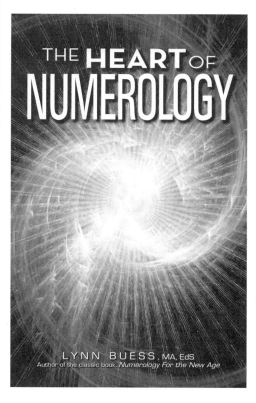

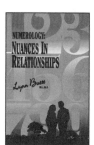

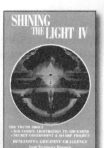

HUMANITY'S GREATEST CHALLENGE

The fourth installment of the series tells of the incredible vehicle traveling with the Hale-Bopp Comet—four times the size of Earth and filled with lightbeings. The book also covers the Montauk project, the HAARP project, and the uncreation of Hitler. Here are forty-nine more chapters in the ongoing process of shining the light on history as it happens—the real truth behind the scenes.

$14.95, 557 PP. Softcover
ISBN 13: 978-0-929385-93-8

HUMANITY IS GOING TO MAKE IT!

Zoosh and others blast the cover off past events and hidden forces at work on this planet and reveal opportunities for immense growth and power. This is a pivotal time as the secrets and mysteries that have long bewildered humanity are at last illuminated by the light of truth.

$14.95, 320 PP. Softcover
ISBN 13: 978-1-891824-00-5

THE END OF WHAT WAS . . .

In this book, the mentors of humanity continue to expose the Sinister Secret Government's nefarious dealings, but they give us step-by-step instructions in the ancient and lost arts of benevolent magic—spiritual wizardry. This enables us as creators in training to blend our hearts, minds, and souls to become creators of our own destinies and thwart the Sinister Secret Government's goals.

$14.95, 316 PP. Softcover
ISBN 13: 978-1-891824-24-1

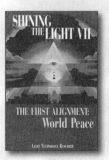

THE FIRST ALIGNMENT: WORLD PEACE

This edition focuses on the first alignment and what we can do to bring light and benevolence to humanity and Mother Earth. The objective is to move through—not jump over—the impossible solutions that have no logical means to explain them. In other words, the solution is located directly in the continuity of your immortal personalities.

$24.95, 532 PP. Softcover
ISBN 13: 978-1-891824-56-2

SHINING THE LIGHT BOOK SERIES
THROUGH ROBERT SHAPIRO

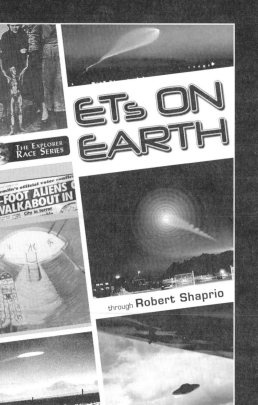

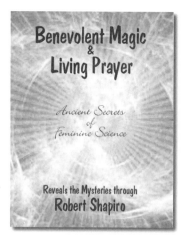

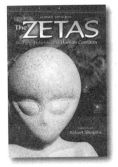

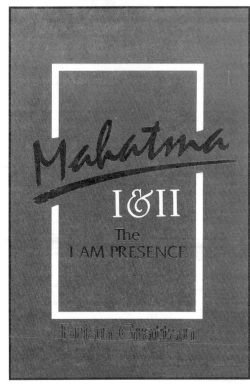

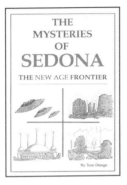

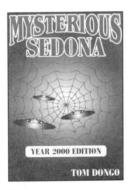

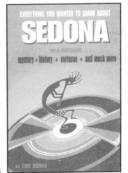

☧ *Light Technology* PUBLISHING

KATHLYN KINGDON

The Matter of Mind

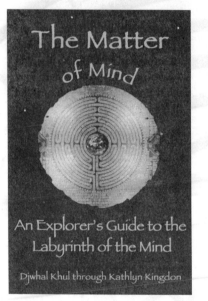

An Explorer's Guide to the Labyrinth of the Mind

Djwhal Khul through Kathlyn Kingdon

$16.⁹⁵

ISBN 1-891824-63-5
Softcover, 184 p.

In this remarkable book, Master Djwhal Khul lays out the dimensions of the mind in a coherent presentation unlike any other available today. Whether you approach the mind from a psychological basis, a spiritual perspective, or simply want fuller disclosure of how it perceives and creates, this book will provide amazing insights. You will discover why those who have attained enlightenment all teach the critical necessity of training the mind as the only means to achieving lasting peace.

In collaboration with Kathlyn Kingdon, Master reveals that the keys to happiness lie within each of us, buried beneath our conditioning and false beliefs, which we mistake for reality. Using this masterful guide, you will discover the importance of dissolving limiting emotional patterns and cutting through the web of illusion, which has held you prisoner in a cage of repeating patterns. The Matter of Mind is an inspiring and lucid treatise created to help you navigate the labyrinth of your mind and open to the experience of your enlightenment. It is hard to imagine reading this classic only once.

Light Technology PUBLISHING

Books by Eileen Nauman

Homeopathy for Epidemics

Homeopathy in Times of Crises

Homeopathy's philosophy is *like cures like.* By potentizing a remedy through a series of dilution steps, only the energy signature of the original substance is eventually left in the alcohol carrier. Quantum physics will one day be able to explain why water has memory; similarly, homeopaths know that each remedy has its own unique frequency, whether there are molecules of the substance left or not.

The homeopathic community knows that in the past, homeopathic remedies have made the difference between life and death during global epidemics. It is my hope that you will pass the information in this book along to your relatives and friends. It might be the greatest gift you ever give them—information that can save their lives.

$25.00 **Softcover 414 p.**
ISBN 1-891824-42-2

Combating deadly viruses with the beauty from nature.

Eileen Nauman holds a doctorate of homeopathic medicine (DHM) from the British Institute of Homeopathy, England. She practiced in Ohio for fifteen years and taught at the Desert Institute of Classical Homeopathy in Phoenix, Arizona, for two years. She is devoted to informing and educating the public on the difference homeopathy can make in people's lives. To that end, she has been busy writing books on homeopathy and has founded her own flower and gem essence company. In addition, she travels around the world lecturing on homeopathy as well as flower and gem essences.

Other Books by Eileen Nauman:

Soul Recovery and Extraction
$9.95 ISBN 0-9634662-3-2

Path of the Mystic
$11.95 ISBN 0-929385-47-0

Medical Astrology
$29.95 ISBN 0-9634662-4-0

Phone: 928-526-1345 or 1-800-450-0985 • Fax: 923-714-1132